This book uses game theory to analyse anticompetitive behaviour among firms and to consider its implications for competition policy. Part I focuses on 'explicit collusion': it is shown that 'four are few and six are many', and how cartels can be enforced under imperfect and incomplete information. Part II on 'tacit collusion' discusses the informational requirements of collusion detection in non-cooperative repeated games. In part III on 'semicollusion', excess capacity is shown to reinforce collusion. Part IV is devoted to the detection of predatory pricing.

In this book, Louis Phlips applies the latest economic theory to a discussion of several European antitrust decisions and empirical studies. The presentation of case studies, combined with a clear exposition of the theory, will make this book invaluable to teachers and students of competition policy.

Competition policy: a game-theoretic perspective

Competition policy:
a game-theoretic perspective

LOUIS PHLIPS
European University Institute

CAMBRIDGE
UNIVERSITY PRESS

Published by the Press Syndicate of the University of Cambridge
The Pitt Building, Trumpington Street, Cambridge CB2 1RP
40 West 20th Street, New York, NY 10011-4211, USA
10 Stamford Road, Oakleigh, Melbourne 3166, Australia

First published 1995

Printed by Bell and Bain Ltd, Glasgow

A catalogue record for this book is available from the British Library

Library of Congress cataloguing in publication data

Phlips, Louis.
    Competition policy : a game-theoretic perspective / Louis Phlips.
      p. cm.
    Includes bibliographical references and index.
    ISBN 0 521 49521 0 (hbk.) – ISBN 0 521 49871 6 (pbk.)
    1. Competition. 2. Cartels. 3. Game theory. 4. Competition –
Europe – Case studies. I. Title.
HB238.P48   1995
338.8–dc 20   95-10651
                                                                   CIP

ISBN 0 521 49521 0 hardback
ISBN 0 521 49871 6 paperback

For
Matthias, who already counts up to five
Louis (the Second), who counts up to two
Lynn, who doesn't count at all but has such blue eyes

Contents

List of figures   *page* xii
List of tables   xiv
Preface   xv

  1   *Preliminaries*   1
1.1   Competition law in the EC   1
1.2   Related topics   4
1.3   Some basic game-theoretic concepts   4
1.4   EC competition policy: 'normal' or 'active' competition   8
1.5   The logic of the book   16

  I   Explicit collusion

  2   *Four are few and six are many*   23
2.1   The model   24
2.2   Stage 3: the supply decision subgame   26
2.3   Stage 2: the cartel bargaining subgame   30
2.4   Stage 1: the participation decision subgame   33

  3   *Cartel laws are good for business*   39
3.1   The model   39
3.2   Stage 3: the (non-collusive) supply subgame   42
3.3   Stage 2: the cartel bargaining subgame   43
3.4   Stage 1: the entry subgames   43

  4   *Cartel enforcement*   47
4.1   Cartel enforcement with imperfect information   49
4.2   Cartel enforcement with incomplete information   56
4.3   Cartels in public procurement markets   66

II   Tacit collusion

5	*Information sharing among oligopolists*	81
5.1	Cournot–Nash equilibrium with uncertain demand and homogeneous goods	83
5.2	Acquisition and transmission of information	85
5.3	Differentiated goods	87
5.4	Uncertainty about costs	88
5.5	Facilitating practices	89
6	*Repeated games with collusive outcomes*	94
6.1	Friedman's balanced temptation equilibrium	94
6.2	The 'Folk Theorem'	99
6.3	The great salt duopoly	101
7	*Price leadership and conscious parallelism*	106
7.1	Static games without uncertainty	107
7.2	Static games with uncertainty	111
7.3	A repeated game	115
7.4	Price parallelism and collusive practices	117
7.5	The basing point system in the ECSC	119
8	*Collusion detection*	124
8.1	Information requirements of collusion detection	124
8.2	A simple Cournot model with seasonal adjustments	126
8.3	The wood pulp case	131
8.4	The ICI–Solvay case	136

III   Semicollusion

9	*Excess capacity and collusion*	151
9.1	The concept of semicollusion	151
9.2	Excess capacity and cartels in an historical perspective	152
9.3	A non-cooperative price-setting game with given capacities	154
9.4	Cartel negotiation with given capacities	159
9.5	Non-cooperative capacity choices with explicit collusion	161
9.6	Collusion detection	164
9.7	Non-cooperative capacity choices with tacit collusion	168
10	*Collusion in R&D*	173
10.1	The basic model	174
10.2	The results	175
10.3	Overinvestment in R&D and collusion	180

IV   Predatory pricing

11   *Predation in theory*   185
11.1   Why predatory pricing is rare and unimportant   186
11.2   The chain store paradox or the impossibility of predation   189
11.3   The lack of common knowledge can generate predation   192
11.4   Reputation and predation   194
11.5   Nash equilibria and predation   198
11.6   Geographical price discrimination and predation   202
11.7   Necessary conditions for predatory pricing   204

12   *Evidence on predation*   206
12.1   Experimental evidence   206
12.2   Antitrust litigation   215
12.3   The historical record   216
12.4   The bus war: a modelling approach   221

13   *Antitrust implications*   230
13.1   Rules   230
13.2   Informational requirements   240
13.3   The AKZO decision   247

References   256
Index   268

Figures

4.1	Joint profit maximisation	*page* 48
4.2	A prisoner's dilemma	50
4.3	The joint profit-maximising quantities	53
6.1	Tacit collusion: a balanced temptation equilibrium	95
7.1	The price leader has the smaller market share	110
7.2	The multiple basing point system with alignment	122
8.1	Duopoly with spatial price discrimination	146
8.2	Price discrimination with a supplement for overseas delivery	146
8.3	Indistinguishability with spatial price discrimination	147
9.1A	$p_1 < p_2$ and industry capacity is very small	156
9.1B	$p_1 > p_2$ and industry capacity is very small	156
9.2A	$p_1 < p_2$ and industry capacity is small	157
9.2B	$p_1 > p_2$ and industry capacity is small	157
9.3	$p_1 > p_2$ and industry capacity is neither very large nor small	158
9.4	Three areas with different threats	159
11.1	Player A's immediate payoffs and player k's payoffs	190
11.2	Player A's immediate payoffs and the payoffs for players 1 and 2	193
11.3	Player A's immediate payoffs and player k's payoffs	195
11.4	No predation in period 1	200
11.5	Predation in period 1	201
11.6	Preying twice to stop all entry	201
12.1	Experimental game without antitrust programme	210
12.2	Experimental game with antitrust programme	211
12.3	Actual and Nash equilibrium profits in Inverness one month after entry	226
12.4	Actual and Nash equilibrium profits in Inverness one year after entry	227

12.5 Bus miles reaction curves in Inverness one month after
     entry   228
12.6 Bus miles reaction curves in Inverness one year after entry 229
13.1 Limit pricing   235

Tables

2.1	Using the fitting-in function for $n = 3$	*page* 29
2.2	Payoffs up to $n = 10$	36
4.1	Numerical calculations with $a = 1$ and $F(v) = v$	65
6.1	Costs and profits of UK salt producers (1980–4)	103
6.2	Gains and losses from deviating of UK salt producers (£000)	105
9.1	The great salt duopoly: excess capacities (in %)	167
9.2	The great salt duopoly: shares in industry output	167
9.3	The great salt duopoly: profits (£000) and profit shares	168
9.4	The great salt duopoly: profits per unit of capacity	168
9.5	Effect of excess capacity, number of firms and inventories on aluminium ingot price–cost margins	171
10.1	Analytical procedure to find subgame perfect R&D effort and output	176
10.2	Results: equilibrium R&D effort and output	177
12.1	Frequencies of soft play by experienced weak monopolists	213
12.2	Frequencies of entry with experienced subjects, games 31–end	214
12.3	Illegal practices alleged in complaints	215
12.4	Cross-tabulation of business relationships and alleged illegal practices	217
12.5	Frequency of alleged illegal practices, by year of filing	218
12.6	Settlements and judgements, by alleged statute violation, alleged illegal practice and business relationships	219
12.7	Competition in the Inverness bus markets: key data for competitors	225
13.1	AKZO's costs	253
13.2	ECS's estimated total average cost	254

Preface

When Patrick McCartan asked me to prepare a second edition of *The Economics of Imperfect Information* for Cambridge University Press, I proposed rather to do a book that would give a coherent presentation of the main game-theoretic contributions to competition policy and include large chunks of the old chapters on oligopoly and collusion and on predatory pricing. I had indeed been writing up lecture notes for a course on applied microeconomic theory that aimed at doing just that. Patrick agreed without hesitation and encouraged me with enthusiasm. Here is the result.

The first colleague to thank is my departmental chairman, Mark Salmon, who talked me into teaching a 'taught' course. Without his bit of arm-twisting I would not have thought of writing another book. Several of my Ph.D. students at the European University Institute in Florence showed a keen interest in the course and started working on my favourite topic: the detection of collusion. Some agreed (or even suggested) to contribute to the manuscript. Barbara Böhnlein accepted to have her work on the informational requirements of collusion detection in the soda-ash market (the ICI–Solvay case) included as section 8.4; Hans-Theo Normann tackled the question of how to distinguish predatory pricing from Stackelberg warfare and normal competition between duopolists in section 13.2; Valeria Fichera wrote section 4.3 on cartels in public procurement contracts. I am sure the reader will pinpoint these sections as particularly interesting and novel contributions.

However, the colleague who contributed most is my dear friend and co-author Ronald Harstad, with whom I had the privilege of writing a number of papers since the days we met at the ZiF in Bielefeld (as members of an interdisciplinary group brought together by Reinhard Selten). One of these papers, on the informational requirements of collusion detection, is included in chapter 8, which I consider as *the* central and novel chapter. It is Harstad who formalised the intuitions I had gathered as a result of my life-long involvement with the enforcement of the Commission's competition policy.

My research assistant, Andrzej Baniak, read the manuscript with a sharp and competent eye. In particular, we worked very hard on the figures that illustrate the Kreps–Scheinkman model in chapter 9 which should make this model understandable for economists who do not have a Ph.D. in mathematics. Since even I now understand it (at least I think so), any reader with courage and patience should also be able to.

Peter Møllgaard and Stephen Martin kindly made many suggestions for improvement and corrected all sorts of errors ('small' errors do not exist). The remaining ones are for the reader to find.

My secretary, Jessica Spataro, not only typed and re-typed the manuscript at an incredible speed. She also continuously checked the references, the footnotes, the English (!) and what not. But above all, she managed to draw the figures on her computer: a glance at the figures in chapter 9 will show that I gave her a hard time indeed. Her dedication is highly appreciated.

A final remark. It is my sincere hope that the antitrust lawyers I had the pleasure of working with on one occasion or another will want to read chapter 1. I wrote it especially for them. Having made that investment, they should have no difficulty in following the critical discussion of the DG IV decisions and the judgements of the European Court of Justice, on the occasion of which we were sometimes on the same side and sometimes on opposite sides.

1 Preliminaries

The purpose of this book is to put together what I see as the main contributions of applied game theory, over the last two decades, to a better understanding of how collusion works and what antitrust authorities should do – and can do – about it. Insights into the economics of collusion detection and prevention should, by the same token, give a better idea of what sort of competition these authorities should aim for.

The results obtained have some general validity, in the sense that they do not depend on the particular legal framework in which competition policy is pursued. However, the choice of topics and of applications to particular antitrust cases refers to decisions taken by the Commission of the European Communities (EC) and judgements made by the European Court of Justice. It is appropriate therefore to start this preliminary chapter with a brief non-technical description of competition law in the EC, the more so as the different parts of the book correspond to different pieces of legislation.

A few basic game-theoretic concepts are then introduced, so as to allow the non-specialised reader to follow a critical discussion of the main features of the policy that appears to have been adopted by the Commission in order to stimulate what is sometimes called 'normal' or 'active' competition. This discussion sets the scene for a more thorough analysis to be developed in the ensuing chapters. The last section gives an outline of the book.

1.1 Competition law in the EC[1]

The basic EC competition rules applying to private undertakings are Articles 85 and 86 of the EC Treaty (the 'Treaty of Rome').

---

[1] The title of this section is also the title of a book by Van Bael and Bellis (1990), which provides a comprehensive and up-to-date (a new third edition is due to appear) analysis of the EC competition rules as developed by the Commission and the Court of Justice. Fifty-six appendices reproduce the text of all relevant articles of the EC Treaty, regulations and Commission notices, plus a list of all Commission decisions and Court orders in particular cases.

Article 85, paragraph 1, prohibits (a) all agreements between under-takings and (b) all 'concerted practices' which may affect trade between Member States and which have as their object or effect the prevention, restriction or distortion of competition. The agreements under (a) include price-fixing agreements, market-sharing agreements, quota cartels and so on. The conditions under which such agreements can arise and can be enforced by the participants are discussed in part I of this book under the heading 'Explicit collusion'. The concerted practices under (b) are what economists call 'tacit collusion' and are analysed in part II. They refer to situations where a concordance of wills leads to collusive outcomes without there being any explicit cooperation between the colluders.[2] These are the situations where problems of collusion detection by the authorities arise, since the existence of collusion has to be inferred from observations on market outcomes (such as parallel pricing over time), in the absence of cooperative behaviour. It is worth emphasising that exchanges of infor-mation between competitors on market conditions and on prices, firm specific production or export deliveries and the like, are considered by the EC authority as proof of tacit collusion. Chapter 5 is devoted to this delicate question.

Paragraph 3 of Article 85 allows for exceptions: the provisions of paragraph 1 may be declared inapplicable in the case of agreements and concerted practices which contribute to improving the production or distribution of goods or to promoting technical or economic progress without imposing unnecessary restrictions or eliminating competition in respect of a substantial part of the products in question. One such exemption was granted for the creation of joint ventures in research and development (R&D), on the condition that the firms involved sell the products resulting from their research efforts competitively. The validity of such an exemption is discussed in part III under the title 'Semicollusion'. Indeed, here is a case where collusion is allowed at the research stage, on the condition that it be followed by competition at the production stage.

Article 86 prohibits any abuse by one or more undertakings in a dominant position within the Common Market or in a substantial part of it in so far as it may affect trade between Member States. It does not define what may constitute an 'abuse' but lists examples of abusive conduct, such as unfair prices, restriction of production, discrimination and tying. Although not listed explicitly, predatory pricing (by a dominant producer) is a case of abuse. Part IV is devoted to the question of how predatory prices

---

[2] If a collusive outcome is reached by non-cooperative behaviour, there is no collusion, in a legal sense, in the US. There is thus a fundamental difference between competition law in the US and in the EC.

can be distinguished from discriminatory prices[3] and from price wars (or 'active' competition).

The Commission of the EC is the authority[4] in charge of implementing these basic rules (it being understood that breach of Articles 85 and 86 may be the subject of a private action in national courts, which retain their full jurisdiction). It is also the only body authorised to grant a negative clearance or an individual exemption from the ban of Article 85(1) and to issue block exemptions for certain categories of agreements on the basis of Article 85(3), as in the case of R&D joint ventures. In fact, the Commission issued several so-called 'Regulations', fixing the procedures to be followed, and 'Notices' which offer guidelines and clarifications on the status of certain agreements and practices in order to promote legal certainty and alleviate the administrative burden on its staff.

In matters of competition policy, the Commission's staff is concentrated in one of its so-called 'Directorates-General' (DGs), namely Directorate-General IV, commonly called DG IV. This directorate is endowed with investigatory, prosecutorial *and* decision-making functions. Except for merger cases, a sole 'rapporteur' or case handler is in charge of all three functions in a particular case, which he may push or not push until a 'decision' is reached (after a vote of all members of the Commission). This accumulation of responsibilities on one man's shoulders is perhaps efficient but certainly does not guarantee objectivity.

Until 1988, an appeal against a Commission decision could be brought directly before the Court of Justice of the EC in Luxembourg. Since then, appeals first go to the Court of First Instance which was attached to the Court of Justice to speed up procedures. An appeal before the Court of Justice from decisions of this Court of First Instance must be brought within two months of this notification.

Three important decisions of the Commission will be critically analysed in some detail: the famous *Wood Pulp decision*, which was annulled by the Court of Justice (section 8.3), the *ICI–Solvay decision* (section 8.4) and the *AKZO decision* (section 13.3). The first two illustrate the informational requirements for the detection of tacit collusion. The third decision shows how difficult it is for an authority to distinguish between predatory and non-predatory price wars.

---

[3] The reader interested in price discrimination is referred to my 1983 book on *The Economics of Price Discrimination*.

[4] National antitrust authorities are competent not only when trade between Member States is not affected but also to apply Articles 85(1) and 86 as long as the Commission has not initiated any procedure.

1.2 Related topics

For a long time, Articles 85 and 86 were interpreted as implying no provisions that would allow the Commission to prevent or control mergers: Article 85 covers agreements and concerted practices between existing firms; Article 86 is concerned with abuses by firms who happen to have a dominant position. Yet, since the early 1970s, the Commission sought and obtained from the Court of Justice the power to control mergers under Article 86: the acquisition of a dominant position in the Common Market or a substantial part of it was thus construed as an abuse. At the end of 1989, after more than a decade and a half of negotiation, the Council of Ministers of the EC finally established a new system of merger control which came into force at the end of September 1990. Merger control is outside the scope of this book. For a critical analysis of the decisions taken by the Commission under this new system, the reader is referred to Neven, Nuttall and Seabright (1993).

In a continuing effort to speed up single market integration, the Commission also 'went on the warpath against any agreement which tended to keep the Common Market partitioned along national boundaries. In particular, it moved against vertical arrangements whereby a manufacturer would entrust the distribution of his product to a separate distributor or licensee in each of the Member States and prohibit "re-exports", thereby preventing parallel "imports".' (Van Bael and Bellis 1990, p. 12). In several block exemption regulations (on motor vehicle distribution and servicing agreements in 1985 or on franchising in 1988) the Commission made it clear that the owner of a property right may not avail himself of such a right to block imports into a Member State of products sold by himself or with his consent in another Member State. Again, I shall not try to cover the relevant literature,[5] which is somewhat outside mainstream competition theory.

1.3 Some basic game-theoretic concepts

The purpose of this section is not and could not be to introduce the reader to modern game theory as applied in industrial economics. Economists are familiar with this theory and its applications in microeconomics: they should skip this section. Non-economists may find the following lines useful. My hope is that a few very basic concepts will thus become familiar and allow them at least to understand the general discussion of the Commission's competition policy presented in section 1.4. Since these

---

[5] An excellent survey can be found in the 1994 OECD report on 'Competition policy and vertical restraints' co-authored by Patrick Rey and Steve Brenner.

concepts will be used over and over again in the following chapters, non-economists may even be willing to try their hands on a few chapters.[6]

Strangely enough, perhaps, the modern approach to the study of collusion is to use *non-cooperative* game theory, in which firms (called 'players') are supposed to maximise their own profit individually, while taking account of the fact that they are in a strategic situation such that what one firm does affects what the others do.

The basic concept is that of a *non-cooperative Nash (1951) equilibrium*. This equilibrium is defined under the assumption that each firm behaves as 'competitively' as possible in the sense that it maximises its own profit individually, yet without ignoring its competitors' actions.

Each firm i is treated as a player in a game,[7] there being n players (so that $i = 1, 2, \ldots, n$). Each has a set of actions available, called 'strategies'. When each player has chosen a strategy, represented by q_i (to be defined in a moment), the resulting vector $q = (q_1, \ldots, q_n)$ is a joint strategy for all n players. A non-cooperative Nash equilibrium is then a joint strategy, call it $q^* = (q_1^*, \ldots, q_n^*)$ such that for *each* player i strategy q_i^* is the best way for it to react to the others' strategies, that is, a 'best reply'. This best reply is found by maximising a player's profit (or 'pay-off') function Π_i with respect to its strategy, given the optimal strategies of its competitors (which are also best replies defined in the same way).[8] A Nash equilibrium is thus a collection of *simultaneous* best replies. As a result, it is characterised by the fact that no player has an interest to deviate from it unilaterally: player i cannot increase its profits by changing its q_i^*, given the strategies of all the other players, and this is true for all other players.[9] Nermuth (1982, p. 49) remarks that

while it does not explain how the players should arrive at an equilibrium, at least it does explain why they should stick with it once they are there. Certainly one can argue that a strategy combination that is not an equilibrium cannot represent a state of affairs in which each player acts rationally: there must be at least one player who could improve his own payoff simply by altering his own strategy, an act nobody can prevent him from committing.

To illustrate, consider the case where there are only two players ($n = 2$) and q_1 is firm 1's rate of production while q_2 is firm 2's rate of production.

---

[6] Or wish to read Friedman's (1983) introduction to oligopoly theory, and especially its chapter 9 where non-cooperative game theory is presented in less than twenty pages.

[7] For more detailed presentations see Friedman (1977, 1983) or Shubik (1982).

[8] Mathematically, $\Pi_i(q^*) = \max\limits_{q_i} \Pi_i(q_i, q_{N-i}^*)$ for all i, or $\Pi_i(q^*) \geq \Pi_i(q_i, q_{N-i}^*)$ for all q_i in the set of available strategies, where q_{N-i} is the vector of strategies of all players except player i.

[9] Johansen (1982) discusses and convincingly rejects a number of critiques of the Nash equilibrium concept, showing that these critiques are based on a misunderstanding of its simultaneous nature.

(Production is equal to sales since there are no stocks by assumption.) We then have Cournot's duopoly model in which the strategies are quantities sold. Cournot's solution turns out to be a non-cooperative Nash equilibrium. Indeed, suppose the market (inverse) demand function is[10]

$$p = \alpha - (q_1 + q_2) \tag{1.1}$$

where p is the market price of the homogeneous commodity produced by the two duopolists. It depends linearly on total sales $(q_1 + q_2)$. The profit functions of the players are $\Pi_1 = [\alpha - (q_1 + q_2)]q_1$ and $\Pi_2 = [\alpha - (q_1 + q_2)]q_2$, that is, the revenues pq_1 and pq_2 respectively, on the simplifying assumption that the costs of production are zero. To find the non-cooperative Nash equilibrium, all one has to do is to simultaneously maximise these revenues with respect to q_1 and q_2, that is, to solve the system of two equations (first-order conditions)

$$\frac{\partial \Pi_1}{\partial q_1} = \alpha - 2q_1 - q_2 = 0$$
$$\frac{\partial \Pi_2}{\partial q_2} = \alpha - 2q_2 - q_1 = 0. \tag{1.2}$$

From the second equation $q_2 = \alpha/2 - q_1/2$ so that $q_1 = \alpha/3$ (from the first equation) and $q_2 = \alpha/3$. This is indeed Cournot's solution. Notice that rewriting the first equation, so that q_1 is expressed as a function of q_2, one obtains the equation of firm 1's 'reaction function'. Rewriting the second equation, so that q_2 is expressed as a function of q_1, gives the equation of the reaction function of firm 2. (In a figure representing these functions, the non-cooperative Nash equilibrium quantities correspond to the point where the two lines cross.) In this simple example, it suffices to know the demand function (1.1) to be able to compute the equilibrium quantities (strategies). Insertion of the sum of these quantities into the demand function gives the non-cooperative Nash equilibrium price.

The concept of a non-cooperative Nash equilibrium is interesting not only because it captures the strategic nature of oligopolistic (small n) competition, but also because the strategies involved can be of a very different nature. In Cournot's duopoly model, they are production rates

---

[10] The market demand function is assumed to be $(q_1 + q_2) = a - bp$. It says that total sales $(q_1 + q_2)$ are a (linear) function of the market price p. Here one wants to write the price as a function of total sales because the quantities sold are the strategies, so that the market price is determined by these quantities. The market demand function is therefore rewritten as $p = a/b - 1/b(q_1 + q_2) = \alpha - \beta(q_2 + q_2)$, with $\alpha = a/b$ and $\beta = 1/b$. To simplify the expressions, β is put equal to 1. This gives equation (1.1). Its graphical representation, with p on the vertical axis and $(q_1 + q_2)$ on the horizontal axis, would be a downward-sloping straight line, starting from α (the intercept) on the vertical axis.

giving rise to a unique market price. But nothing prevents us from defining the strategies as prices (one for each firm) when the competitors sell differentiated goods for example, or as different product qualities (one for each firm).

Rather paradoxically, we will discover (in chapter 6) that a set of non-cooperative Nash equilibrium strategies could imply collusive profits, when the game is not a one-period ('single-shot') game as in the Cournot model but is supposed to be repeated over time. In such a 'repeated game', the players compare the discounted value of the future profits they could make by deviating from a tacitly collusive outcome with the discounted value of the future profits they could make if they do not deviate. When this comparison shows that it is not profitable in the long run to deviate, then the collusive outcome is itself a non-cooperative Nash equilibrium! Such strategies give a precise meaning to what is often loosely referred to as tacit collusion or concerted practices.

This is not to suggest, however, that non-cooperative Nash equilibrium strategies can imply collusive outcomes only in repeated games. The Nash equilibrium concept is a general one and is being used whenever one has to find a set of strategies such that no player has an interest to deviate from it. In fact, chapter 2 will show that an explicit cartel agreement can turn out to be a non-cooperative Nash equilibrium, in the sense that accepting a production quota, for example, can be a best reply. Care should therefore be taken to always make it clear what sort of market outcome (competitive, collusive, ...) a particular non-cooperative Nash equilibrium refers to.

A further basic concept that will be used repeatedly is that of a *subgame perfect* (or simply 'perfect') equilibrium as coined by Selten (1965). Suppose a game is played in several stages. For example, firms invest in R&D in a first stage, and then sell their products in a second stage. Or firms sign a quota cartel agreement in a first stage, and sell their quotas (or more) in a second stage. An equilibrium is then called subgame perfect when the equilibria of the subgames considered separately coincide with the equilibrium of the entire game. A subgame is the game starting at a particular stage. When the stages correspond to successive time periods, subgame perfectness implies that strategies selected in a period turn out to still be best replies when reconsidered in the next period: there is time consistency. Analytically, this is obtained by solving the game backwards: start solving the last stage subgame, for given strategies in earlier stages, and then proceed to solving the previous subgame, using the equilibrium values obtained for later stages. In the game with R&D in a first stage and selling in a second stage, the trick is to find the second-stage equilibrium sales first, conditional on given R&D expenditures, and then to find the equilibrium R&D expenditures using the equilibrium sales quantities obtained for the second stage.

1.4 EC competition policy: 'normal' or 'active' competition

We should now be able to enter a general preliminary discussion of what appears to me to be the general principles underlying the competition policy worked out by the Commission in recent years. The point of reference used consistently by DG IV and the Court of Justice is the concept of 'normal' or 'active' competition. To make this concept more precise, as it emerges from a reading of a number of decisions and judgements, I have written down eight propositions, then scrutinised these from a game-theoretic point of view and finally come up with alternative formulations. This confrontation should convince the reader that game theory has something to contribute to a better understanding of what antitrust authorities can and should do and that the matter is worth pursuing in greater detail in the chapters to come.

In the Commission's view, normal competition is characterised by the following ingredients.

Proposition 1: Normal competition implies the freedom, for each individual firm, to change its prices independently.

Anything that affects this freedom is an illegal restriction of competition. This includes price agreements, needless to say, but also any discussion, between competitors, of their current or future prices and of the market conditions that make it possible for a firm to change or not to change its prices.

Proposition 2: Price competition between oligopolists typically takes the form of secret rebates, given for particular transactions, on list prices.

Secrecy of the rebate is the feature that prevents oligopolistic competitors from reacting immediately to a price reduction by one of them and thus makes price competition effective. Without secrecy, the reaction would be immediate and therefore the price reduction would not be granted. In addition, these rebates should be 'real' rebates, not just payment facilities granted to a select group of large customers. (The fact that such rebates imply price discrimination, which is illegal, is not stressed.)

Proposition 3: Normal competition is not compatible with simultaneous moves of transaction prices (and thus of secret rebates) or list prices.

Indeed, if each firm is free to change its prices, simultaneous moves are not to be expected. Each firm will act according to its own individual interest, changing its list price or its transaction price at the point in time that is privately optimal. As a result, if oligopolistic prices display parallel moves, this very fact proves that there is collusion.

Proposition 4: Imperfect information among sellers strengthens the bargaining position of their customers and thus leads to lower transaction prices.

Indeed, it is costly for a firm to check whether a competitor is quoting a low price, as claimed by its customers, so that it will more readily concede a price reduction. When customers are able to play this game simultaneously, average price will go down.

Proposition 5: Perfect information among competitors is not only a necessary condition for collusion but also a sufficient condition, because oligopolists want to collude.

Without market transparency about prices or quantities, colluders cannot enforce a price agreement, that is, punish the cheater. With market transparency, they will maximise joint profits overtly or tacitly or follow the price leader's moves without delay.

Proposition 6: Multilateral information transmission among oligopolists is therefore per se evidence of collusion.

The transmission of information about current prices or quantities is a substitute for a formal price agreement because this information is all that is needed for collusion to work.

Proposition 7: Multilateral information transmission about future prices is, *a fortiori*, per se evidence of collusion.

To discuss or communicate current prices or production rates is bad. To discuss or communicate future prices or production rates is even worse, since the freedom to change in the future is thus also restricted. More or less simultaneous announcements are substitutes for dinner meetings of colluding oligopolists.

Proposition 8: Unilateral information transmission about future prices is also per se evidence of collusion, because it could have no other purpose.

Why, indeed, would an individual firm bother to announce a price change publicly (by issuing a press release, circulating a new price list, sending telexes to customers or agents) if not to make sure that competitors be informed in time to be able to make similar moves?

The possibility of non-cooperative equilibria

These propositions leave one with uneasy feelings. First, there obviously is no reference to a possible non-cooperative equilibrium. Normal competition is seen as implying independent moves by individual firms resulting from bargaining between a particular seller and a particular buyer and leading to price undercutting.[11]

Second, no mention is made of a lower limit at which there would be no possibility of further price decreases. Theoreticians will no doubt emphasise that the lower limit is price equal to marginal cost. But marginal cost is not generally taken as a legal criterion in court discussions or in official decisions by the Commission of the EC. Admittedly, the idea that a price is above marginal cost and therefore too high may pop up occasionally, but it seems fair to say that Pareto optimality is not the stated objective of current antitrust policy.

Third, the implicit assumption seems to be that the only conceivable oligopolistic equilibrium is a collusive one. If prices do not move, there must be a collusive equilibrium. If prices move simultaneously, or almost simultaneously, this must be a move from one collusive equilibrium to another collusive equilibrium. If one firm changes its price, and the others follow immediately or almost immediately, this must be interpreted as a defensive reaction to maintain the agreed market shares. Consequently, competition among oligopolists is possible only through (what game theorists call) cheating. Therefore cheating has to be encouraged by all means. And the best encouragement is to create or maintain imperfect information among competitors.

The time has come to turn towards game theory and to throw in the now trivial idea that an oligopolistic industry can be in equilibrium, so no firm has any incentive to change its price or production rate, without there being any collusion. There is no cooperation whatsoever neither tacit nor explicit and yet no firm actively tries to increase its market share! There is competition, and yet no firm actively fights its competitors, because it is in no firm's individual interest to engage in 'active' competition! Needless to say, I am referring to a competitive non-cooperative Nash equilibrium as defined in section 1.3, for example the Cournot equilibrium.

The least I hope for is that it should be clear that antitrust authorities,

[11] This clearly implies that normal competition does not mean perfect competition in the classroom sense. For example, in perfect competition firms cannot change their prices independently.

lawyers, judges and experts cannot continue to ignore the concept of a Nash equilibrium (which is at least as much a theoretical possibility as the equality of price and marginal cost), though I know that much work remains to be done on practical questions, such as how a given industry can be identified as being in a Nash equilibrium, how it gets into such an equilibrium, how it gets out of it, and how it moves from one such equilibrium to another one. Progress in this direction will be made only to the extent that the people involved in antitrust cases begin to take the concept seriously.

Even if many of these questions cannot yet be answered in practice, I am arguing that the present state of the art allows us to go a few steps further. The first thing we can do – and I shall make an effort in that direction in a moment – is to study the properties of a competitive Nash equilibrium and compare these with those of a collusive equilibrium, to see for example which types of behaviour or which informational requirements, if any, are typical for the latter and can thus be identified clearly as implying collusion. If both equilibria turn out to have the same informational requirements or to imply the same behaviour, it should be doubtful that parallel behaviour and information transmission are per se evidence of collusion.

The next step is a more difficult one to agree on. I consider active competition as one way to get an industry out of a collusive equilibrium and move it into a competitive Nash equilibrium. I therefore am ready to argue that the competitive Nash equilibrium provides the equilibrium concept that is missing in the propositions listed above and defines the lower limit to which active competition should reduce industry prices or the upper limit to which active competition should push industry production. Once this limit is reached, no oligopolist has an incentive to break through it. To break through it would be against everybody's interest. Perhaps this is what industry circles call 'ruinous competition' (although the same word could designate the collapse of a collusive equilibrium). At any rate, nothing allows us to interpret such terminology as obviously referring to the breakdown of collusion. The words could have their true meaning. Now that the concept of a Nash equilibrium exists, and that the possibility of its occurring in the real world must be granted, it seems unfair not to allow for this possibility.

My last step is likely to meet strong opposition. To state it bluntly: To reach a competitive Nash equilibrium of a single-shot game is the best antitrust policy can hope for in oligopolistic markets (which is a far-reaching statement, given that most real life markets are oligopolistic). Therefore, if normal competition is the objective of antitrust policy, it should be defined as and have the properties of a competitive Nash equilibrium.

Let me make this statement a bit more precise and insist that, given the multiplicity of possible Nash equilibria, I mean a 'perfect' competitive Nash equilibrium (in quantities or prices, according to the strategies chosen by the industry). Such a perfect Nash equilibrium is part of a two-stage equilibrium,[12] in which the other stage implies a market structure that is endogenously determined by the given technology and given tastes. If, at a point in time, demand is such and technology is such that, with free entry, there is room for say only two firms with a given number of products each, and if prices and quantities are at the competitive Nash equilibrium levels, what more can antitrust authorities ask for? Should it call for active competition that would bring prices down to even lower levels? Should it object to the absence of price changes if market conditions are such that no price changes are called for?

Pervasive to the entire argument is the idea that antitrust authorities are *not* social planners. A social planner wants price equal to marginal cost, plus optimal taxes or subsidies. Antitrust authorities want the best possible market structure given technology and tastes, and, given this market structure, as much competition as is compatible with it and with entrepreneurial freedom. But that is precisely, it seems to me, what is described by a perfect competitive Nash equilibrium.

It should be clear, therefore, that the Nash equilibrium referred to is a particular one: It is a perfect non-cooperative and non-collusive Nash equilibrium (whether static or dynamic). To avoid tedious repetition, this particular equilibrium will be designated in what follows as an NE.

Again, such an NE may be a set of quantity strategies or a set of price strategies. This should not trouble us, contrary to a still widespread opinion, because the nature of the product (the extent of product differentiation and storability) or more generally the production technology (the necessity to plan production in advance and the presence of excess capacity) determines which of these strategies (quantity or price) is relevant.

New insights

To check whether all this is more than loose speculation, I suggest the following exercise. Let us consider such an NE and write down a set of propositions that correspond, one by one, to the propositions 1–8 and describe their relevant properties. I will have reached my objective if the simple juxtaposition of these makes you doubt the truth of at least one proposition stated above. I must confess I have doubts about several.

---

[12] See Shaked and Sutton (1987).

Proposition la: In an NE, each individual firm is free to change its prices (or quantities), but it is in the interest of none to do so independently.

To raise or lower one's price makes sense only if all other competitors do the same, because one firm is in NE only on the condition that all others are. To act independently is foolish because no firm is independent of the others.

Proposition 2a: In an NE, there is no room for secret rebates.

Cheating makes sense only if there is collusion. Since there is no collusion here, there is no need for competitors either to prevent cheating or to make secret moves to prevent the others from reacting immediately. On the contrary, if one firm moves it expects its competitors to move in the same direction. If they don't, it must conclude that it misinterpreted the market situation. Yet, nothing prevents the firms involved from giving 'genuine' rebates in the open; that is, price discrimination is compatible with an NE.

Proposition 3a: Successive Nash equilibria are compatible with simultaneous moves of list prices and transaction prices.

Although there are no secret rebates, transaction prices can differ from list prices, for example if a rebate is required in a particular transaction (for a particular location, say, or for a particular delivery date). At any rate, if market conditions change in the same direction for all (aggregate demand increases or falls, or wage rates move up in the same way for all), simultaneous moves are to be expected. If the first to move makes the correct decision, one should expect all competitors to follow within days or hours: what looks like price leadership develops. Simultaneous moves are not per se evidence of collusion.

Proposition 4a: An NE requires neither perfect nor complete information.

Analytically, the NE of a game can be found (by game theorists) even if the players do not know each other's profit functions or strategies with certainty (this is a game with 'incomplete' information). The same is true for games in which the history of the game, including today's moves, is not perfectly observable (these are games with 'imperfect' information). Hopefully, real-life oligopolists are able to find their NE in the same circumstances using some rule of thumb such as cost-plus or normal costing. It is doubtful, therefore, that the strengthening of the buyers' bargaining position (emphasised in proposition 4) must lead to a price war.

Proposition 5a: The implementation of tacit or explicit collusion requires perfect information, because colluders have an incentive to cheat. In addition, however, the difficulties due to incomplete information have to be solved.

Proposition 5 ignored the fact that potential colluders may not be able to observe each other's preferences (profit functions), and reduced the problem of implementing collusion to the detection and punishment of cheating. Proposition 5a recognises the importance of perfect information, but insists that, even if information is perfect, collusion does not automatically result. If potential colluders are not able to observe each other's profit functions, they each have private information and must be given an incentive to reveal it correctly. While proposition 5 gives the impression that collusion is easy and therefore ubiquitous, proposition 5a reminds us that collusion is not only difficult to implement, once reached, because of the prisoner's dilemma,[13] but is also difficult to achieve because there are two types of information involved. To be well informed about how competitors are currently behaving is not the same thing as being well informed about the competitors' decision parameters.[14] Market transparency therefore does not guarantee that there is collusion. The presumption that market transparency (among oligopolists) is evidence of collusion should rather be based on the following proposition.

Proposition 6a: In an NE, it is not in the oligopolists' interest to share information, but it is in their individual interest to acquire more information.

This proposition will be discussed at length in chapter 5. If information sharing leads to perfect information, if perfect information is a necessary ingredient of collusion, and if a non-cooperative equilibrium provides no incentive for such information sharing (or even an incentive not to share information), then the current distrust of information sharing agreements can be given a sound theoretical foundation. However, this conclusion is valid for schemes that systematically pool all current information available to all colluders, so information is perfect. A case in point is the agreement between OPEC and an independent agency that will collect complete daily information on oil extraction and shipments by OPEC members.

I wonder whether proposition 6a applies to the transmission of price or quantity data, by individual firms, via press releases, telexes, or letters or even to meetings where competitors discuss their price or production

---

[13] See section 4.1.   [14] See section 4.2.

policies. When a pooling scheme is in operation, such messages or meetings are superfluous. Couldn't these messages or meetings simply reflect everybody's interest in getting more information, the more so as one cannot presume that more information is all that is needed for collusion to work?

Proposition 7a: Communication about future prices may be a way of getting better information about a new NE.

Suppose industry demand displays seasonal fluctuations, as in the wood pulp industry.[15] Under explicit collusion, the cartel would collectively announce in advance a price schedule covering the entire year. (The announced price changes would be smaller or larger, depending on the possibility of building up inventories and depending on whether inventories are built up at the producer or at the customer level).[16] Perfect intertemporal information (complete certainty) about prices is thus obtained, in the same way as a pooling scheme provides perfect information about current prices, and the freedom to change prices in the future is collectively restricted.

If, now, firms individually announce prices valid for the next quarter only, not the next year, and do this in rapid succession within hours or days, this is a substitute for a discussion at a meeting. (In an explicit collusive arrangement, such signalling would be superfluous.) A price announcement may be a way of implementing 'conscious parallelism', that is, tacit collusion. But the message may as well be that a firm thinks the old NE needs to be changed and wishes the others to confirm or contradict. If firms go through the trouble of announcing future quarterly prices in advance, so that competitors have time to confirm or not, this is therefore not evidence of collusion. And if the same first is always first, there is price leadership, but even that is not collusion.

Proposition 8a: Advance notice of price changes may serve all sorts of purposes.

Advance notice of a price increase is a classic device to encourage customers to buy now rather than later: The flow of orders is smoothed over time so that the cost of carrying inventories is shifted from the seller to the buyer. Advance notice of a price decrease provides an incentive to buy later and smoothes the rate of production over time. A better understanding of intertemporal profit maximisation and of the economics of inventory building may take away some of the current distrust.

[15] See section 8.3.   [16] See Phlips and Thisse (1981).

To sum up, we cannot avoid the conclusion that the current antitrust attitude with respect to information acquisition and pooling rests on shaky grounds, to the extent that it considers any communication between oligopolists as evidence of collusion. Careful distinctions have to be drawn. The quest for perfect information on current behaviour has to be distinguished from transmission of information about 'preferences' (i.e., the quest for 'complete' information about profit functions and strategies). Pooling schemes are not synonymous with discussions about current or future prices or quantities: the former are proof of collusion; the latter may occur between non-cooperating competitors. Advance notification cannot be said to be bad as such. And information about prices should not, in principle, be considered more 'dangerous' than information about quantities, because quantity can be a strategic variable as well as price, especially for homogeneous goods.

Are we to conclude that per se rules are to be avoided and that we should more carefully weigh the pros and cons in each case? I would hate such a conclusion, not only because it is no conclusion at all, but especially because it leaves business with no indication about what is legal and what is not. We must, somehow, sharpen our economics to the extent that per se illegal behaviour can be defined.

1.5 The logic of the book

A very old idea in industrial economics is to say that explicit collusion is likely to occur in markets where competitors are 'few'. But what number corresponds to 'few'? It turns out that four are few and six are many: if there are less than five competitors in a market, they will find it profitable to form a cartel; if there are more than five, it becomes more advantageous to stay out of a cartel formed by others. So antitrust authorities should keep a close eye on industries with less than five competing firms. This result was obtained by Selten (1973) in an important but highly technical paper. Chapter 2 aims at presenting its main arguments in a non-technical way. All my efforts in that direction notwithstanding, the result is a chapter which is probably the most difficult but also the most rewarding of the book.

Chapter 3 is complementary to chapter 2 and considers the effects of competition laws which make cartels illegal. It is generally thought that such laws are bad for business, because they reduce the profits firms can expect to make. Selten (1984), again, shows that the opposite may be true when there is free entry into an industry. Indeed, collusive profits (made in the absence of an active competition policy) attract new entrants. When cartel laws are enforced, to the contrary, there might be fewer competitors with the result that total expected profits in the industry are larger!

After this provocative interlude, chapter 4 digs into the problems cartel members face when they try to enforce an existing agreement. The policing of a collusive agreement is a problem in the theory of *imperfect* information, since deviations from the agreement (such as secret price cutting or shipments in excess of production quotas) must be detectable for retaliation to be possible and for a threat of retaliation to be credible. This is a central problem in oligopoly theory, since the 'prisoner's dilemma' emphasises that it is always in the interest of one member of the agreement to cheat if it can do so without detection. One way to police an agreement is then to adopt a rule saying that if one member deviates, all the others will deviate in such a way that each member keeps its market share.

The policing of a collusive agreement is also a problem in the theory of *incomplete* information, when some cartel members are more efficient than others so that side-payments are necessary. Side-payments must be based on the costs of production of the individual members. But these costs must be revealed by the members themselves. Is it possible to give them an incentive to reveal their costs truthfully so that the agreement is viable? The answer is yes, if there are (again!) less than five competitors in the market.

Public procurement markets, where a public authority buys goods or services, are often organised as auctions. The enforcement of collusive 'rings' among the bidders creates special problems which are discussed in section 4.3.

Part II is dedicated to situations where explicit collusion is illegal and is vigorously attacked, so that firms that wish to collude have to look for ways of colluding tacitly, while antitrust authorities have to look for ways of detecting this tacit collusion. (In part I, collusion detection was no problem in the sense that it suffices to find a copy of a cartel agreement to have proof of collusion.)

We saw that the current EC policy is based on the presumption that the transmission of information is proof of collusion, because it is seen as a necessary and sufficient means to facilitate tacit collusion. In chapter 5, the problem is reformulated in game-theoretic terms. The (correct) formulation is: would oligopolists in a situation of incomplete information want to share their private information (on market demand or on costs of production) in a competitive Nash equilibrium? If yes, then information transmission is not proof of collusion, since it could be a natural way of finding out what the competitive equilibrium is. If not *and* if we observe that they do share, then collusion is to be suspected. The case of a homogeneous commodity is considered first with the help of the basic model by Novshek and Sonnenschein (1982). Then Vives' (1984) findings for differentiated goods are reported. In both cases, the uncertainty is about the level of market demand. The rather different problem of information sharing about costs is tackled next. The conclusions differ according to whether uncertainty is about 'common' values (such as market demand or industry-wide costs) or about 'private' values such as firm-specific costs.

The fundamental question, however, is to understand how tacit collusion can be enforced when competitors meet repeatedly over time and what remains of the prisoner's dilemma when competitors are given a time horizon, so that they can evaluate what would happen tomorrow if they were to deviate from a collusive situation today. The answer is in Friedman's seminal (1971) paper, which shows that a collusive outcome can be sustained (as a non-cooperative Nash equilibrium) in a repeated game when competitors use 'trigger strategies' such that, if one of them deviates from a collusive equilibrium, they all shift to the competitive Nash equilibrium (chapter 6). No deviation will occur if the discount factor is high enough, that is, if a big enough weight is placed on future losses resulting from punishment by the others. The study of the salt duopoly in the UK gives an empirical application of this theory.

The next step is to introduce a preplay convention in the repeated game, as postulated by MacLeod (1985), according to which (1) a price increase, announced by any competitor, will be followed if it is profitable to do so and if the others do the same; (2) a price decrease, announced by any competitor, will be followed if it does not go below the competitive Nash equilibrium; (3) any deviation from rules (1) and (2) by a rival will be met by a move to the competitive Nash price. This leads to collusive profits that are somewhere between the competitive Nash and the joint profit maximisation profit level. Chapter 7 surveys the literature on price leadership to prepare the reader for this repeated game approach and also draws a rather fascinating analogy with the multiple basing point system of the European Coal and Steel Community (replacing temporal by spatial considerations).

Chapter 8 asks the question whether an antitrust authority can detect such collusive behaviour when it is at an informational disadvantage relative to oligopolistic firms that are playing this sort of repeated game. Joint work with R. Harstad has shown that knowledge of some parameters by firms but not by antitrust authorities makes non-collusive and collusive behaviour indistinguishable in simple models of Cournot oligopolies with seasonal variations in demand and costs, and also in Bertrand oligopolies (using price strategies) characterised by multimarket contact over space. The *Wood Pulp* and *ICI–Solvay* decisions by DG IV are used as illustrations of these two situations. It is shown in particular that the Court of Justice was right in concluding that parallel pricing is *not* proof of collusion, contrary to DG IV's position. This concludes the discussion of tacit collusion.

Part III is devoted to what is becoming a rapidly growing new area in competition theory, namely 'semicollusion'. Here account is taken of the fact that competitive strategies may be chosen to reach, say, investment decisions with the understanding that the output resulting from such decisions will be sold in a collusive way (chapter 9) or, alternatively, that collusive investment decisions may be made with the understanding that the resulting output will be sold competitively (chapter 10). Such a two-stage approach is particularly relevant to an evaluation of the block exemption, given under Article 85(3) by the EC Commission to joint R&D ventures on the condition that the products resulting from these cooperative R&D investments be sold in a competitive way.

Part IV raises the question how to distinguish between predatory and non-predatory price wars. Chapter 11 is based on the rather recent and perhaps surprising insight that predatory pricing is a problem in the theory of information. Common sense suggests that predatory price cutting is irrational, at least in the framework of a single-market monopoly situation. In addition, 'the chain store paradox' – which gives a game-theoretic treatment of multimarket monopoly – suggests that predation cannot occur in equilibrium under complete information. As long as both the potential predator and the potential prey know each other's situation (in terms of foregone profits) and each other's moves, and as long as it is clear to both that the issue is one of predatory pricing, the potential prey will enter the market without fear and the established firm will prefer normal competition, that is, a competitive Nash equilibrium with both firms in the market.

However, if the potential victim has incomplete information and is, as a result of it, in doubt whether predation could occur, then its entry can meet a predatory response in equilibrium. One approach supposes that the entrant entertains the possibility (however small) that the established firm may be irrational (a fanatic predator or a fanatic pacifist). The established firm may then risk preying in order to establish a reputation of aggressiveness, since if it ever fails to prey the entrant will conclude that it will never prey. An alternative approach uses less restrictive assumptions and supposes that the entrant entertains the possibility that a price cut by the established firm could be either predatory or an implication of a non-cooperative Nash equilibrium. It is not sure, therefore, whether there is room for it in the market it entered in. By cutting its price, a predator then makes it look as if, indeed, there is no room for an additional firm in the market, when in fact there is. This seems to be the characteristic feature of the majority of actual cases of alleged predation.

Chapter 12 collects some evidence, however fragmentary, on alleged cases of predation and also on experimental results. To find evidence of predation seems to be as difficult in experiments as in real life. And what looks like predation may in fact be just Stackelberg warfare, that is, a struggle between two firms who both pretend to be price leaders or simply normal competition, leading to the exit of a firm for which there was no room in the market. It will be shown that it *is* possible to actually compute the Nash equilibrium for a particular market, using observed data, and to infer from it whether a price war is predatory or not.

The implications for antitrust policy are clear (chapter 13). One cannot conclude, as is often done, that the policy standards presented in the literature (such as pricing below marginal cost, an increase of output above the pre-entry level or a price increase after the entrant has been forced to cease operations) can be used as evidence of predation. Each case has to be evaluated on the basis of all evidence relevant to the question of whether there is room for the alleged victim in the market in a competitive Nash equilibrium. A detailed discussion of the AKZO case illustrates the informational requirements of predation detection by an antitrust authority. It is argued that this was a case of Stackelberg warfare, not of predation.

I

Explicit collusion

2   Four are few and six are many

From a methodological point of view, the message of this chapter is that explicit collusion can and should be analysed as the solution of a non-cooperative game. A cartel will appear as a non-cooperative Nash equilibrium: each cartel member decides to join the cartel because joining is his best reply strategy. In particular, to accept a production quota is a best reply. In part II, tacit collusion will also appear as a non-cooperative Nash equilibrium (of a repeated game) and so will partial collusion in part III: the non-cooperative approach thus appears as *the* general methodology appropriate for an analysis of collusive as well as non-collusive equilibria, for the simple reason that one has to explain why each firm has an individual interest to use the collusive strategy.

There is an important proviso, however: in this chapter, problems of imperfect information and of incomplete information are ignored. When *imperfect* information is allowed for, so that the players cannot observe the actual behaviour of their competitors, it becomes possible to cheat on an agreement. Then the cheater has to be identified and punished: this is the problem of cartel enforcement tackled in section 4.1. When there is *incomplete* information about a parameter of the players' profit functions, for example uncertainty about the cost of production of individual cartel members, then a mechanism has to be designed that gives an incentive to truthfully reveal one's own cost to the others and provides for an efficient allocation of the production quotas of the members. This is the problem of cartel enforcement with incomplete information discussed in section 4.2.

From a policy point of view, this chapter answers a fundamental question: in what sort of industries is explicit collusion likely to occur? It is generally thought that cartels are to be found in concentrated industries, where competitors are 'few'. This is a very vague statement, however. As shown by Selten (1973) in his paper entitled 'A simple model of imperfect competition where four are few and six are many', non-cooperative game theory gives a clear-cut answer: If there are less than five competitors, they

23

will *all* find it profitable to collude explicitly; if there are more than five competitors, it becomes more advantageous to stay out of a cartel formed by others, that is, the position of an outsider becomes relatively more attractive as the number of competitors increases. Note that Selten's point is very different from the one which says that the more competitors there are, the more difficult it is to enforce an agreement. Indeed, in Selten's model there is no room for cheating or untruthful cost reporting, since cartels appear as non-cooperative Nash equilibria with perfect and complete information.

This chapter is entirely devoted to an exposition of Selten's 1973 paper. I shall avoid the game-theoretic technicalities which make the paper very long and very difficult to read for the general economist and try to concentrate on the details of the economic analysis for their own sake. The basic result (that four are few and six are many) can be obtained in a very simple way, using the cartel stability analysis of d'Aspremont *et al.* (1983), as shown in Martin (1993a, chapter 5). My purpose is to emphasise the non-cooperative modelling technique.

2.1 The model

Selten considers a symmetric Cournot model with linear cost and demand. There are n players. Firm i is called player i $(i = 1, \ldots, n)$. They all supply the same homogeneous commodity. The supply of firm i is denoted $q_i \geq 0$.

Symmetry means that all firms have the same cost function

$$K_i = C + cq_i \tag{2.1}$$

for $q_i > 0$, $C > 0$, and $c > 0$. (Nothing is gained by supposing cost differences: such differences are of interest when there is uncertainty about firm specific costs as in section 4.2.)

Total industry supply is

$$Q = \sum_{i=1}^{n} q_i \tag{2.2}$$

and the market price, p, is determined by it according to the inverse market demand function

$$p = \begin{cases} \alpha - \beta Q & \text{for} \quad 0 \leq Q \leq \dfrac{\alpha}{\beta} \\ 0 & \text{for} \quad Q > \dfrac{\alpha}{\beta} \end{cases} \tag{2.3}$$

with $\alpha > C$ and $\beta > 0$.

To simplify the algebra, the following normalisation is adopted

$$\beta = 1 \tag{2.4}$$

$$\alpha = 1 + c. \tag{2.5}$$

This normalisation allows one to write the profit margin, which is

$$g = p - c, \tag{2.6}$$

as

$$g = \alpha - \beta Q - c = 1 + c - Q - c = 1 - Q. \tag{2.7}$$

The gross profit of firm i, which ignores fixed costs C, is

$$\Pi_i = q_i g. \tag{2.8}$$

In what follows, fixed costs are supposed to be sunk. Note that gross profit is non-negative, that is, $\Pi_i > 0$ if $1 - Q \geq 0$ or

$$Q \leq 1. \tag{2.9}$$

Given these cost, demand and profit functions, the n firms play a game that has three successive stages: (1) a 'participation decision' stage, in which the firms decide whether they want to participate in the bargaining to reach a cartel agreement; (2) a 'cartel bargaining' stage, during which quota proposals are made, which may lead to a cartel agreement or not; (3) a 'supply decision' stage, in which each firm selects a supply quantity q_i. These stages are modelled as follows.

The *participation decision* is the selection of a zero-one variable z_i. Either $z_i = 0$, which means that firm i does not want to participate, or $z_i = 1$, in which case firm i wants to participate. The participation decision is a simultaneous one. Each firm has to decide without knowing the participation decisions of the other players. The set of all firms who select $z_i = 1$ is denoted Z. At the end of this stage, Z is made known to all players, who are thus perfectly informed about who is going to participate in the bargaining in the next stage and who is not.

In the *cartel bargaining* stage, each 'participator' $i \in Z$ proposes a quota system

$$Y_i(y_{ij})_{j \in C}. \tag{2.10}$$

Y_i is a vector of non-negative quotas (quantities to be produced) proposed by i for all those players, including himself ($i \in C$), who belong to a particular coalition C, which is a subset of $Z(C \subseteq Z)$. A player who participates is thus free to propose a quota allocation for any subset of Z. All such proposals are made simultaneously without knowing the proposals of the other participants.

A binding cartel agreement is reached when all members of a coalition propose the same vector of quotas, that is, when unanimity is reached, or

$$Y_c = (y_j)_{j \in C} = Y_i \tag{2.11}$$

for all $i \in C$. The system of individual proposals

$$Y = (Y_i)_{i \in Z}$$

contains the proposals made by each $i \in Z$ and gives a complete description of the course of the game up to the end of the bargaining stage. At the end of this stage, Y is made known to all n players, who are thus perfectly informed about who is a member of which partial or full cartel and what his quota is.

In the *supply decision* stage, each player i selects independently a supply quantity q_i such that

$$0 \le q_i \le y_i, \tag{2.12}$$

y_i being the agreed quota when i joined a cartel. (Since there is no cheating, q_i cannot be larger than the agreed y_i.) For firms that did not join a cartel, $y_i = \infty$ since their supply is not restricted.

Subgame perfect equilibrium is the solution concept, so that the game has to be solved backwards: First solve the supply decision subgame for given $y = (y_1, \ldots, y_n)$ and Z; then solve the cartel bargaining subgame, for given Z, using the equilibrium supply decisions found for stage 3; finally, determine Z using all previous subgame equilibrium results. This procedure guarantees that the solution to a subgame is also the solution to the entire game.

2.2 Stage 3: the supply decision subgame

Consider what may have happened in stage 2. If no agreement was reached or if there was an agreement on quotas that do not restrict individual supplies, then clearly the individual supply decisions are simply the Cournot–Nash equilibrium quantities. With $\beta = 1$ and $\alpha = 1 + c$, these quantities[1] are

$$q_i = \frac{1}{n+1} \tag{2.13}$$

for all i, and the corresponding profits are

$$\Pi_i = \frac{1}{(n+1)^2}. \tag{2.14}$$

---

[1] Without the normalisation, the Cournot–Nash quantities are $q_i = (\alpha - c)/\beta(n+1)$.

All firms supply the same quantity since they have the same cost function and nobody has a binding quota.

If there was an agreement, then the quotas may be binding for some firms but not for others: one has to find out for each firm what the best reply quantity is, given the quota allocation. Participators are free to produce less than their quota, if that is the profit-maximising solution. They supply their quota only if it is smaller than the individual profit-maximising quantity.

The reaction function of firm i gives its best reply to the production of its competitors $Q_i = \sum_{j=1}^{n} q_j (j \neq i)$. With a given quota vector y, this reaction function is

$$\varphi_i(Q_i) = \max\left[0, \min\left(\frac{1-Q_i}{2}, y_i \right) \right]. \tag{2.15}$$

To understand this, remember first that profits are non-negative for $Q = Q_i + q_i \leq 1$ according to equation (2.9). If the competitors' supply $Q_i > 1$, so that $(1 - Q_i) < 0$, the only way for firm i to avoid negative profits is to produce nothing, or $q_i = 0$. If, to the contrary, $Q_i < 1$, then q_i must not be larger than $1 - Q_i$. Why should it be $(1 - Q_i)/2$ in the absence of quotas? Simply because this quantity maximises profit $\Pi_i = q_i g = q_i(1 - Q) = q_i(1 - Q_i - q_i)$, as the reader will verify. The quota is i's best reply only if it is smaller than $(1 - Q_i)/2$.

The reaction function (2.15) gives the best reply to the production of i's competitors. Selten (1973) proposes to use another function, which gives the best reply to the industry's *total* production Q. He calls it the 'fitting-in' function (from the German word 'Einpassungsfunktion').[2] This function facilitates the computation of the Cournot equilibrium outputs in cases where there are more than two firms with unequal outputs. In our problem, such non-symmetric equilibria arise, although all firms have the same cost function, because some firms may have their outputs restricted by their quotas. The fitting-in function allows one to make sure that the output of each firm is consistent with both profit maximisation and total output Q in an easy way. This consistency must be assured, since all firms face the same total output in equilibrium. When the reaction function (2.15) is used, it is not clear how this is to be achieved, since Q_i may differ from $Q_j = \sum_{k=1}^{n} q_k (k \neq j)$ for j different from i.

---

[2] This function has appeared in the literature under different names. Novshek and Sonnenschein (1978, p. 240) call it the 'backward map'. Novshek (1984) uses the term 'backward reaction mapping'.

The fitting-in function of firm i is

$$\eta_i(Q) = \max [0, \min (1 - Q, y_i)]. \tag{2.16}$$

In equilibrium, total output must be the sum of these best replies, or

$$\sum_{i=1}^{n} \eta_i(Q) = Q. \tag{2.17}$$

An equilibrium exists because $\sum_i^n \eta_i(Q)$ is decreasing in Q, positive for $Q = 0$ and zero for $Q = 1$. The fitting-in function is also a reaction function, but defined with respect to i's competitors' output after making sure that this output is consistent with total output, or

$$\eta_i(Q) = \varphi_i(Q - \eta_i(Q)).$$

To see this, remember that the model is symmetric: all firms have the same constant marginal cost c. In the absence of quotas, they would have the same equilibrium output. Let us compute their reaction function, ignoring quotas, for $n = 2$. Partial differentiation of $\Pi_i = (p - c)q_i = [1 - (q_i + q_2)]q_i$ gives the reaction functions

$$q_1 = \frac{1}{2}(1 - q_2) \quad \text{for firm 1}$$

$$q_2 = \frac{1}{2}(1 - q_1) \quad \text{for firm 2}$$

and the equilibrium quantities $q_1 = q_2 = \frac{1}{3}$, as already indicated in equation (2.13). Now replace q_2 by $(Q - q_1)$ in the reaction function of firm 1, to obtain

$$q_1 = \frac{1}{2}(1 - Q + q_1)$$

or

$$q_1 = 1 - Q.$$

Replacing q_1 by $(Q - q_2)$ in the reaction function of firm 2 gives

$$q_2 = 1 - Q.$$

In the absence of quotas or when quotas are not restrictive, the best reply to total output is $1 - Q$, as indicated in (2.16). To find the equilibrium outputs, use (2.17):

Table 2.1. *Using the fitting-in function for n = 3*

Q	$1-Q$	$\eta_1(Q)$	$\eta_2(Q)$	$\eta_3(Q)$	$\sum_{i=1}^{3} \eta_i(Q)$
0	1	$y_1 = 0.6$	$y_2 = 0.4$	$y_3 = 0.1$	1.1
0.1	0.9	$y_1 = 0.6$	$y_2 = 0.4$	$y_3 = 0.1$	1.1
0.4	0.6	$y_1 = 0.6$	$y_2 = 0.4$	$y_3 = 0.1$	1.1
0.5	0.5	$1-Q = 0.5$	$y_2 = 0.4$	$y_3 = 0.1$	1.0
0.6	0.4	$1-Q = 0.4$	$y_2 = 0.4$	$y_3 = 0.1$	0.9
0.7	0.3	$1-Q = \underline{0.3}$	$1-Q = \underline{0.3}$	$y_3 = \underline{0.1}$	$\underline{0.7}$
0.9	0.1	$1-Q = 0.1$	$1-Q = 0.1$	$y_3 = 0.1$	0.3
1	0	$1-Q = 0$	$1-Q = 0$	$1-Q = 0$	0

Note: The given vector of quotas is $y = (0.6, 0.4, 0.1)$.

$$2(1-Q) = Q$$

or

$$Q = \frac{2}{3}$$

so that (as before) each firms supplies $\left(1 - \frac{2}{3}\right) = \frac{1}{3}$ in equilibrium.

Suppose, to the contrary, that some quotas are restrictive. Selten (1973, p. 125) proposes the following illustration. Let there be three firms with the same marginal cost c. Let the inverse market demand function be $p = (1+c) - (q_1 + q_2 + q_3)$ and let the agreed quotas be $y_1 = 0.6$, $y_2 = 0.4$ and $y_3 = 0.1$. What will each firm supply in equilibrium?

Now the usefulness of the fitting-in function becomes apparent. Simply apply equation (2.16) to determine $\eta_i(Q)$ for different values of Q between 0 and 1, since Q cannot be larger than 1 with non-negative profits according to equation (2.9). (Notice that the sum of the quotas is $0.6 + 0.4 + 0.1 = 1.1$, so that some firms will want to produce less than their quota.) In table 2.1, the equilibrium individual supplies are those for which the sum in the last column is equal to the value of Q in the first column, so that equation (2.17) is satisfied.

The equilibrium value of Q is 0.7. It is composed of the equilibrium supplies $q_1 = 0.3$, $q_2 = 0.3$ and $q_3 = 0.1$. Firms 1 and 2 supply less than their quota. For firm 1, $1 - Q$ is smaller than its quota for $Q \geq 0.5$. For firm 2, this is the case for $Q \geq 0.7$. In the absence of binding quotas, each of these three firms would have produced $q_i = 0.25$ according to equation (2.13) and total production would have been 0.75. The binding quota y_3 allowed firms 1 and 2 to produce a bit more. Yet, total industry supply is somewhat smaller.

2.3 Stage 2: the cartel bargaining subgame

The solution of this subgame depends on the number of *non*-participators, that is, of those who decided (in the previous stage) to stay out of the cartel bargaining process and chose $z_i = 0$. Designate this number by k. There are thus k firms in the set of non-participators $N - Z$. In this second stage, k is given since it was determined in stage 1. The problem is to find out which quotas will be agreed on by the participators who know the solution of the supply decision subgame: they know that, and how, quotas affect all individual supply decisions and therefore total supply (and the market price). Before solving the cartel bargaining game, it is therefore useful to note a number of implications of the results derived in stage 3.

Consider the *non-participants* first. We know that their outputs are not restricted by quotas. In the n vector of quotas y, they have $y_i = \infty$ for $i \in N - Z$. Therefore their best reply is $q_i = \eta_i(Q) = 1 - Q$. With given k, total supply Q can be decomposed in

$$Q = Q_Z + Q_{N-Z}$$

where

$$Q_Z = \sum_{i \in Z} q_i$$

and

$$Q_{N-Z} = \sum_{i \in N - Z} q_i.$$

Since all non-participators supply the same quantity $q_i = 1 - Q$, their total supply is

$$Q_{N-Z} = k(1 - Q_Z - Q_{N-Z})$$

$$= \frac{k}{k+1}(1 - Q_Z)$$

so that

$$q_i = 1 - Q_Z - \frac{k}{k+1}(1 - Q_Z)$$

or

$$q_i = \frac{1}{k+1}(1 - Q_Z) \qquad \text{for } i \in N - Z. \tag{2.18}$$

Next consider the *participators*. They supply a quantity $1 - Q$, if that is smaller than their quota, or else their quota. So

$$q_i \leq 1 - Q$$

for $i \in Z$ and their total supply Q_Z is

$$Q_Z \leq (n-k)(1-Q).$$

Using equation (2.18), we also have

$$(n-k)(1-Q) = \frac{n-k}{k+1}(1-Q_Z)$$

so that

$$Q_Z + \frac{n-k}{k+1} Q_Z \leq \frac{n-k}{k+1}$$

or

$$Q_Z \leq \frac{n-k}{n+1}. \tag{2.19}$$

Finally, the *joint profit* of the participators $\Pi_Z = \sum_{i \in Z} \Pi_i$ is

$$\Pi_Z = Q_Z g = Q_Z(1-Q)$$

using equation (2.8), or

$$\Pi_Z = \frac{1}{k+1} Q_Z(1-Q_Z) \tag{2.20}$$

using equation (2.18). This joint profit reaches its maximum at

$$Q_Z = \frac{1}{2}. \tag{2.21}$$

With equations (2.18)–(2.21) in hand, we can now demonstrate that the number of non-participators k plays a crucial role in the success of a cartel agreement. We shall see that if $k \geq \frac{n-1}{2}$ a quota agreement has no effect in the sense that the participators will behave like the non-participators. This is the case for a market with, say, five firms when $(5-1)/2 = 2$ or more do not participate in the cartel bargaining. To the contrary, if $k < \frac{n-1}{2}$, there are quotas which are best replies according to the fitting-in function. This is the case for a market with five firms when at least four participate in the cartel.

We begin with the case where $k \geq \dfrac{n-1}{2}$. Take the lower bound of k, that is, $k = \dfrac{n-1}{2}$. (What is true for this value of k must be true for any higher value.) Inserting this value into equation (2.19) shows that the participators together supply

$$Q_Z \leq \frac{n - \dfrac{n-1}{2}}{n+1} = \frac{1}{2}.$$

However, in the relevant interval $0 \leq Q_Z \leq \dfrac{1}{2}$, the joint profit Π_Z is increasing monotonically (check using equation (2.20)). Therefore the highest attainable joint profit corresponds to the highest possible value of Q_Z, which is

$$Q_Z = \frac{n-k}{n+1}$$

according to equation (2.19). But then, each participator produces

$$q_i = \frac{Q_Z}{n-k} = \frac{n-k}{(n-k)(n+1)} = \frac{1}{n+1}$$

(for $i \in Z$). From equation (2.13) we know that is the Cournot–Nash equilibrium quantity! Intuition suggests that the non-participators also supply that quantity. This can be verified by inserting $Q_Z = (n-k)/(n+1)$ into equation (2.18). The entire industry is thus in the Cournot–Nash equilibrium. Quota proposals in order to maximise joint profit are meaningless, since they would not affect the participants' behaviour.

The situation is completely different when $k < \dfrac{n-1}{2}$. (With five firms, for example, at most one does not participate). Suppose that the participators propose equal quotas, namely

$$y_{ij} = \frac{Q_Z}{n-k} = \frac{1}{2(n-k)}, \tag{2.22}$$

that is, an equal part of their total supply $Q_Z = \dfrac{1}{2}$ that maximises their joint profit. According to the fitting-in function, these quotas are best replies to total industry output

$$Q = k(1-Q) + (n-k)\min\left[1-Q, \frac{1}{2(n-k)}\right]$$

since $1 - Q$ can be shown to be larger than $1/2(n-k)$. For all cartel participants $i(i \in Z)$, the best response is thus to supply the agreed quota, or

$$q_i = \eta_i(Q) = \frac{1}{2(n-k)} \quad \text{for } i \in Z. \tag{2.23}$$

What are the individual supplies of the non-participants in equilibrium? Since the participants maximise their joint profit, Q_Z is equal to $\frac{1}{2}$, so that for $i \in N - Z$

$$q_i = \frac{1}{k+1}(1 - Q_Z) = \frac{1}{k+1}\left(1 - \frac{1}{2}\right) = \frac{1}{2(k+1)}. \tag{2.24}$$

The resulting profit for the participants $(i \in Z)$ is

$$\Pi_i = \frac{1}{4(n-k)(k+1)} \tag{2.25}$$

when $k < (n-1)/2$. The non-participators $(i \in N - Z)$ get

$$\Pi_i = \frac{1}{4(k+1)^2}. \tag{2.26}$$

We shall need these profit expressions to solve the participation decision subgame.

2.4 Stage 1: the participation decision subgame

It remains to find out how many players participate in a cartel agreement and, in particular, whether this agreement will include all players or only a subset of them. We will discover that if there are up to $n = 4$ firms in a market, for *all* of them to participate is a subgame perfect equilibrium. That is why 'four are few'. When there are more than four firms, cartel equilibria with less than the total number of firms participating can be found. However, if the number of non-participants is $k \geq (n-1)/2$, then every player receives the unrestricted Cournot–Nash equilibrium profit.

Consider player i, who has to decide whether to participate ($z_i = 1$) or not ($z_i = 0$). We wish to distinguish the case where this player is one of the k non-participants from the case where he is not. We therefore introduce m, the number of non-participants in $N - \{i\}$. In words, m is the number of non-participants other than player i. If i decides not to participate ($z_i = 0$), $k = m + 1$ by definition. If i does participate ($z_i = 1$), $k = m$.

To find i's equilibrium strategy in this subgame that is also an equilibrium for the entire three-stage game, all the results obtained so far in stages 2 and

3 must be used. This can be done by collecting all possible equilibrium profits i can make and rewriting these in terms of m instead of k.

If i decides $z_i = 0$, so that $k = m + 1$, he gets either the profit defined by equation (2.26) when others form a cartel, that is

$$\Pi_i = \frac{1}{4(m+2)^2} \qquad \text{for } m < \frac{n-3}{2} \qquad (2.27)$$

or the Cournot–Nash equilibrium profit

$$\Pi_i = \frac{1}{(n+1)^2} \qquad \text{for } m \geq \frac{n-3}{2}. \qquad (2.28)$$

If, to the contrary, i chooses $z_i = 1$, so that $k = m$, his profit is either

$$\Pi_i = \frac{1}{4(n-m)(m+1)} \qquad \text{for } m < \frac{n-1}{2} \qquad (2.29)$$

from equation (2.25), or the Cournot–Nash equilibrium profit

$$\Pi_i = \frac{1}{(n+1)^2} \qquad \text{for } m \geq \frac{n-1}{2}. \qquad (2.30)$$

It is now an easy (though tricky) task to determine whether player i ($i = 1, \dots, n$) will participate or not in equilibrium. He will participate if payoff (2.29) is larger than the payoff he would get – either (2.27) or (2.28) depending on the value of m – as a non-participator. This happens to be the case for all firms in the market up to $n = 4$.

Indeed, for $n = 2$, the difference between payoff (2.29) with $k = m = 0$ and payoff (2.28), $m = k - 1 = 0$ being larger than $(2-3)/2$, is

$$\frac{1}{4(2-0)(0+1)} - \frac{1}{(2+1)^2} = \frac{1}{8} - \frac{1}{9} = 0.12500 - 0.11111 > 0.$$

With $n = 3$, player i wants to participate in a cartel that includes all three firms. Subtracting the non-participator's payoff (2.28) from (2.29), since $m = 0$ is equal to $(3-3)/2$, gives

$$\frac{1}{4(3-0)(0+1)} - \frac{1}{(3+1)^2} = \frac{1}{12} - \frac{1}{16} = 0.08333 - 0.06250 > 0.$$

With $n = 4$ and a cartel that includes all four firms, player i would get payoff (2.27) if he were the only non-participator, since then $m = 0$ is smaller than $(4-3)/2$. We have

$$\frac{1}{4(4-0)(0+1)} - \frac{1}{4(0+2)^2} = \frac{1}{16} - \frac{1}{16} = 0.06250 - 0.06250 = 0.$$

Player i has no interest in deviating from the cartel he is a member of. If he were one of two non-participators, then $m = 1 > (4-3)/2$ and each of the non-participators would make a profit of only $1/(4+1)^2 = 1/25 = 0.04000$. We may conclude that cartels which include all firms are equilibria up to $n = 4$.

However, the situation changes drastically as soon as $n = 5$. Indeed, when there are five or more firms (and $k < (n-1)/2$ so that cartel agreements can be effective), i would want to be the outsider to a cartel that includes all firms: please check that his payoff (2.29) as a participator would always, that is, for any $n \geq 5$, be smaller than the payoff $1/4(0+2)^2 = 0.06250$ he would receive as the only outsider. However, *partial* cartel equilibria, which both participators and non-participators have no incentive to modify, are possible: a participator in such a partial cartel has no incentive to leave it, while a non-participator has no incentive to join it.

Consider $n = 5$. For a partial cartel to be effective, we must have $k < (n-1)/2$. Since $(5-1)/2 = 2$, k must be equal to 1 and the cartel must have four members. Let us verify that such a partial cartel is an equilibrium. If player i is one of the four cartel members, would he want to become an outsider to the cartel? Having chosen $z_i = 1$, equation (2.29) defines his payoff with $k = m = 1$: the non-participator must be a firm other than i. If i were also a non-participator, there would be two outsiders so that $k = 2 = (n-1)/2$ and i would receive the Cournot–Nash profit (2.28). Subtracting payoff (2.28) from payoff (2.29) gives

$$\frac{1}{4(5-1)(1+1)} - \frac{1}{(5+1)^2} = \frac{1}{32} - \frac{1}{36} = 0.03125 - 0.02778 > 0.$$

It is in player i's interest to stick to the partial cartel agreement. Suppose, to the contrary, that this player has chosen $z_i = 0$ so that he is an outsider to the cartel. Would he want to join it? Being the only non-participator (since $k = 1$: otherwise the cartel would not exist), $m = k - 1 = 0$ in payoff (2.27). If he were to join, he would receive payoff (2.29) with $k = m = 0$. Subtracting the former from the latter

$$\frac{1}{4(5-0)(0+1)} - \frac{1}{4(0+2)^2} = \frac{1}{20} - \frac{1}{16} = 0.05000 - 0.06250 < 0.$$

Player i would not want to join the cartel. A partial cartel with four members out of five is an equilibrium.

Table 2.2 tabulates the numerical values of the payoffs defined by equations (2.27) to (2.30) up to $n = 10$. With the help of the previous discussion, the reader should have no difficulty in interpreting the numbers given up to $n = 5$. With more than five firms in the industry, the question

Table 2.2. *Payoffs up to n = 10*

Number of players	Number of non-participators	Payoff of a participator	Payoff of a non-participator
$n = 2$	$k = 0$	0.12500	—
	$k \geq 1$	0.11111	0.11111
$n = 3$	$k = 0$	0.08333	—
	$k \geq 1$	0.06250	0.06250
$n = 4$	$k = 0$	0.06250	—
	$k = 1$	0.04167	0.06250
	$k \geq 2$	0.04000	0.04000
$n = 5$	$k = 0$	0.05000	—
	$k = 1$	0.03125	0.06250
	$k \geq 2$	0.02778	0.02778
$n = 6$	$k = 0$	0.04167	—
	$k = 1$	0.02500	0.06250
	$k = 2$	0.02083	0.02778
	$k \geq 3$	0.02041	0.02041
$n = 7$	$k = 0$	0.03571	—
	$k = 1$	0.02083	0.06250
	$k = 2$	0.01667	0.02778
	$k \geq 3$	0.01562	0.01562
$n = 8$	$k = 0$	0.03125	—
	$k = 1$	0.01786	0.06250
	$k = 2$	0.01389	0.02778
	$k = 3$	0.01250	0.01562
	$k \geq 4$	0.01235	0.01235
$n = 9$	$k = 0$	0.02778	—
	$k = 1$	0.01562	0.06250
	$k = 2$	0.01190	0.02778
	$k = 3$	0.01042	0.01562
	$k \geq 4$	0.01000	0.01000
$n = 10$	$k = 0$	0.02500	—
	$k = 1$	0.01389	0.06250
	$k = 2$	0.01042	0.02778
	$k = 3$	0.00893	0.01562
	$k = 4$	0.00833	0.01000
	$k \geq 5$	0.00826	0.00826

Source: Table 1 in Selten (1973).

arises how the equilibrium number of cartel members evolves. A discussion of the case $n=6$ should make it clear how the reasoning goes for $n>6$.

When $n=6$, $(n-1)/2=2.5$ so that k must be equal to 1 or 2 for partial collusion to be effective. Is a partial cartel with five members an equilibrium? No. Suppose player i is one of the five $(z_i=1)$. So $k=m=1$ in payoff (2.29). If i became a non-participator, there would be two outsiders and equation (2.27) applies with $m=1$. The difference is

$$\frac{1}{4(6-1)(1+1)} - \frac{1}{4(1+2)^2} = \frac{1}{40} - \frac{1}{36} = 0.02500 - 0.02778 < 0.$$

Player i prefers to be a non-participator. If, to the contrary, player i was the non-participator, he would not want to join. If he were to join the five cartel members, we would have $k=m=0$ in payoff (2.29). If he remains an outsider, $m=k-1=0$ in payoff (2.27). The difference is negative

$$\frac{1}{4(6-0)(0+1)} - \frac{1}{4(0+2)^2} = \frac{1}{24} - \frac{1}{16} = 0.04167 - 0.06250 < 0.$$

A partial cartel with four members is an equilibrium, however. If player i is one of the four $(z_i=1)$, then $k=m=2$ in payoff (2.29). If i were to join the two other non-participants $(z_i=0)$, he would only make profit (2.28). The difference is positive

$$\frac{1}{4(6-2)(2+1)} - \frac{1}{(6+1)^2} = \frac{1}{48} - \frac{1}{49} = 0.02083 - 0.02041 > 0.$$

Player i remains a member of the partial cartel. If $z_i=0$, to the contrary, i is one of the two non-participators. So $m=k-1=1$ in payoff (2.27). If he were to join the four cartel members, his payoff would be given by equation (2.29) with $k=m=1$. He prefers to remain an outsider

$$\frac{1}{4(6-1)(1+1)} - \frac{1}{4(1+2)^2} = \frac{1}{40} - \frac{1}{36} = 0.02500 - 0.02778 < 0.$$

A similar analysis for higher numbers of firms shows that partial equilibrium cartels include five members for $n=7$ and $n=8$, and six members for $n=9$ and $n=10$. This should be clear from a careful look at table 2.2. The implication is that the position of an outsider becomes relatively more attractive as n grows, starting from $n=5$. One out of five is 20 per cent. Four out of ten is 40 per cent.

It is therefore of some interest to consider the probability w_i that a player participates in a (full or partial) cartel. Selten shows that this probability is the same for all players because of the symmetry of the game, so that $w_i = w_1$ for $i=2,\ldots,n$. For $n\leq4$, $w_i=1$. For $n>4$, $0<w_1<1$. This 'participation probability' depends on the number of players and goes to zero as n goes to infinity.

Whether full or partial, equilibrium cartel agreements occur only when $k < (n-1)/2$. Define the 'cartel probability' as the probability that $k < (n-1)/2$. This probability is clearly equal to 1 for $n \leq 4$. Selten shows that, for $n = 5$, it is only 0.221 and that for $n > 5$ it is approximately 1 per cent or smaller.

Our discussion of the cases where $n < 5$ made it clear why 'four are few'. The results for $n > 5$ show that 'six are many' indeed.

It might seem that the model is very particular and this conclusion is therefore model specific. I think it is quite general. The normalisation adopted in equations (2.4) and (2.5) is just a convenient choice of units of measurement. The linearity assumptions can be seen as simplifying approximations: nothing essential is lost by making them. The same is true for the assumption that the firms are symmetric when they are perfectly informed of all decisions at the end of stages 1 and 2. The only problem is to know whether four are still few and six are still many when the firms have different costs and do not know their competitors' costs. We will discover in chapter 4, section 4.2, that Selten's result still holds under incomplete information!

3 Cartel laws are good for business

Cartels that affect trade between Member States are illegal in the EC, according to Article 85 of the Roman Treaty. Member States have their own competition law that makes cartels affecting trade inside their countries illegal. These 'cartel laws' are being actively enforced by EC and national authorities. This is certainly in the interest of the consumers, since prices can be expected to be lower in an environment where binding agreements are not permitted. At first sight, the producers should suffer, since they have a reduced opportunity to increase profits by collusion.

Selten (1984) argues that this intuition is not necessarily correct. Joint profit maximisation is likely to attract new entry. When collusion is effectively prevented (explicit as well as tacit collusion: tacit collusion is ignored for the sake of exposition), there may be fewer competitors around, with the result that producers make higher profits on average than when they collude. This 'entry effect', that is, the influence of cartel laws on the number of competitors, counteracts the advantages of collusion in terms of individual profits. Is this counter-influence sufficiently strong to make cartel laws desirable for business from the point of view of profit maximisation? Under reasonable assumptions it is, because cartel laws increase the expected sum of all profits.

This question is tackled here rather than at the end of the book, because the model used to answer it is very close to the one discussed in the previous chapter. In fact, this short chapter can be seen as an extension of or an afterthought to chapter 2.

3.1 The model

The general framework is again that of a non-cooperative Cournot model with linear costs and linear demand, in which cartels are the result of non-cooperative decisions. We must compare two games: (a) a non-cooperative game in the absence of cartel laws, called the collusive game, and (b) a non-cooperative game under cartel laws, called the non-collusive game, in which firms are not free to collude.

The *collusive game* is a modified version of the game analysed in chapter 2, which had three stages: the participation decision stage, the cartel bargaining stage and the supply decision stage. In the first stage, a given number of firms had to decide whether to participate in a cartel agreement or not. Here, the number of firms is not given. The assumption is that there is a large number of firms waiting for the opportunity to enter an oligopolistic market characterised by Cournot strategies, linear costs and linear market demand. We now have the following three stages: the entry decision stage, the cartel bargaining stage and the supply decision stage.

In the *entry decision* stage, firms decide whether to enter the oligopoly or not. The order in which they decide to enter or not is determined by a random ranking. All rankings are equally probable. Once the ranking is chosen, it is made known to all players, who decide in turn. More precisely, the kth player i_k in the ranking $r = (i_1, \ldots, i_N)$ either selects $z(i_k) = 1$ or $z(i_k) = 0$. All players $1, \ldots, N$ know the cost and demand parameters. Each entry decision is immediately made known to all players. The set of the players who decided to enter (all players i with $z(i) = 1$) is denoted by Z. Profits obtained during the entry stage are neglected.

In the *cartel bargaining* stage, every firm in the market independently and simultaneously proposes a quota system for *every* member in Z. (No partial cartels are allowed, in contradiction with the results of chapter 2, to simplify the analysis!) If there is unanimity, the agreement is binding. The proposals of all players $i \in Z$ are made known to all players after the bargaining stage. If a binding agreement is reached, then the game ends. The individual supplies are the agreed quotas.

If no binding agreement is reached in the bargaining stage, then the *supply stage* follows. Every firm in the market independently and simultaneously selects a supply quantity.

In the *non-collusive game*, stage 2 drops out. The entry stage is immediately followed by the supply stage. In both games, the players that do not enter receive zero payoffs.

The solution concept is again subgame perfect equilibrium. The solution of the collusive game will be a symmetric cartel agreement for the maximal number of competitors such that cartel profits are non-negative. The solution of the non-collusive game will be a Cournot–Nash equilibrium for the maximal number of competitors such that profits are non-negative. Then the sum of profits in both solutions will be compared, since these joint profits determine the chances that a particular entrant will be able to survive in the market. Indeed, each potential entrant has the same profit expectation, namely the sum of profits divided by the number of firms in the market.

Agreements to restrict entry are excluded from consideration, since the purpose of the analysis is to find the maximum number of firms *compatible with positive profits*. That is why it is supposed that new firms can be formed just for the purpose of entering a new market or, equivalently, that there is a large number of firms waiting for the opportunity to enter. In such a situation agreements to restrict entry would not be effective.

N is the given number of players waiting for the opportunity to enter the market. It should not be confused with the number of players *in* the market, which is now endogenous and has to be determined by the play of the game. Let Z be this endogenous number of players in the market. (In chapter 2, Z was the number of participators in a cartel agreement.) The supply of firm $i \in Z$ is denoted by $q_i \geq 0$. All firms have the same cost function

$$K_i = C + cq_i \tag{3.1}$$

for $q_i > 0$, with $C > 0$ and $c > 0$.

Total supply is

$$Q = \sum_{i \in Z} q_i. \tag{3.2}$$

The market price p is determined by total supply according to the inverse market demand function

$$p = \begin{cases} \alpha - \beta Q & \text{for} \quad 0 \leq Q \leq \dfrac{\alpha}{\beta} \\ 0 & \text{for} \quad Q > \dfrac{\alpha}{\beta} \end{cases} \tag{3.3}$$

with $\alpha > c$ and $\beta > 0$. Note that if $\alpha \leq c$ there is no incentive to enter since p would be below marginal cost.

The profit margin is

$$g = p - c = \alpha - \beta Q - c \tag{3.4}$$

for $p > 0$. The gross profit of firm i is

$$G_i = q_i g \quad i \in Z \tag{3.5}$$

while its net profit is

$$\Pi_i = G - C \quad i \in Z. \tag{3.6}$$

In this model *net* profits are introduced (so that Π_i is defined differently from chapter 2) since entry entails a fixed cost C which cannot be ignored.

The sum of gross profits for all $i \in Z$ is

$$G = Qg \tag{3.7}$$

and the maximal value M of G is

$$M = \max_{Q \geq 0} Q(\alpha - \beta Q - c).$$

$dM/dQ = \alpha - 2\beta Q - c = 0$ implies $Q = (\alpha - c)/2\beta$, which is the total monopoly supply, so that

$$M = \left(\frac{\alpha - c}{2\beta}\right)(\alpha - c) - \beta \left(\frac{\alpha - c}{2\beta}\right)^2 = \frac{(\alpha - c)^2}{4\beta}. \tag{3.8}$$

M is called monopoly gross profits.

The 'size' of the market is defined as

$$s = \frac{M}{C}. \tag{3.9}$$

To make sure that entry is not restricted by a lack of potential competitors waiting for the opportunity to enter, it is supposed that

$$N > s > 0. \tag{3.10}$$

The size of the market and monopoly gross profit are going to be the key variables. The sums of the profits to be compared will be expressed in terms of M and s. In the collusive game, the sum of the profits obtainable by a cartel is $M - nC$ where n is the number of firms. The equilibrium value of n will be the largest integer not greater than s. Since $C = M/s$, the joint cartel profits can be written as $M - n(M/s) = M(s - n)/s$. We will see that the sum of the profits obtainable in the non-collusive game (the joint Cournot profits) can also be written as a product of M and a factor which depends only on s. This will facilitate the comparison.

3.2 Stage 3: the (non-collusive) supply subgame

Suppose $Z = (i_1, \ldots, i_z)$ is the set of players who decided to enter the industry in stage 1. The industry is a symmetric Cournot oligopoly, so for $i \in Z$ the Cournot solution is for each player to supply

$$q_i = \frac{\alpha - c}{\beta(z + 1)}. \tag{3.11}$$

The equilibrium net profits are, using $Q = z(\alpha - c)/\beta(z + 1)$ and equations (3.3), (3.4) and (3.6)

$$\Pi_i = \frac{(\alpha - c)^2}{\beta(z+1)^2} - C \tag{3.12}$$

or

$$\Pi_i = \left(\frac{4M}{(z+1)^2} - \frac{M}{s}\right) = \left(\frac{4}{(z+1)^2} - \frac{1}{s}\right) M \tag{3.13}$$

using equations (3.8) and (3.9). The players who decided not to enter receive zero profits, as mentioned before.

3.3 Stage 2: the cartel bargaining subgame

The only symmetric equilibrium quota proposal is such that all players in Z get an equal share of the total monopoly profit, and therefore an equal share of the total monopoly quantity $Q = (\alpha - c)/2\beta$ or

$$y_j = \frac{\alpha - c}{2\beta z} \tag{3.14}$$

for every $j \in Z$ with a corresponding net profit of

$$\Pi_i = \frac{M}{z} - C = \frac{(\alpha - c)^2}{4\beta z} - C \tag{3.15}$$

or

$$\Pi_i = \frac{M}{z} - \frac{M}{s} = \left(\frac{1}{z} - \frac{1}{s}\right) M. \tag{3.16}$$

3.4 Stage 1: the entry subgames

There are two entry subgames to be considered: one for the non-collusive game and one for the collusive game.

For the *non-collusive game*, the question to be answered is: what is the maximal number of players, z, who are entering in the presence of cartel laws? This is the number z such that $\Pi_i \geq 0$. Using equation (3.13), we have that

$$\Pi_i = \left(\frac{4}{(z+1)^2} - \frac{1}{s}\right) M \geq 0 \tag{3.17}$$

if

$$\frac{4}{(z+1)^2} \geq \frac{1}{s}$$

or

$$\frac{2}{(z+1)} \geq \frac{1}{\sqrt{s}}$$

or

$$z \leq 2\sqrt{s} - 1.$$

For $\Pi_i = 0$, $z = 2\sqrt{s} - 1$. Note that s is not necessarily an integer. Let m be the greatest integer not greater than $2\sqrt{s}$. Then

$$z = m - 1 \tag{3.18}$$

is the maximal number of entrants compatible with non-negative Cournot net profits. So the entry decision is to enter as long as,[1] after my entry, $z \leq m - 1$.

Now consider the entry subgame for the *collusive game*. In the absence of cartel laws, z is defined by the condition that

$$\Pi_i = \left(\frac{1}{z} - \frac{1}{s}\right) M \geq 0 \tag{3.19}$$

using equation (3.16). This condition is satisfied if $1/z \geq 1/s$ or

$$z \leq s.$$

Therefore

$$z = n \tag{3.20}$$

where n is the largest integer not larger than s. The entry decision is now to enter as long as, after my entry, $z \leq n$.

We have a first result: *in the non-collusive game, the number of entrants is smaller than in the collusive game*. Entry is smaller in the presence of cartel laws than in the absence of cartel laws. Indeed[2]

$$m - 1 < n.$$

The main result is that the *expected sum of profits is larger in the presence of cartel laws* (in the non-collusive game) than in the absence of cartel laws (in the collusive game). Cartel laws are good for business.

The sums of profits can easily be computed with the help of equations (3.13) and (3.16) respectively. If the non-collusive game were actually

---

[1] If the size of the market is $s = 1$, then $m = 2$ and $z = 1$. There is room for one firm only. If $s < 1$, m has to be redefined as $m = 1$ to get $z = 0$.

[2] Please check. For example, with $s = 9$, $m = 6$ and $n = 9$.

played, the industry would end up having $z = m - 1$ firms in it. The sum of
their Cournot profits Π_c would be

$$\Pi_c = (m-1)\Pi_i = \left[(m-1)\left(\frac{4}{m^2} - \frac{1}{s}\right) \right] M. \qquad (3.21)$$

The term between brackets measures the proportion of the maximal value
of gross profits G realised by the industry as a whole. At the end of the
collusive game, to the contrary, there would be $z = n$ firms in the industry
and their joint cartel profits Π_M would be

$$\Pi_M = n\Pi_i = \left(1 - \frac{n}{s}\right) M. \qquad (3.22)$$

The proportion[3] of the maximal value of gross profits realised is $(1 - n/s)M$.

Each joint profit is expressed as a function of s and M. For some values of
this pair of parameters Π_c is larger than Π_M. For other values, the opposite
is true.[4] To compare them in a meaningful way, it is necessary to consider
their expectation defined on a joint probability distribution of the pair
(s, M) conditional on $s \geq 1$. Selten therefore defines the expected joint
profits as

$$E(\Pi_c) = \int_1^{\bar{s}} \int_0^{\bar{M}} \Pi_c f(s, M) dM \, ds$$

$$E(\Pi_M) = \int_1^{\bar{s}} \int_0^{\bar{M}} \Pi_M f(s, M) dM \, ds$$

where $f(s, M)$ is the joint probability bounded by $1 \leq s \leq \bar{s}$ and $0 \leq M \leq \bar{M}$.
The proof that the expected joint non-collusive profit is larger than the joint
collusive profit, or

$$E(\Pi_c) > E(\Pi_M)$$

[3] Notice that if $2\sqrt{s}$ is an integer, so that m is equal to it, and if s is an integer, so that n is equal
to it, then $\Pi_C = \Pi_M = 0$ and no solution can be given to the entry subgames. Decisions to
enter or not to enter both yield zero profits. Selten therefore excludes these cases, which do
not affect the comparison of joint profits. Note also that, when $0 < s < 1$, there is no entry in
both games and the sums of profits are zero, since all players earn zero profits. Therefore the
sums in equations (3.21) and (3.22) are computed under the assumption that $s \geq 1$. Indeed,
Selten is only interested in markets which are *profitable*.

[4] Please check. For example, compute the difference $(m-1)(4s/m^2 - 1) - (s - n)$ for different
values of s such as $s = 2$, $s = 2.2$, $s = 4.1$, $s = 4.9$, $s = 9$. The difference is sometimes positive,
sometimes negative, sometimes zero.

is unfortunately too long and too difficult[5] to be given here. The intuition is that, *on average* (over the different possible market sizes s), the proportion $(m-1)(4/m^2 - 1/s)$ is larger than $(1 - n/s)$.

A larger expected joint profit in the absence of collusion implies that the expected profit *per producer* is also larger in the presence of cartel laws, or

$$\frac{E(\Pi_c)}{m-1} > \frac{E(\Pi_M)}{n},$$

since $m - 1 < n$.

---

[5] The difficulty of the proof stems from the fact that m and n (the numbers of entrants) are integers while s is continuous.

4   Cartel enforcement

In chapter 2, all players were perfectly informed of the choices made by all other players (at the end of each stage of the games considered). All players also knew the demand parameters and had the same cost parameters: there was 'complete' information. These strong assumptions are appropriate when the problem is to find out under what market structure it is profitable for a firm to be a member of a cartel. The firms' decision was to join or not to join. And this decision depended crucially, for a particular firm, on how many *other* firms decided not to join. To join implied sticking to the agreed quota or supplying *less*.

In this chapter, the internal functioning of a given cartel is studied. Now the problem arises to what extent cartel members may want to deviate from an agreement by selling *more* than their quota. Such a deviation is called 'cheating', because the deviation is profitable only if it can be done *secretly* to avoid immediate punishment. It is then necessary to suppose that information is imperfect. For the cartel to be viable, however, it must be possible to punish the cheater and to threaten the deviator with retaliation in a credible way. This in turn implies that the deviation must be detectable. Section 4.1 shows how a credible deterrent to individual cheating can be worked out.

Section 4.2 is devoted to collusion enforcement under perfect but incomplete information about the firms' cost parameters. This problem arises when the firms operate with different costs of production and are uncertain about the cost of their competitors. To work out a cartel agreement, an allocation of total industry production *and* of joint profits is to be found such that joint profits are maximised and such that cartel members stick to the agreement. This implies that production be carried out by the firms with the lowest cost, on the one hand, and that side-payments be made to less efficient firms, on the other hand. For this to be possible, individual costs must be truthfully revealed. We will discover that such a

47

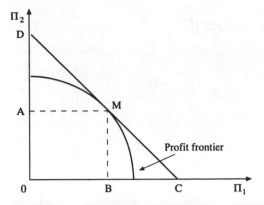

Figure 4.1 Joint profit maximisation

scheme works only when an industry comprises up to four firms. Selten's result, that four are few and six are many is thus reinforced.

Before we proceed, the implications of joint profit maximisation have to be clarified.

Joint profit maximisation

The aim of explicit collusion is to maximise the joint profit of the colluding firms, that is, the sum of their profits. When joint profit is maximised, it is not possible to increase the profit of one firm without reducing the profit of some other firm. (Indeed, away from the maximum, joint profit is smaller. If nevertheless one firm gets more, some other firm must get less.) The maximum joint profit must therefore be a point on the profit frontier, such as point M in figure 4.1, which represents the profits of two firms.

All points on the profit frontier[1] are, by definition, such that it is impossible to strictly increase the profits of all firms. In that (restricted) sense, these points are said to be Pareto optimal. Point M in addition is assumed to have the property that the joint profit is maximised. The other points on the profit frontier therefore are below the straight line DC, which represents the profit combinations that give the same joint profit as M. (To find DC, given point M, add OA to OB to find point C, and add OB to OA to find point D, so that OC = OD = OA + OB.) Obviously, the same maximum joint profit can be allocated very differently among the colluding firms. An agreement to collude in order to reach point M does not imply that there is agreement about the allocation of the joint profit among the

---

[1] The profit frontier is postulated to be concave. See Friedman (1972).

colluders. They may have to pool all profits and have these redistributed in order to reach some other point along DC.

4.1 Cartel enforcement with imperfect information

Firms that wish to maximise joint profits face (at least) three problems. First, although it is in their common interest to do so (i.e., to reach point M), each firm has an individual interest to cheat (i.e., to secretly deviate from point M in the direction that increases its individual profit). This is the well-known 'prisoner's dilemma'. Second, a way must be found to deter cheating. Third, the implementation of a deterring mechanism requires information about the actual behaviour of the colluding firms. The conclusion will be that perfect information on the actual behaviour of the partners is a condition sine qua non for the agreement to be operational. We consider each problem in turn.

A prisoner's dilemma

Consider an agreement to maximise joint profits at M. Each member of the agreement could increase his individual profit by secretly deviating from it (moving away from it along the profit frontier). However, if all were to do so, they would end up at a point below the profit frontier, so that all would make smaller profits! This is clearly a situation that can be described as a prisoner's dilemma. Shubik (1982, p. 254) formulates its usual verbal scenario as follows:

Two prisoners who are suspected of having committed a crime are interrogated separately by the police. If both maintain silence, at most they can be booked on a minor charge. Each is encouraged to incriminate the other with a promise of leniency if he is not himself incriminated. If they double-cross each other, they are both in trouble.

Osborne (1976) illustrates the dilemma as follows (in the quantity domain). Instead of measuring profits on the axes, let us use the quantities produced and let q_i^0 ($i = 1,2$) be the production quotas agreed on, so that they correspond to a point O on the contract curve in figure 4.2. This point implies tangency of two isoprofit curves and may or may not maximise joint profits. (It is clear, though, that the corresponding profits must be on the profit frontier.)

Notice that the profit realised by firm i is higher along the isoprofit curve Π_i^1 than along the curve Π_i^2, along the curve Π_i^2 than along Π_i^3 and so on, because each of these curves corresponds to a higher production of the other firm for any value of q_i. Let $F_i(q_1^0, q_2^0)$ be the profit of firm i at point O. Clearly

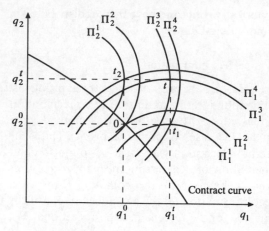

Figure 4.2 A prisoner's dilemma

$$\frac{\partial F_i(q_1^0, q_2^0)}{\partial q_i} > 0. \tag{4.1}$$

Each firm can increase its profit by producing more than its quota q_1^0.

Second, a comparison of points[2] t_1 and t_2 with point O shows that

$$F_1(q_1^t, q_2^0) > F_1(q_1^0, q_2^0) \tag{4.2}$$

for firm 1, because t_1 is on Π_1^1 and O is on Π_1^2, and

$$F_2(q_1^0, q_2^t) > F_2(q_1^0, q_2^0) \tag{4.3}$$

for firm 2, because t_2 is on Π_2^1 while O is on Π_2^2. In words: if firm i expects its competitor to stick to its quota q_j^0, firm i can increase its profit by producing q_i^t instead of q_i^0. It is profitable to cheat, if one expects the other not to cheat.

Third, compare point t with point O. This amounts to considering that each competitor expects the other to observe the quota they agreed on, so both end up cheating. Then

$$F_1(q_1^0, q_2^0) > F_1(q_1^t, q_2^t) \tag{4.4}$$

and

$$F_2(q_1^0, q_2^0) > F_2(q_1^t, q_2^t). \tag{4.5}$$

Both make less profits when they both cheat than if they had both refrained from cheating.

---

[2] Point t_1 gives the highest profit if firm 1 deviates from point O, because it is located on the isoprofit curve with the highest profit. Similarly for t_2.

Nevertheless, if the other cheats, it is better for each firm also to cheat than to observe the quota! On comparing point t with point t_2, one finds that, for firm 1

$$F_1(q_1', q_2') > F_1(q_1^0, q_2'). \tag{4.6}$$

Similarly, a comparison of points t and t_1 gives, for firm 2

$$F_2(q_1', q_2') > F_2(q_1', q_2^0) \tag{4.7}$$

because t is on Π_2^3 and t_1 is on Π_2^4. The conclusion is that, whether the other cheats or not, cheating dominates observing the quota for any particular firm.

The situation can also be described as a game in which each of, say, two players has two strategies (observe the agreement or cheat) and the profits are the payoffs. The following payoff matrix, with conveniently chosen numbers (representing each firm's profit for a given pair of strategies), illustrates points O, t_2, t_1, and t numerically. The profits of firm 1 are in the upper-left corners. The profits of firm 2 are in the lower-right corners.

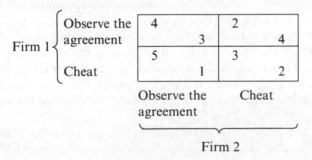

Whether member 2 cheats or not, member 1 prefers to cheat, because cheating gives the highest profit (5 or 3). Whether member 1 cheats or not, member 2 prefers to cheat, because that strategy gives the highest profit (4 or 2). When both cheat, both lose (they get only 3 and 2, respectively), while they would have made 4 and 3, respectively, if they had both observed the agreement. The strategy pair (cheat, cheat) is off the profit frontier, because both profits could be increased by shifting to another strategy pair. In this sense, it is said to be Pareto dominated. The other three strategy pairs are on the profit frontier (or Pareto optimal), because one profit cannot be increased without decreasing the other firm's profit. Since the pair (cheat, cheat) is inside the profit frontier, it could be a Cournot–Nash equilibrium. In the three Pareto-optimal pairs, at least one firm refrains from using a more profitable strategy (cheating).

How to deter cheating?

Is there a way out of the dilemma? A dilemma is a dilemma, and cannot have a solution. Yet, in real life, collusive agreements sometimes are successful, in the sense that they are not only signed but also enforced over several years. Firms thus seem to find a way out.

Pooling of revenues in order to make interfirm compensations may be one of those ways. This amounts to making side-payments, i.e., to redistributing the joint profit $4 + 3 = 7$ obtained in the payoff matrix when both observe the agreement. Perhaps member 2 would refrain from cheating (cheating gives an additional profit of $4 - 3 = 1$ or $2 - 1 = 1$) if he or she were offered a 50–50 redistribution (each would get 3, 5) or some analogous split of the joint profit. And similarly for member 1, for whom cheating also brings in an additional $5 - 4 = 1$ or $3 - 2 = 1$. However, member 1 is somehow capable of making more profits than member 2, so 50–50 may not be acceptable, and so on.

This kind of profit-sharing agreement, on top of an agreement on production quotas, was long thought to be the only means by which cartels could survive.[3] Since it is difficult to negotiate, cartels should not have a long life. Yet, Osborne (1976) observed that the OPEC cartel of oil-producing countries was created in October 1973 and was still very powerful three years later. In 1983 OPEC saw its share of the world oil market reduced drastically and internal disagreements were more and more frequent (cheating occurs more and more frequently). Yet, it still very much existed and continued to have a strong stabilising[4] influence on the world oil price.

Osborne then goes on to show that the dilemma can be 'solved' or overcome without pooling of revenues if each firm is assigned an operating rule incorporating a deterrent to cheating which keeps all firms at the joint profit maximising point. This 'best reply' rule to cheating is for the loyal firms to increase output in the same proportion as the cheaters increase theirs.

To understand this, one has to know how to find the vector (q_1^0, q_2^0) that maximises joint profit. Osborne shows that it corresponds to that tangency point of two isoprofit curves (on the contract curve) at which the tangent $L(q^0)$ to these two curves passes through the origin. (This is generally not a 45° line, of course.) Along this line, market shares are constant because q_2/q_1 is constant (see figure 4.3).

---

[3] See Patinkin (1947), Fellner (1960) and section 4.2.

[4] Why and in what sense OPEC tries to stabilise the world oil price can be explained with reference to a model proposed by Hotelling. See Phlips (1983, chapter 7).

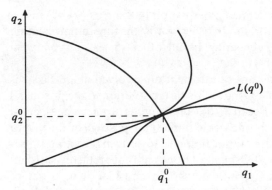

Figure 4.3 The joint profit-maximising quantities

The idea is then to make sure that each firm is kept on the tangent $L(q^0)$ and has an incentive to stay at point (q_1^0, q_2^0). Let

$$s_i^0 = \frac{q_i^0}{\sum_{j=1}^{n} q_j^0}$$

be the market share of firm i at that point, when there are n cartel members. Then it suffices for the cartel to assign to each of its members the rule

$$\max \left\{ q_i^0, q_i^0 + \frac{s_i^0}{s_j^0} \Delta q_j \right\} \tag{4.8}$$

when the production of member j deviates from his quota q_j^0 by Δq_j. Then the vector of productions moves in such a way that each member keeps his or her market share.

This is a deterrent to cheating, because member j will not cheat when he knows that the others will follow this rule. Indeed, cheating would then put him on a point above (q_1^0, q_2^0) on $L(q^0)$ where his profit is smaller (remember, from figure 4.2, how the isoprofit curves are positioned). And it is a credible deterrent, because with n of these rules operating simultaneously, nobody can normally[5] win by deviating unilaterally from these rules. For example, if member i were to stay at q_i^0 when j moves to $q_j^0 + \Delta q_j$, she would lose more, according to equations (4.6) and (4.7), than if she applied the rule. When these rules are interpreted as strategies, we thus see

---

[5] Holahan (1978) has shown that following rule (4.8) may leave loyal members worse off if sufficiently large differences exist between the profit functions of loyalists and cheaters. Rothschild (1981) identifies conditions under which loyal firms are worse off than they would have been if they had stood pat, even when all firms have identical profit functions.

that the vector of strategies defined by equation (4.8) turns (q_1^0, q_2^0) into a non-cooperative Nash equilibrium. In other words, the threat that cheating by one member will lead to cheating by all others gives everybody an incentive not to cheat.

Before considering the amount of information involved in all this, it is important to ask in what sense Osborne's rule is a solution to the prisoner's dilemma as defined earlier. Because that dilemma occurs in a one-period game by definition, while Osborne's rule implies the passage of time, with some cheaters increasing their output first and loyal firms reacting subsequently, it should be clear that Osborne's rule is not theoretically satisfactory. A rigorous theoretical treatment should consider it as a set of strategies in a game that is played over several time periods. Section 6.1 will show how this can be done for an alternative set of strategies (according to which, if one cheats, all will jump to a Cournot–Nash equilibrium). May it suffice to stress the dynamic nature of the problem for the time being. Going through Osborne's analysis had the advantage of clarifying the economics involved and provides a better understanding of the solution of a truly dynamic game.

Cheating and imperfect information

An implicit assumption in the discussion of Osborne's rule (4.8) should now be made explicit: This rule works only if cheating is detected. Only under that condition can the rule be said to deter cheating. For if cheating goes undetected, the n strategies (4.8) cease to be a Nash equilibrium, because the threat that others will retaliate ceases to be credible.

Stigler (1964) discusses different ways by which a cartel member can detect price cutting by other members, the basic method of detection being the fact that the cheater is getting business he or she would otherwise not obtain. One method is to check whether one is losing more old customers than is statistically probable. Another method is to verify whether the suspected cheater is not keeping more customers than is statistically justified. A third method[6] is to watch the number of new customers attracted by a competitor. Though interesting, these methods are not directly relevant in the present context. First, we have been considering Cournot strategies, that is, firms determining their rates of production while the price is determined by the market. Second, Stigler's methods do not reveal the identity of the cheater with certainty.

Osborne therefore discusses the information structure in terms of individual quantities produced. The information structure required for his

---

[6] The model constructed by Rees (1985) is based on this method.

operating rule to be totally effective would be one of perfect information about the production rates of each cartel member. In a real-life situation, information is often less perfect. Consider the realistic case where the cartel knows the total production of its members, taken together, but has no way of knowing the output of individual members. A second-best solution, that will have some deterrent effect, is then to suppose that the cheater has the average quota share and to tell the cartel member to produce

$$\max \left\{ q_i^0, q_i^0 + \frac{s_i}{1/n} \Delta q \right\} = \max\{q_i^0, q_i^0 + n s_i \Delta q\} \qquad (4.8a)$$

where Δq is the deviation of total output from $\sum_{i=1}^{n} q_i^0$ (total output under joint profit maximisation). This rule will deter cheating on the average, because it keeps the *expected* output vector on $L(q^0)$. A drawback is that it will not deter cheating by a member with a particularly small quota who could increase its market share enough to overmatch the price depressing effect of the greater cartel output. Clearly, the more market shares are equal, the better rule (4.8a) will work. But it cannot be more than a second-best solution.

Even worse, from the cartel point of view, is a third situation where it knows total industry output only, not the total output of the cartel. A fourth case is when it does not even know total industry output. In both cases explicit collusion is doomed to failure. Such situations can arise in the case of international agreements such as OPEC, which appears to be in the third situation.

In 1976, Osborne (pp. 842–3) wrote down the following scenario, describing what might happen to OPEC. Today that prediction appears as a very realistic description of what actually happened to oil prices:

With only the shortest of lags, world shipments of crude oil are known by all interested parties. The information is collected and reported by trade journals and various national and international agencies, and could in any case be inferred from a number of sources (for example, tanker charterings). All producers know their current market shares to a high degree of accuracy, and can thus learn if someone is cheating; they cannot so easily learn who is cheating. The members are sovereign states; they can attempt to keep their sales statistics secret if they wish. And some important producers (for example, Mexico) remain outside the cartel. OPEC thus finds itself in the third of the four positions. The likely consequences are a matter for speculation, but the following events are possible.

An increase in world shipments reduces the market shares of the loyal members who, however, cannot detect its source. If they assume the source to be external and remain at x_i^0 [i.e., q_i^0], they will, in effect, demonstrate the profitability of cheating; those loyal to the cartel will then secretly increase their output. On the other hand, if the loyal members assume the source to be internal and obey their quota rules (however modified), they will risk a needless increase in cartel output. With either choice the additional cartel output, added to the original increase from the unknown source, reduces prices. Distrust grows. Discipline weakens generally, and can be expected ultimately to disappear. Each member must look out for himself. Plenty of business can be done at a dollar under the cartel price; but it must be done quickly, for the buyers are daily demanding better terms. There is a general scurry for orders, and long-term commitments are made at $1, then $2, then $5 and $6 under the cartel price. The cartel has collapsed.

The antitrust implications are clear. Public policy must place firms in a situation where they do not know each other's output and refrain from publishing individual output statistics. In a similar vein, consuming nations facing an international cartel such as OPEC should refrain from establishing a central purchasing agency (through which all orders are funnelled) in order to present a 'united front'. Such an agency would strengthen the cartel, since sellers will be identified and undetected cheating would become impossible.

4.2 Cartel enforcement with incomplete information

In his seminal 1985 paper, Roberts noted that the problem of detecting cheating in a situation of imperfect information (which he calls 'moral hazard') has to be distinguished from problems of incomplete information (or 'adverse selection') which arise[7] when firms have private information on some parameter of their profit functions, for example their cost of production, but are not sure about the corresponding parameters of their competitors.

If there was no such uncertainty, firms could work out a cartel agreement even if they cannot observe their competitors' production (see chapter 2): there is no need for direct communication. With incomplete information, 'attention must focus on the fact that if the implementation of a cartel rule depends upon the use of information private to one firm, that firm must be given an incentive to correctly reveal the information' (Roberts 1985, pp. 402–3).

Duopoly

Roberts considers two firms who have one of two possible (constant) marginal costs, high or low. In other words, each firm can be of one of two 'types': high-cost or low-cost. Ignoring the issue of side-payments in a first approach, he finds that monopoly collusion cannot be achieved if the firm

---

[7] On moral hazard and adverse selection, see Phlips (1988b, chapter 3).

types are sufficiently similar, because then the incentive constraint (that a low-cost firm must not prefer to misreport itself as being high-cost) is binding, so that the joint profit-maximising solution cannot be reached.

Side-payments increase the set of opportunities available to the colluding firms, since the sharing out of profits can be divorced from production decisions. The cartel agreement becomes a combination of production quotas and side-payments to make or receive. The latter have, in addition, the role of an incentive device, since the sharing out of profits depends upon what a firm reports. Conceptually, the cartel functions like an auction.[8] Production should be undertaken by the low-cost firm and this can be ensured by allowing the firms to bid for the right to produce. Side-payments correspond to such bids when the auction is a second-price (Vickrey) auction where the highest bidder wins but only pays the second highest price. The bids are final commitments: no recontracting is possible. In such a scheme, a collusive outcome with truthful reporting is possible.

Kihlstrom and Vives (1989) work this out in full detail for the relatively easy duopoly case. Going through this analysis is helpful for a better understanding of the more interesting case where there are more than two firms, possibly many, so that the question raised in chapter 2 whether five is still a critical number (below which four is 'few' and above which six is 'many') can be reconsidered.

So let there be two firms. Firm i knows its marginal cost c_i, which is unknown to the other firm. (This cost is constant, so that the question whether merging – to exploit economies of scale – is not a better policy than colluding is ignored.) Each firm knows that the other firm's marginal cost can take one of two possible values, θ_1 or θ_2, with $\theta_1 < \theta_2$. $\tilde{c} = (\tilde{c}_1, \tilde{c}_2)$ is the vector of random marginal costs of firms 1 and 2, which are identically and independently distributed. This does *not* mean that one firm is low-cost and the other firm is high-cost. It does mean that the following four possibilities arise:

$$\tilde{c} = (\theta_1, \theta_2)$$
$$\tilde{c} = (\theta_2, \theta_1)$$
$$\tilde{c} = (\theta_1, \theta_1)$$
$$\tilde{c} = (\theta_2, \theta_2).$$

The distribution of $\tilde{c}_i$, which is common knowledge, is

$$\mu = (\mu_1, \mu_2)$$

which means that μ_1 is the probability that $\tilde{c}_i = \theta_1$ and μ_2 is the probability that $\tilde{c}_i = \theta_2$. The inverse market demand function is $p(Q)$ where p is the price

---

[8] A summary of auction theory can be found in Phlips (1988b, chapter 4).

of the homogeneous good produced by the two firms and $Q = q_1 + q_2$ is total output.

The two firms attempt to form a cartel with the aid of a cartel manager to whom they report their marginal costs. The cartel manager announces and implements a rule for allocating total output and making side-payments, that is, announces the pair

$$\langle q, s \rangle$$

where $q = (q_1, q_2)$ is the vector of output quotas allocated to firms 1 and 2 and $s = (s_1, s_2)$ is the vector of side-payments to be *received* by firms 1 and 2. These side-payments must satisfy

$$s_1(c) + s_2(c) \leq 0 \tag{4.9}$$

where $c = (c_1, c_2)$ is any vector of marginal costs reported to the cartel manager. (The payment received (a positive number) by one firm cannot be larger than the amount contributed by the other firm, so the sum of the two cannot be positive.) The pair $\langle q, s \rangle$ is called the cartel contract.

Knowing the cartel contract announced by the cartel manager, the firms decide what to report as their marginal costs. Their strategies are therefore cost reports and the strategy set is $\{\theta_1, \theta_2\}$ since both firms know that these are the only two possible values. (In this way a game with incomplete information is transformed into a game with complete information on the distribution of two values.) A specific report is denoted c_i^*.

The objective function of firm i ($i = 1,2$) can now be written as

$$\Pi_i(c_i, c^*) = [p(Q(c^*)) - c_i]q_i(c^*) + s_i(c^*)$$

where $Q(c^*) = q_1(c^*) + q_2(c^*)$, c^* is the vector of costs reported by the two firms and c_i is the true cost of firm i. Firm i will reveal its true cost if

$$E\Pi_i(c_i, (c_i, \tilde{c}_j)) \geq E\Pi_i(c_i^*, (c_i, \tilde{c}_j)) \tag{4.10}$$

for *both* possible reports c_i^* and for *both* possible true marginal costs c_i.

Equation (4.10) is the *incentive compatibility* constraint. It induces firms to reveal their marginal costs when they know that their cost report will be used to implement the production allocation. The problem is whether it is possible for the cartel manager to find a cartel contract that maximises the joint (or monopoly) profit and induces the firms to reveal their costs truthfully. The answer is yes: in this simple duopoly case, there always exists a vector of side-payments such that firms will reveal their true costs when they know that their cost reports will be used to implement the joint profit-maximising output allocation.

Before proceeding with the proof, Kihlstrom and Vives (1989) consider a situation with complete cost information, so that the constraint (4.10) can be ignored. The cartel contract would be simple: all output is allocated to the firm with the lowest marginal cost $\underline{c} = \min\{c_1, c_2\}$ and is equal to the quantity that maximises the monopoly profit for this firm, that is

$$\hat{q}_i = q^M(\underline{c}) = \arg\max_q [p(q) - \underline{c}]q \quad \text{if } c_i = \underline{c}.$$

The other firm produces nothing. The total monopoly profit is

$$\Pi^M(\underline{c}) = [p(q^M(\underline{c})) - \underline{c}]q^M(\underline{c}).$$

Note also that if firm i had a cost c_i but reported $\underline{c}$ instead and was instructed by the cartel manager to produce $q^M(\underline{c})$, its profits would be

$$\Pi_i(\underline{c}, c_i) = [p(q^M(\underline{c})) - c_i]q^M(\underline{c}) = \Pi^M(\underline{c}) + (\underline{c} - c_i)q^M(\underline{c}) \quad (4.11)$$

where $(\underline{c} - c_i) < 0$.

We are now well equipped to show that the allocation of production $\hat{q} = (q^M(\underline{c}), 0)$ between the two firms can always be implemented because there exists a side-payment function $\hat{s}(c)$ such that the cartel contract $\langle \hat{q}(\cdot), \hat{s}(\cdot) \rangle$ is incentive compatible, so that truthful revelation is an equilibrium strategy.

The function $\hat{s}(c)$ is defined as follows. Let $\bar{s} \geq 0$ be the side-payment received (by the high-cost firm) and $-\bar{s}$ the payment made (by the low-cost firm). Then

$$\hat{s}_i(c) = \begin{cases} -\bar{s} & \text{if } c_i = \theta_1 \text{ and } c_j = \theta_2 \\ \bar{s} & \text{if } c_i = \theta_2 \text{ and } c_j = \theta_1 \\ 0 & \text{otherwise,} \end{cases}$$

that is, the low-cost firm which is instructed to produce pays $\bar{s}$ to the high-cost firm which is instructed not to produce, if the firms have different costs. If they have the same marginal costs, there are no side-payments.

Consider a *low-cost* firm. So let $c_i = \theta_1$. What side-payment will induce firm i to reveal that it is low-cost? In other words, what is the *largest* payment it is willing to make to the other firm (which could be also low-cost)? We must compare i's expected profit when it reveals its true cost and when it does not.

If i reports truthfully θ_1, or $c_i^* = \theta_1$, the other firm j is either high-cost or low-cost. If it is high-cost and reveals it, then i is the sole producer, earns $\Pi^M(\theta_1)$ and pays $\bar{s}$. If j is low-cost and reveals it, then they each produce $q^M/2$, earn $\Pi^M(\theta_1)/2$ and make no side-payments. However, i doesn't know c_j! Suppose i expects j to reveal the true c_j. Then i's expected profit is

$$E\hat{\Pi}(c_i, (c_i^*, \tilde{c}_j)) = (\Pi^M(\theta_1) - \bar{s})\mu_2 + \frac{\Pi^M(\theta_1)}{2}\mu_1$$

$$= \Pi^M(\theta_1)\left(\frac{\mu_1}{2} + \mu_2\right) - \bar{s}\mu_2.$$

(4.12)

On the other hand, if i untruthfully reports $c_i^* = \theta_2$, the other firm can again be high-cost or low-cost. If j reveals that it is high-cost, both appear to have the same high cost. They each produce half the monopoly output $q^M/2$ and there are no side-payments. Firm i earns $[\Pi^M(\theta_2) + (\theta_2 - \theta_1)q^M(\theta_2)]/2$ in accordance with equation (4.11). Alternatively, if j reveals that it is low-cost, then it is the sole producer and i receives $\bar{s}$. Again, i doesn't know c_j. When i expects j to reveal its true c_j, then i's expected income is

$$E\hat{\Pi}(c_i,(c_i^*,\tilde{c}_j)) = [\Pi^M(\theta_2) + (\theta_2 - \theta_1)q^M(\theta_2)]\frac{\mu_2}{2} + \bar{s}\mu_1. \qquad (4.13)$$

The incentive compatibility constraint (4.10) is satisfied if the expected profit under truthful reporting, defined by (4.12), is larger than its expected profit with untruthful reporting, defined by (4.13). The cartel contract is incentive compatible (so that i will report that it is low-cost) if

$$E\Pi^M(\theta_1)\left(\frac{\mu_1}{2} + \mu_2\right) - \bar{s}(\mu_2) \geq [\Pi^M(\theta_2) + (\theta_2 - \theta_1)q^M(\theta_2)]\frac{\mu_2}{2} + \bar{s}\mu_1.$$

$$(4.14)$$

This equation can be rewritten as

$$E\Pi^M(\theta_1)\left(\frac{\mu_1}{2} + \mu_2\right) - [\Pi^M(\theta_2) + (\theta_2 - \theta_1)q^M(\theta_2)]\frac{\mu_2}{2} \geq \bar{s}(\mu_1 + \mu_2) = \bar{s}.$$

$$(4.15)$$

The left-hand side of equation (4.15) is the *largest* payment a low-cost firm is willing to make when it reveals that it is low-cost. Call this payment $\bar{f}$.

By a similar reasoning, Kihlstrom and Vives (1989) show that a *high-cost* firm will reveal this if it receives at least

$$\underline{f} = [\Pi^M(\theta_1) + (\theta_1 - \theta_2)q^M(\theta_1)]\left(\frac{\mu_1}{2} + \mu_2\right) - \Pi^M(\theta_2)\frac{\mu_1}{2}. \qquad (4.16)$$

The cartel contract must therefore stipulate a side-payment $\bar{s}$ such that

$$\bar{f} \geq \bar{s} \geq \underline{f}.$$

For this to be possible, it suffices to show that $\bar{f} > \underline{f}$. This is indeed the case, since

$$\bar{f} - \underline{f} = (\theta_2 - \theta_1)\{[q^M(\theta_1) - q^M(\theta_2)]\mu_2 + q^M(\theta_1)\}/2 > 0,$$

because $\theta_2 > \theta_1$ and because $\theta_2 > \theta_1$ implies that $q^M(\theta_1) > q^M(\theta_2)$.

After this discussion of incentive compatibility, Kihlstrom and Vives go on to discuss *individual rationality*. This requires that a low-cost firm will cooperate, that is, accept to pay the side-payment or share the monopoly profit with another low-cost firm, only if it cannot make higher profits by staying out of the cartel. The maximum payment makes it indifferent between staying in or not. For a high-cost firm, the individual rationality condition requires that it will cooperate, that is, accept not to produce or share the monopoly profits with another high-cost firm, only if it cannot make higher profits by staying out. The minimum payment to receive makes it indifferent between staying in or not. This constraint can always be satisfied, since it turns out that the maximum payment that makes the low-cost firm indifferent is larger than the minimum payment that makes the high-cost firm indifferent. We shall go into more details about individual rationality in the case where there are more than two firms: there the situation will be more complicated.

All I want to do here is to draw attention to a distinction between 'interim' and '*ex post*' individual rationality. When a cartel contract is signed before the cost of the competitor(s) is revealed, this contract is said to be 'interim individually rational'. This is the appropriate concept for the study of a legally enforceable contract from which the parties cannot withdraw. It is the concept used in what precedes. To the contrary, a contract is '*ex post* individually rational' when firms cannot be prevented from withdrawing from the contract after the true costs are revealed. This is the case in a legal environment where cartel contracts are illegal and therefore void. In such a situation, *ex post* individual rationality has to be imposed in addition to interim individual rationality if each duopolist is to adhere to the agreement. This may remain possible but it is also possible that the two constraints conflict with each other.

More than two firms with a continuum of types

To study the case where there are more than two firms, Cramton and Palfrey (1990) use the same general approach as the one used in the duopoly case, but with important modifications. A *continuum of types* is now introduced, with the result that, while firm i knows c_i privately, the other firms know that the private cost parameter of firm i is drawn independently from a continuous distribution F with positive density f on $[\underline{c}, \bar{c}]$ with $\bar{c} \leq a$, where a is the intercept of the inverse market demand function $p(q)$

$$= a - \sum_{i=1}^{n} q_i, \quad q = (q_i, ..., n) \text{ and } i \in N = (1, ..., n). \text{ The form of the market}$$

demand function, the cost functions and the distribution F are common knowledge. We also have $c = (c_1, ..., c_n)$ and $r(c) = (r_1(c), ..., r_n(c))$, r_i being firm i's share of the industry revenue from producing q_i. These shares include the (positive or negative) side-payments and must satisfy

$$\sum_{i=1}^{n} r_i(c) = \left[a - \sum_{i=1}^{n} q_i(c) \right] \sum_{i=1}^{n} q_i(c) \qquad (4.17)$$

for all possible values of c_i between $\underline{c}$ and $\bar{c}$ for all $i = 1, \ldots, n$. In words, the sum of the revenue shares must equal total industry revenue. The cartel contract is now a pair $\langle q, r \rangle$.

Ex post profits are $r_i - c_i q_i$. Expected production,[9] when firm i announces c_i, is $\bar{q}_i(c_i)$ and expected revenue is $\bar{r}(c_i)$. The firms maximise their expected profit $\bar{\Pi}_i(c_i) = \bar{r}_i(c_i) - c_i \bar{q}_i(c_i)$. The cartel contract is *incentive compatible* if all types of all firms want to report their private information truthfully, that is

$$\bar{\Pi}_i(c_i) \geq \bar{r}_i(v) - c \bar{q}_i(v)$$

for all firms i and for all values of c_i and v between $\underline{c}$ and $\bar{c}$.

To define *individual rationality*, it is necessary to consider what happens to a cartel agreement when one firm defects. In what follows I consider only the case[10] where (a) defection by one firm leads to the complete breakdown of the cartel, which is another way of saying that unanimous interim consent is required and (b) the breakdown implies that all firms choose the Cournot–Nash equilibrium. Under these two assumptions, the cartel $\langle q, r \rangle$ is individually rational if

$$\bar{\Pi}_i(c_i) \geq \bar{\Pi}_i^c(c_i)$$

for *all* firms and all values of c_i. $\bar{\Pi}_i^c(c_i)$ is the expected profit at the Cournot–Nash equilibrium.

Checking individual rationality was easy with two firms and only two types. With n firms and a continuum of types, one has to verify whether the *worst-off* type prefers the expected cartel profit to the expected Cournot–Nash equilibrium.

With constant marginal costs, efficiency requires that the lowest-cost firm produces the monopoly output and that all other firms produce nothing. The monopoly output is $(a - c)/2$ in this linear world. The expected monopoly quantity is $\bar{q}^M(c) = \left(\dfrac{a - c}{2} \right)[1 - F(c)]^{n-1}$, since $[1 - F(c)]^{n-1}$ is the probability that a firm with cost c has the lowest cost.

Can such an efficient cartel be incentive compatible and individually rational, when defection leads to the Cournot–Nash equilibrium? To simplify the presentation as much as possible, let the distribution of types be

---

[9] The expectation is taken over the possible costs of the other firms.
[10] A general treatment is to be found in Cramton and Palfrey (1990). It is too technical to be presented here.

uniform, so that $F(v) = v$ and the density $f(v) = \dfrac{dF}{dv} = 1$, and put the intercept of the demand function a equal to 1. Suppose also that the cartel is symmetric, so that the expected productions and revenues are equal among firms. (Supposing asymmetry gives no new insights.) Suppose finally that firms' costs are uniformly distributed between 0 and 1. Then the monopoly output is $(1 - c)/2$ and the *ex post* monopoly profit is

$$\Pi^M(c) = \left(1 - \frac{1-c}{2} - c\right)\left(\frac{1-c}{2}\right) = \frac{(1-c)^2}{4}$$

for a firm with cost c.

Let us start with incentive compatibility and use the general result[11] that *in a symmetric, ex post efficient, incentive compatible cartel, the expected profit (and revenue) to the highest-cost firm (with $\bar{c} = 1$) is an equal share of the expected industry profit if the second most profitable firm were to produce its monopoly output.* Indeed

$$\bar{\Pi}^M(1) = \bar{r}^M(1) = \int_0^1 \frac{1}{4}(1-v)^2[(n-1)v(1-v)^{n-2}]dv > 0 \tag{4.18}$$

implying profits for a firm with cost c of

$$\bar{\Pi}^M(c) = \Pi^M(1) + \int_c^1 \bar{q}^M(v)dv. \tag{4.19}$$

The integral in (4.18) is an equal share of the expected monopoly profit if the *second* most profitable firm were the only one to produce, since $n(n-1)v(1-v)^{n-2}$ is the probability that a firm with a cost v has the second-lowest cost under the assumptions made. In (4.18) this expression is divided by n. Equation (4.19) says that all lower-cost firms must be paid strictly more than the highest-cost firm.

There is, again, an analogy with the auction literature. Suppose that the firms in our industry are bidding for the right to be the monopolist. The value of this right is $v_i = (1 - c_i)^2/4$ for a firm with cost c_i. In an efficient equilibrium of a private value auction, the total expected surplus is $E[v_1]$ and the expected profit for the winning bidder is $E[v_1 - v_2]$ where v_k is the kth order statistic of the n values v_i. The remaining profit $E[v_2]$ is split equally among the n firms.

[11] See lemma 4 in Cramton and Palfrey (1990).

Equations (4.18) and (4.19) suggest that it becomes more and more difficult to combine incentive compatibility with efficiency as the number of firms grows. Indeed, when n gets larger the integral in (4.18) converges to an equal share of what the expected monopoly profit would be if the lowest-cost firm were to produce the monopoly profit. This is what the highest-cost firm will tend to get. However, equation (4.19) says that all lower-cost firms must receive even more: at some point not enough money will be available given the budget constraint (4.17).

Solving the integrals in equations (4.18) and (4.19) gives

$$\bar{\Pi}^M(c) = \frac{n-1}{4(n+1)(n+2)} + \frac{(1-c)^{n+1}}{2(n+1)}. \tag{4.20}$$

The next step is to impose (interim) individual rationality with the Cournot–Nash equilibrium as the reference point. In a Cournot game, firm i's profit is

$$\bar{\Pi}^c(c_i) = [1 - (n-1)\bar{q} - \bar{q}_i]\bar{q}_i - c_i\bar{q}_i$$
$$= (\tilde{c} - c_i - \bar{q}_i)\bar{q}_i$$

where the expected production $\bar{q}$ is treated as given for the other firms and

$$\tilde{c} = 1 - (n-1)\bar{q}.$$

Maximisation of $\bar{\Pi}^c(c_i)$ with respect to $\bar{q}_i$ gives

$$\bar{q}_i = \frac{1}{2}(\tilde{c} - c_i) > 0 \text{ for } c_i < \tilde{c}.$$

In equilibrium

$$\bar{\Pi}^c(c) = \left[\tilde{c} - c - \frac{1}{2}(\tilde{c} - c)\right]\left(\frac{\tilde{c} - c}{2}\right) = \frac{1}{4}(\tilde{c} - c)^2 \tag{4.21}$$

for a firm with cost $c < \tilde{c}$.

Let the worst-off type of firm have a cost $\hat{c}$. For this type to be indifferent between staying in and defecting, its expected production as a cartel member $\frac{1}{2}(1 - \hat{c})(1 - \hat{c})^{n-1} = \frac{1}{2}(1 - \hat{c})^n$ must be equal to its expected production in a Cournot–Nash equilibrium $\frac{1}{2}(\tilde{c} - \hat{c})$, according to lemma 2 of Cramton and Palfrey (1990). Consequently, $\hat{c}$ can be computed by finding the first positive root of the equation

$$\frac{1}{2}(1 - \hat{c})^n = \frac{1}{2}(\tilde{c} - \hat{c}). \tag{4.22}$$

Table 4.1. *Numerical calculations with* $a = 1$ *and* $F(v) = v$

n	2	4	8	16
$\hat{c}$	0.21995	0.15371	0.10290	0.06629
$\tilde{c}$	0.82843	0.66667	0.52241	0.40000
Ex ante *industry quantity*				
Cartel	0.33333	0.40000	0.44444	0.47059
Cournot	0.34315	0.44444	0.54582	0.64000
Ex ante *industry profit*				
Cartel	0.12500	0.16667	0.20000	0.22222
Cournot	0.09476	0.09877	0.09505	0.08533
n times net payoff of cartel for worst-off type				
	0.01476	0.01052	-0.02916	-0.10273
Proportion of firms who prefer cartel to Cournot competition				
	1.00000	1.00000	0.85005	0.83898

Source: Cramton and Palfrey (1990, table 1).

An incentive compatible cartel is individually rational if this worst-off type of firm prefers to stay in the cartel, that is, if

$$\bar{\Pi}^M(\hat{c}) \geq \bar{\Pi}^c(\hat{c})$$

or, using (4.20) and (4.21), if

$$\frac{n-1}{4(n+1)(n+2)} + \frac{(1-\hat{c})^{n+1}}{2(n+1)} \geq \frac{1}{4}(\tilde{c} - \hat{c})^2, \tag{4.23}$$

c being replaced by $\hat{c}$. It remains to find $\tilde{c}$, which is implicitly defined by

$$\tilde{c} = 1 - (n-1)\bar{q} = 1 - \left(\frac{n-1}{2}\right)\int_0^{\tilde{c}} v\,dv.$$

The solution is

$$\tilde{c} = \frac{2}{\sqrt{n+1}}. \tag{4.24}$$

Table 4.1 shows how the values of $\hat{c}$, $\tilde{c}$ and the expected outcomes with an efficient incentive compatible cartel and Cournot competition change when the number of firms n increases from two to four, eight and sixteen respectively. It also shows how the net payoff for the worst-off type, $\bar{\Pi}^M(\hat{c}) - \bar{\Pi}^c(\hat{c})$, decreases with n. As long as this net payoff is positive, all firms are better off joining the cartel than defecting and the cartel contract is individually rational. As soon as this net payoff becomes negative, the cartel ceases to be enforceable, since some firms will prefer to defect (see the last row of the table).

Selten's result, that four are few and six are many (see chapter 2), is reinforced: with incomplete information about firm specific costs, the monopoly outcome is enforceable if and only if $n \leq 5$!

A final remark: Cramton and Palfrey (1990) also show that if the uncertainty is about a *common* cost, so that all firms are equally efficient, the cartel problem is simply to determine aggregate production on the basis of the information reported by its members about their common cost. All members then produce an equal share of that total. With such an agreement, a *large* cartel can successfully attain the monopoly solution. The distinction between firm-specific or 'private' costs and 'common' costs is therefore an important one.

4.3 Cartels in public procurement markets[12]

A specific interest in public procurement markets results from a peculiar situation that might and does arise in some of these markets. When the public sector acts as a buyer in a specific industry, and faces a supply side made up of a small number of firms, the resulting interaction can be described as one between a group of oligopolists and a very special buyer. The interest for this particular trade relation arises when the public sector itself represents the biggest buyer in the market, covering a large share of market demand. In such a situation, the resulting market interaction becomes even more peculiar. In a game-theoretic setting this case has to be modelled as the strategic interaction between a limited number of firms (an oligopoly) and a 'special' monopsonist.

What can be deemed the peculiarity of the public buyer with respect to a private one, concerns the distinct strategies spaces available to each of them. Whereas the private buyer can choose his strategic actions inside a wider choice set, the public sector is constrained not only by the general law, but also by very detailed administrative regulations and procedures. On the one hand, those rules were set as an attempt to avoid any abuse of discretion by the agent of the public sector.[13] On the other hand, the lack of flexibility

[12] This section was written by Valeria Fichera.
[13] The standard justification points to the 'capture' issue, that is, the possibility that the agent of the public buyer be captured by the interests of a seller, or a coalition of sellers. In the case

hinders the public buyer from reacting strategically, when confronted with an agreement among potential contractors that aims at reaping a bigger profit out of taxpayers' money.

Two main theoretical approaches can be identified in the analysis of public procurement. To the first belong mechanism design theorists, who focus on the design of optimal awarding mechanisms, for given information structures. In that framework the interaction between the players is captured by a multiple-stage game. In the mechanism design game both the buyer and the potential sellers can act strategically. The buyer is entitled to decide the awarding procedure at the initial stage of the game and commits himself to it. Afterwards, the players on the other side of the market determine their optimal strategies, which depend on the awarding rules and the information available to them (both private and public). The 'normative' goal of this approach consists in identifying the contract, or class of contracts, that are optimal for the public buyer. The optimal contract will depend on the information structure, given the public objective of getting 'the best value for money', and the profit-maximisation objective driving firms' behaviour.

The alternative approach, more a complement to the first than a substitute, can be considered as an in-depth focus on the second stage of the stylised game structure. The standard rules to allocate public contracts in the real world are quite stiff. The agent of the public sector does not enjoy any freedom in choosing an allocation rule for the contract at stake, and she must stick to the one fixed by law for that class of transactions. Of course laws can be changed, but this is normally the result of a time-consuming political procedure, only partially grounded on economic rationale. Hence, in a short-term perspective, the public buyer is hindered from reacting strategically to a specific realisation of the public procurement game. The game-theoretic models following this second approach focus on the strategic behaviour of potential bidders facing a given allocation rule. Since the most widespread rule in the real world is the first price sealed bid auction, the majority of existing studies concentrate on that mechanism.

From a theoretical point of view, the tools to investigate the existence and functioning of collusive agreements on the *supply* side of markets for public contracts are those developed in auction theory to deal with bidding rings on the *demand* side of an auction market. As illustrated by McAfee and

---

of capture, the agent uses her discretion to the advantage of those sellers that have entered an agreement with herself. On their side, the capturing sellers will adequately pay the agent's service. The rigidity of the regulations is aimed at limiting discretion and it should prevent capture. The recent discovery of widespread corruption in several European countries witnesses to the failure of the existing laws in realising this objective.

McMillan (1992) in an auction context, the decision whether to establish a ring, and the details of the collusive agreement, are both dependent on how the following four crucial problems are dealt with by the members of the constituting coalition:

1 Collusive agreements are illegal. It is not possible to enforce them by using standard enforcing procedures.
2 A sharing rule for the gains from collusion needs to be agreed upon.
3 High profits gained by cartel participants attract new entrants, undermining the stability of the cartel which is inversely related to the number of participants.
4 The victim of collusion, on the other side of the market, may take actions to destabilise the cartel.[14]

With minor modifications the same problems are relevant for the design of a collusive agreement among firms participating in public procurement. Information issues, crucial in modelling bidding rings in auction models, show as much prominence in any attempt to model collusive behaviour in public procurement games. While points 1 and 3 are already illustrated in the wider framework of cartel agreement in standard oligopolies, points 2 and 4 need to be treated more specifically in the public procurement context.

To look closer into the issue of collusion in public procurement games, however, we need a more structured starting point. Since collusion is a deviation from competition, we begin our formal analysis with a simple model of a competitive procurement game.

A standard competitive model

To remain as close to reality as possible and to maintain a comprehensible level of normalisation, we choose as our benchmark model the allocation of a generic public contract by first price sealed bid auction.

More specifically, we make use of the symmetric independent private value model and its assumptions as they were first outlined by Vickrey in his seminal 1961 paper on auctions. A few modifications are needed to adapt

---

[14] In the case of standard auctions, the victim of a collusive agreement is the seller. A typical reaction from a seller facing collusive bidders is to make strategic use of his minimum reserve price (see Phlips 1988b, chapter 4), or to introduce 'phantom' bids. In the case of public procurement, the designated victim is the public buyer. Because of the stiff legal regulations, the public buyer cannot react strategically if the auctioning procedure is already taking its official course. The only reaction the public buyer can enforce is the annulment of the contract, if he can show the contract is vitiated. Annulment, however, is normally a costly and time-consuming procedure.

the standard structure of a first price sealed bid auction to the procurement game.[15] The basic assumptions are:

1 The bidders are risk neutral, which implies that the objective of bidder i ($i = 1, \ldots, N$) is the individual maximisation of his expected profit $E\Pi_i$.
2 Each firm's cost of realising the project is independent and private, that is to say, the cost of the project for firm i does not affect other firms' costs. Furthermore, each firm participating in the game knows its own cost and the distribution from which the costs of its competitors are drawn.
3 The bidders are symmetric. Their costs are drawn from the same distribution.
4 The public buyer assigns the contract to the lowest bidder worth the amount of his bid, according to the rules of a fixed-price contract.[16]

In our context we need a supplementary assumption concerning the maximum price the public buyer is allowed to pay for the contract at stake. Although it is very similar to an auctioneer's reservation price, here the limiting value is externally given and cannot be fixed strategically by the buyer.

5 The public buyer fixes an upper limit c_h to the final payment. This upper limit is publicly revealed.[17]

In what follows we consider the price as the only criterion driving the process of evaluating the bids by the buyer.[18]

---

[15] In what follows, the solution for the optimal strategies in the competitive model of the procurement game is a straightforward adaptation of the general solution for the optimal bidding strategies in a first price sealed bid auction as reported in McAfee and McMillan (1987) or Phlips (1988b, chapter 4).

[16] In a fixed-price contract the firm is the residual claimant for its cost savings. The buyer pays only the amount of the winning bid and does not reimburse any of the costs. For more details see Laffont and Tirole (1993).

[17] This last condition is not very different from the usual practice, followed by several awarding authorities in most Western countries, of explicitly announcing the maximum amount of money allocated to each single project.

Less understandable, and hard to justify, is another practice used until very recently by most Italian awarding authorities, and outlawed by the European Court of Justice. According to Italian national law, the awarding authorities, in the case of public works, were allowed to fix a secret minimum bid and reject all the bids below that minimum. The justification for this rule was that a 'too low' bid is more a consequence of bad quality, rather than the outcome of genuinely competitive behaviour.

[18] This is clearly a restriction with respect to the possibilities admitted by existing regulations at all levels. The EC Public Procurement Directives, for example, include the criterion of 'the most advantageous economic offer' among the admitted ones, as an attempt to give consideration to quality issues. According to this criterion, the price is only one of the elements to be considered for the awarding of a contract. The weight given to each element in the evaluation procedure, however, is to be explicitly stated in the announcement of the competition. In a recent paper, Branco (1992) models an auction procedure which is a good

The object of the contract is fully specified, and each firm's cost for its execution is c_i. Each c_i, known only by firm i, is a realisation from the density function $f(c)$, defined on the interval $[c_l, c_h]$, and with cumulative distribution $F(c)$. The density f, the distribution F and the support are common knowledge.

In the competitive setting each firm looks for the optimal-bidding strategy, i.e., the one that maximises its expected profit

$$E\Pi_i(c_i) = (b_i - c_i)p(b_i < b_j) \quad \forall j \neq i. \tag{4.25}$$

In equation (4.25) b_i is firm i's bid and the second term, $p(b_i < b_j)$ represents the probability for firm i of posting the lowest bid, hence of winning the contract. Each firm's profit expectation depends on this firm's cost parameter and on the distribution of the cost parameters of its competitors. The expected value is calculated on the joint distribution of the other firms' cost parameters. A potential contractor has to find the optimal bid (b_i^*) which maximises his expected profit as expressed in equation (4.25).

Since a first price sealed bid auction does not have an equilibrium in dominant strategies, we look for a Bayesian–Nash equilibrium of the game. According to the definition of such an equilibrium, each player chooses his optimal strategy given his beliefs (consistent in equilibrium) about the decision rules followed by the other bidders. In our framework bidder i conjectures that his opponents j are using as a decision rule a function $B(c_j)$ in order to determine b_j. Assume that B is monotonically increasing in c_j.

Equation (4.25) can then be written

$$
\begin{aligned}
E\Pi_i(c_i) &= (b_i - c_i)p(b_i < B(c_j)) \quad \forall j \neq i \\
&= (b_i - c_i)p[c_j > B^{-1}(b_i)] \\
&= (b_i - c_i)\left[1 - F(B^{-1}(b_i))\right]^{(N-1)}.
\end{aligned} \tag{4.26}
$$

The maximisation of the expected profit implies

$$\frac{\partial E\Pi_i(c_i)}{\partial b_i} = 0. \tag{4.27}$$

By differentiating $E\Pi_i(c_i)$, and applying the Envelope Theorem we get

$$\frac{dE\Pi_i(c_i)}{dc_i} = \frac{\partial E\Pi_i(c_i)}{\partial c_i} + \frac{\partial E\Pi_i(c_i)}{\partial b_i}\frac{\partial b_i}{\partial c_i} = \frac{\partial E\Pi_i(c_i)}{\partial c_i} \tag{4.28}$$

hence

formal representation of that criterion. In the model, the firms submit bids, specifying both price and a few 'quality' parameters. The government then calculates a unified score for each bid and ranks the firms accordingly. The firm with the highest score is assigned the contract.

$$\frac{dE\Pi_i(c_i)}{dc_i} = -\left[1 - F(B^{-1}(b_i))\right]^{(N-1)}. \tag{4.29}$$

The Nash condition of a symmetric game implies that if $B(c_j)$ is the optimal-bidding function for bidder j, the same must hold for player i, hence

$$b_i = B(c_i). \tag{4.30}$$

Equation (4.26) then becomes

$$E\Pi_i(c_i) = (b_i - c_i)[1 - F(c_i)]^{(N-1)} \tag{4.31}$$

and equation (4.29)

$$\frac{dE\Pi_i(c_i)}{dc_i} = -[1 - F(c_i)]^{(N-1)}. \tag{4.32}$$

To solve for the optimal-bidding function we need a boundary condition, which can be derived from the following reasoning: if a bidder's cost is equal to the maximum accepted bid he cannot do better than bidding his true cost, that is $B(c_h) = c_h$. In this case his profit expectation $E\Pi_i$ will, by necessity, be zero.

By integrating (4.32) and setting it equal to (4.31) we get

$$\int_{c_h}^{c_i} -\left(1 - F(z)\right)^{(N-1)} dz = (b_i - c_i)[1 - F(c_i)]^{(N-1)} \tag{4.33}$$

which is equivalent to

$$\int_{c_i}^{c_h} \left(1 - F(z)\right)^{(N-1)} dz = (b_i - c_i)[1 - F(c_i)]^{(N-1)}. \tag{4.34}$$

Thus the optimal bid b_i^* is given by

$$b_i^* = c_i + \frac{\displaystyle\int_{c_i}^{c_h} \left(1 - F(z)\right)^{(N-1)} dz}{\left(1 - F(c_i)\right)^{(N-1)}}. \tag{4.35}$$

It has been shown that the optimal bid of equation (4.35) is equivalent to the expected value of the second lowest cost conditional upon c_i being the lowest cost in the sample.[19]

[19] See Mougeot and Naegelen (1993, chapter 2).

The second term on the r.h.s. of equation (4.34) represents the profit for a firm with cost parameter c_i, *if it wins the contract*. The expected profit $E\Pi_i$ for each firm is thus that value, weighted by the probability of winning the auction

$$E\Pi_i(c_i) = \frac{\int_{c_i}^{c_h} (1 - F(z))^{(N-1)} dz}{(1 - F(c_i))^{(N-1)}} (1 - F(c_i))^{(N-1)} \tag{4.36}$$

so that its expected profit is

$$E\Pi_i(c_i) = \int_{c_i}^{c_h} (1 - F(z))^{(N-1)} dz. \tag{4.37}$$

In spite of its simple setting, this model shows that the auction procedure stimulates competition. As can be easily checked from equation (4.37), the bigger the number of firms participating in the auction, the lower the expected profit of the final contractor. A large number of firms makes everybody bid more aggressively and allows the public buyer to extract as much rent as possible from the winning firm, given the firms' informational advantage. However, the device successfully achieves its goal only if the firms do really compete among each other and do not manage to collude and reap the profit of the informational asymmetry. Thus our next question is: given the awarding rules, do the firms have an interest in colluding? If yes, what kind of agreement can they reach?

The collusive alternative

Collusive agreements among firms participating in the market for public contracts are not a peculiarity of our time. The Prussian Penal Code of 1851 already provided for criminal penalties for tendering cartels. In times of big public expenditures as in the recent past in most Western countries, the lack of competition in the assignment of public contracts might have been partially responsible for the unusual growth of public expenditures. Of course, a cartel agreement represents only one possible violation of competition, and likely a minor one when compared with the economic consequences of corruption in the public sector.[20]

---

[20] Starting with the well-known Italian 'Tangentopoli' case in 1992, Europe has seen in the last year the discovery of widespread corruption in several countries. The Italian case, which is entering its third year of investigation, has shown that the usual practice for the awarding of big public works implied the payment of a bribe. The 'standard bribe' paid by public

A simple example of the distortionary effect of a cartel is given by the US Department of Justice. The antitrust chief in an interview to the *New York Times*, a few years ago, maintained that bid-rigging by highway contractors increased the cost of building roads by 10 per cent or more. An even more fascinating example, reported by all economists dealing with collusion in public contracts, is the 'Electrical Conspiracy' case. More than thirty companies participated in the cartel. The method they invented to allocate contracts was an ingenious one. According to the 'phases of the moon system'[21] it was impossible to detect that the winning bid was the result of a collusive agreement. The antitrust action was eventually successful only because federal antitrust officers managed to get hold of the documentation on the agreement.

Let us now set up a stylised analysis of how a cartel forms and operates in the public contracts market. Once the awarding rules are fixed by existing law, the potential contractors have first to decide whether they are going to compete or to cooperate at the expense of the public buyer. By taking the awarding rules as exogenously given, we are partially abandoning the mechanism design framework. We do not make any analysis of the role of the public buyer, who will not be allowed any strategic action. His actions will be in the form of notarial deeds. A simple mechanism design approach is however used in the analysis of coalition formation among potential contractors.

The decision in favour of cooperation will depend on:

1 How the contract is allocated among the members of the coalition (an internal allocation rule).
2 How to share the profit arising from cooperation among cartel members (a profit-sharing rule).
3 How to enforce the agreement if it is not self-enforcing (a detection and punishment procedure).

Most models only consider coalition involving all bidders. We too are going to consider only this special class of coalitions. One must acknow-

contractors falls in the range between 5 and 15 per cent of the value of the contract. It seems that this practice had become an accepted system from the beginning of the 1980s. For the time being, the estimates of the effects of this system on the Italian public finances are still provisional, but they are rarely below 1 point of the percentage ratio between the budget deficit and GDP, for every single year belonging to the time period considered.

[21] The peculiar assignment mechanism inside the cartel worked according to a rotating-bid arrangement. The mechanism used an intricate device to establish which bidder's turn it was to bid. The mechanism was such that every two weeks a firm was 'phased' into a priority position. This firm was asked if it wanted the contract for the highest price the buyer was ready to pay. If it did it would face only token opposition from the fellow cartel members, if not the next bidder on the list was asked. For more details on the Electrical Conspiracy case, see Smith (1961).

ledge, however, that the game would be rather different if not all firms took part in the cartel. A more complete (but possibly too complex) model would be necessary to explain both the decision and the behaviour of those firms not joining the cartel.

The advantage of an all-inclusive bidder coalition is that the cartel may aim at realising the equivalent of monopoly profit. In the procurement game, monopoly profit coincides with having the public sector pay the *ex ante* fixed c_h. Remember that c_h represents the highest amount an administration has been assigned for the realisation of a given contract.

The main problem that colluding bidders have to solve is incomplete information: they do not know the individual cost parameter of their fellow cartel members.[22] If individual cost parameters were known by all potential contractors (but still obscure to the public administration auctioning the contract), the optimal strategy for the cartel would be straightforward. In such a full-information setting, had the firms competed with each other, the most efficient firm would be awarded the contract, but for a price close to the cost parameter of the second lowest-cost firm. By making a collusive agreement, the potential contractors are able to reach a much better outcome. The most efficient firm, the one with the lowest c_i, bids c_h. The other firms abstain from bidding. Thus, the lowest-cost firm is awarded the contract at the highest price the public buyer is willing to pay. The coalition has then to share the collusive profit amongst its members, according to a rule accepted by all colluding firms. To agree to collude, the most efficient firm must receive at least its competitive profit. The extra profit due to the agreement is thus the difference between c_h and the cost parameter of the firm with the second lowest cost. This extra profit has to be shared among all cartel members. The final individual advantages are clear: the contractor is still the one who receives the higher profit; but all other firms, which could not make any positive profit in a competitive environment, receive a profit from cooperation.[23]

In the more interesting case of incomplete information, our potential cartel members have a much harder life. At present the only results available come once again from auction theory. In the rest of the section, we will adapt the analytical results by McAfee and McMillan (1992) concerning bidding rings to the public procurement context. McAfee and McMillan start by building a descriptive classification of collusive mechanisms.

[22] The informational problem of the bidders is very similar to the one described in the last part of section 4.2.

[23] There are a few recent articles on the sharing of collusive gains among members of bidder coalitions in English auctions and second-price sealed bid auctions. Graham *et al.* (1990) design a special mechanism that make expected payments to coalition members equal to their exact contribution to cooperative profit.

The mechanisms they describe are chosen to maximise *ex ante profits* prior to the realisation of valuations.

Four categories are ordered according to the ease of detection by outsiders. The first is a tacit mechanism which does not give rise to any transfer. Each bidder's bid depends only on his own cost parameter. No contact among bidders is needed to operate this form of collusion. The second, the coordinative agreement, is again a no-transfer mechanism, but individual bids may depend upon the entire vector of the cost parameters of potential contractors. In that case the bidders need to meet to coordinate their behaviour. In the sequel these two collusive forms are put together in the class of '*weak cartels*', characterised by the absence of side-payments among coalition members. The last two mechanisms make up the '*strong cartels*' category. This includes the transfer mechanism and the budget-breaking mechanism. In the simple transfer mechanism, side-payments among cartel members are allowed, but they must sum to zero for every realisation of the cost vector. In the budget-breaking mechanism, the constraint is relaxed and the side-payments need sum to zero only on average. The budget-breaking cartel, however, needs the presence of an external budget breaker, thus the risk of detection substantially increases.

In their analysis of *weak cartels*, McAfee and McMillan reach the conclusion that the impossibility of transfers prevents the achievement of efficiency.[24] The optimal strategy under tacit collusion does not ensure the assignment of the contract to the lowest-cost firm. Thus, tacit collusion prevents profit maximisation at the cartel level. Indeed, they show[25] that optimal tacit collusion implies the following bidding strategy

$$B(c_i[c_{-i}]) = \begin{cases} 0 & \text{if } c_i > c_h \\ c_h & \text{if } c_i \leq c_h. \end{cases} \qquad (4.38)$$

In this formulation $[c_{-i}]$ is the vector of the cost parameters of all potential contractors excluding i. In words, if a firm has a cost parameter higher than the reservation price set by the public buyer (c_h), its optimal bidding strategy is to abstain from bidding (bidding zero). Otherwise, optimal bidding implies to bid exactly the buyer's reservation price c_h. From equation (4.38) it results that all firms with costs parameters smaller than

---

[24] See lemma 1 in McAfee and McMillan (1992). Notice the difference with the model of collusion in oligopoly with more than two firms and cost uncertainty of section 4.2. In that model, achievement of efficiency depends upon the number of firms: with less than five firms the monopoly outcome is enforceable. In the case of tacit collusion in public procurement, the monopoly outcome cannot be achieved irrespective of the size of the cartel.

[25] See theorem 1 in McAfee and McMillan (1992).

the reservation price bid identically. This result is shown to hold for most continuous distributions.[26]

This theoretically optimal tacit mechanism of collusion has a striking real-world counterpart. As mentioned by Scherer (1980): '*Each year the federal and state governments receive thousands of sets of identical bids in the sealed bid competitions they sponsor.*'

A plausible interpretation of this apparently naive form of coordination is the following. In environments where detective activities by antitrust authorities are very efficient, side-payments might be too risky, thus a strong cartel would not be viable. A coordinative agreement, on the other hand, would leave traces of its existence in the documents used to coordinate cartel members' behaviour. In those cases, the mechanism described in equation (4.38) might be the only alternative to competition available to potential contractors, who do not want to leave any 'hard' evidence of the existence of a collusive agreement.

The second kind of weak cartel mechanism, the coordinative one, avoids identical bidding, but cannot achieve better results in terms of efficiency. The advantage, in the real world, of coordinative agreements is that identical bidding normally raises suspicions and may cause the reaction of the awarding administration (which in the model is excluded). Further-more, a coordinative agreement makes it possible to assign different shares of a market for public contracts to different members of a cartel.[27] While a coordinative mechanism creates the risk of cartel communications being detected, it reduces the immediate evidence of identical bidding.

Moving to the case of *strong cartels*, the possibility of side-payments among cartel members enables the coalition to achieve efficiency. More-over, efficient cartels with transfers manage to maximise cooperative profits.

McAfee and McMillan show that a workable mechanism to achieve this outcome is to hold a prior first price sealed bid auction. In this prior auction potential contractors bid non-cooperatively. The winner (who is the lowest-cost firm!) is assigned the right to be awarded the contract at the regular procurement auction with a tender equivalent to c_h. At the regular auction, the other cartel members either abstain from bidding or make token bids above the reserve price. At the end of the game, the winner shares with all coalition members an amount equivalent to the difference between the final price at the legitimate auction (that is the limit price c_h) and the lower one he

---

[26] A significant exception is the exponential density function.

[27] The 'phase of the moon' mechanism of the electrical conspiracy took into account the need to assign different quotas of contracts to different cartel members. For example, circuit-breaker contracts were allocated so that General Electric got 45 per cent, Westinghouse got 35 per cent and two smaller producers were assigned 10 per cent each (see Smith 1961).

bid at the cartel private auction. This difference exactly represents the gain from collusion.

The amount transferred to each fellow cartel member by the winning bidder is[28]

$$\Pi(0) = \frac{E[c_h - c_{(2)} | c_{(1)} \leq c_h]}{N}. \tag{4.39}$$

In equation (4.39) $\Pi(0)$ stands for the expected profit of a losing bidder that belongs to the cartel. In the function, the argument '0' serves the purpose of reminding us that, in a competitive auction, all the bidders but the winner would receive zero profit. The $c_{(k)}$ terms represent the kth order statistics. The expectation is taken over the distribution of the first-order statistics, that is, the distribution of the lowest element in a sample.[29]

The expected profit of the winning bidder is composed of two parts. The first is the expected profit of the lowest bidder in the competitive auction. *Ex ante*, this profit expectation is equivalent to the expected difference between the second lowest and the lowest cost of the potential contractors.[30] The second part of the winning bidder's expected profit is an equal share of the gain from collusion, as expressed in (4.39).

An example of a similar mechanism used in the real world is given by Stigler (1966). Six cast-iron pipe manufacturers operated a knockout[31] to allocate the contracts in those cities not reserved for a particular firm. The reservation price was fixed by a central committee constituted by the firms themselves. The committee received the bids from the cartel members for the right to the contract. The lowest bidder then bid the prearranged price in the legitimate auction, and the others submitted higher bids. Periodically, the gain from collusion was allocated among cartel members according to their production capacities. The members of the cast-iron pipe cartel were the first contractors to be convicted under the Sherman Antitrust Act of 1890.

McAfee and McMillan (1992) choose to develop their analysis of bidding rings in *ex ante* terms. This choice leads them to neglect the enforcement problem. In their model, detection of deviations from the actions

---

[28] For the proof, see theorem 4 in McAfee and McMillan (1992).

[29] The essential features and properties of order statistics can be found in most statistics handbooks (e.g., Mood, Graybill and Boes 1974, chapter VI). For a detailed treatment see David (1981).

[30] For technical details on this result see McAfee and McMillan (1987).

[31] This is the technical term used to indicate an illicit auction held among the members of a bidding ring to determine the internal allocation of the good and the amount of the transfers.

prescribed by the different forms of collusive agreements is straight-forward:[32] what is needed is simply the identity and the bid of the winning bidder. In the public contract case this information is routinely released. To enforce a cartel agreement, however, the detection of cheating is necessary but not sufficient. In viable cartels, cheaters must be punished. With respect to the punishment issue, McAfee and McMillan do not go into details. They just mention two possible solutions: an external one, exemplified as the organised crime approach; and the classical grim trigger strategy of repeated games.

In the first case an external enforcer is hired, who does not even need to intervene materially, to the extent that his threat is credible and extremely unpleasant. The second solution is more appropriate in a dynamic context of repeated auction games. However, the hypothesis of an infinite number of repetitions of the same stage game, which is an appealing argument in standard oligopoly games[33] (as well as in some auction markets for artworks), has limited application in the context of public procurement. Particularly in the case of big public works, it is impossible to foresee the number of similar contracts that will be assigned in the medium term. Hence, the repeated game argument is deemed to fail precisely for those contracts that would permit a cartel to reap huge profits.

Looking at recent events in several European countries, we may add another very strong and popular enforcement mechanism. As mentioned above, the agreements between the holders of political power and stable groups of potential contractors (mainly national and well-established firms) in several countries, resulted in a constant violation of competition and in a completely organised sharing of the most substantial part of the market for public contracts.

[32] Notice the difference with the detection of deviations in standard oligopoly, as illustrated in section 4.1.   [33] See chapter 6.

II

Tacit collusion

5 Information sharing among oligopolists

In the preceding chapter, the transmission of information appeared as an essential ingredient of cartel enforcement when the colluding firms have imperfect information about their current production rates or incomplete information about each other's cost of production. An efficient allocation of the production quotas implies side-payments. These in turn require truthful cost revelation since they depend on the cost reports. Efficient cartel agreements can be enforced with an appropriate combination of production quotas, side-payments and information transmission.

The next chapter is devoted to the enforcement of tacit collusion. It will be shown that collusive outcomes can be sustained as equilibria of a repeated game that is played non-cooperatively, that is, without explicit collusion and therefore without communication. The enforcement is based on credible threats of punishments imposed on a deviator. The detection of deviations and the carrying out of threats requires the passage of time: that is why firms must be supposed to meet over and over again in the marketplace. In chapter 7, collusive outcomes will be shown to result from announcements, by a leading firm, of price changes that are matched by the competitors. Finally, chapter 8 will draw attention to the informational disadvantage that makes it difficult, and often impossible, for antitrust authorities to detect tacit collusion and easy for tacitly colluding firms to untruthfully report demand or cost parameters such that collusive outcomes appear as competitive outcomes.

This chapter addresses a preliminary question: is the exchange, among oligopolists, of information related to demand or cost parameters an indication that these firms are trying to collude? The assumption is that there is no explicit collusion. In addition, the question of how to enforce tacit collusion is left aside, so that there is no need to reason in a repeated game framework.

Antitrust authorities often take the simple view that, when oligopolists communicate their views on the state of the market or on the evolution of costs of production to each other, this is proof of collusion. Given the difficulties of collusion enforcement, it is clear to me that the simple exchange of information cannot, as such, be construed as implying that a collusive *outcome* is being achieved. All it could show is that there is collusive *conduct*, in the sense that the oligopolists are *trying* to achieve a collusive outcome. In this restrictive sense, information sharing could play the same role as 'meeting competition' or 'most-favoured-customer' clauses, which are often called practices that 'facilitate' tacit collusion. The final section of this chapter briefly discusses these practices.

Experimental results[1] indicate that communication between competitors indeed facilitates collusive conduct. Experimental games conducted by Hoggatt (1959 and 1967), Fouraker and Siegel (1963), Friedman (1963, 1969, 1970), Dolbear *et al.* (1968) and Sauermann and Selten (1967) show that when information about competitors is limited, and in the absence of communication between players, (posted) prices actually tend to a competitive equilibrium when Bertrand price strategies are played, even with very few players. With quantity decisions, the outcome is most often a non-cooperative Cournot–Nash equilibrium.[2] The accuracy of the joint maximisation model was found to decrease with a reduction of information about other agents' actions. But joint profit maximisation was the outcome under perfect information with experienced players (Stoecker 1980 and Friedman and Hoggatt 1980). Notice that under imperfect information

the number of sellers becomes a very important treatment variable in that an increase in the number destroys the accuracy of the joint maximum model. In the duopoly markets, significant (but less than perfect) cooperation occurs, but, with an increase in the number of firms, it vanishes almost completely and the Cournot model is very accurate by comparison. (Plott 1982, pp. 1516–17)

The theory of information sharing when the competitors are few reformulates our problem in the following way. Would oligopolists who have private information on the parameters of their profit function want to share this information in a non-cooperative (static) Nash equilibrium? If they would, then information sharing cannot be said to indicate collusive conduct: it might be a means of making a non-collusive equilibrium easier to find. If, to the contrary, they have no incentive to share information in a

---

[1] Excellent reviews of experiments in this field can be found in Selten (1979) and Plott (1982, 1989).

[2] The distinction between Bertrand price strategies and Cournot quantity strategies appears as less fundamental once it is realised that the Cournot outcome is also a perfect equilibrium in a two-stage game in which the players choose their capacity in the first stage and compete in prices in the second stage, as shown by Kreps and Scheinkman (1983). See also MacLeod (1984). The Kreps–Scheinkman game is discussed in section 9.3.

non-cooperative Nash equilibrium while we observe that they, in fact, do share, then we have good theoretical reasons to believe that tacit collusion is in the air.

A correct theoretical approach is therefore to first work out a non-cooperative Nash equilibrium with incomplete information and then check whether it is profitable to transmit or acquire information. Section 5.1 sets up the basic Cournot duopoly model with homogeneous goods and uncertainty about market demand to which most of the literature refers as a benchmark. Section 5.2 derives the basic answer: while they want more information, these duopolists will not pool their private information. They will share only if they are allowed to cooperate! Further results for the case of differentiated goods are given in section 5.3, while section 5.4 briefly reports on information sharing in non-cooperative duopoly games when there is uncertainty about costs of production.

5.1 Cournot–Nash equilibrium with uncertain demand and homogeneous goods

Let us start by showing how a Cournot–Nash equilibrium under incomplete information can be worked out and let us follow Novshek and Sonnenschein (1982). Imagine that duopolists producing a homogeneous good do not know each other's profit functions because they are uncertain about the position of their industry's inverse demand function, which is specified as

$$p = \alpha - q = \alpha - (q_1 + q_2) \tag{5.1}$$

by a suitable choice of units. The uncertainty is about the numerical value of the random intercept α, about which each duopolist receives a signal $s^i (i = 1,2)$ in each period.

Each firm has to determine an output strategy σ^i by maximising its expected profit with respect to it, given the signal received and the optimal strategy of its competitor. This expected profit $E(\Pi_i | s^i, \sigma^1, \sigma^2)$ is defined on a distribution which is supposed to be known, so as to transform the problem into one that can be solved. Here the trick is to suppose that each player knows the joint distribution of his or her signal s^i and the residual intercept $\alpha - \sigma^j$. The Cournot–Nash equilibrium is then such that, for each firm i and for each signal s^i, outputs σ^i maximise the expected individual profits.

Notice that the assumption about the players knowing a joint distribution does not imply that the signals about the true value of α turn out to be correct. The assumption made here implies however that, given the equilibrium, the expected joint evolution (the joint distribution) of a signal and the intercept on which it provides information is correct. In this sense, expectations are said to be 'fulfilled'.

What is the equilibrium? If intercept α were perfectly known, the equilibrium strategies would be $q_1 = q_2 = \alpha/3$. Indeed, the profit functions would be $\Pi_1 = [\alpha - (q_1 + q_2)]q_1$ and $\Pi_2 = [\alpha - (q_1 + q_2)]q_2$ respectively, and the system of first-order conditions to be solved would be

$$\frac{\partial \Pi_1}{\partial q_1} = \alpha - 2q_1 - q_2 = 0,$$

$$\frac{\partial \Pi_2}{\partial q_2} = \alpha - 2q_2 - q_1 = 0.$$

From the second equation $q_2 = \alpha/2 - q_1/2$ so that $q_1 = \alpha/3$ (from the first equation) and $q_2 = \alpha/3$. In the Novshek–Sonnenschein model, the equilibrium pair is simply $\sigma^1 = s^1/3$ and $\sigma^2 = s^2/3$. The true value of α is replaced by the signal perceived by each duopolist.

To prove this, Novshek and Sonnenschein (1982) suppose that the conditional expectation of α, for firm 1, is

$$E(\alpha|s^1) = s^1 = E(s^2|s^1)$$

for all values of signal s^1, and similarly

$$E(\alpha|s^2) = s^2 = E(s^1|s^2)$$

for firm 2, for all values of signal s^2. This amounts to assuming that the signals are unbiased. This is not too unrealistic, if one admits that small errors can be neglected.

Suppose firm 1 chooses strategy $\sigma^1 = s^1/3$. Then, for all values of s^2, the expected profit of firm 2 is

$$q_2 E[(\alpha - \sigma^1 - q_2)|s^2] = q_2 E[(\alpha - \sigma^1)|s^2] - q_2^2.$$

The maximisation of this expected profit with respect to q_2 gives

$$E[(\alpha - \sigma^1)|s^2] - 2q_2 = 0$$

or

$$q_2^* = \frac{1}{2} E[(\alpha - \sigma^1)|s^2]$$

$$= \frac{1}{2} E\left[\left(\alpha - \frac{s^1}{3}\right)|s^2\right]$$

$$= \frac{1}{2}\left(s^2 - \frac{s^2}{3}\right) = \frac{s^2}{3}$$

because $E(\alpha|s^2)=s^2$ and $E(s^1|s^2)=s^2$ by assumption.[3]

5.2 Acquisition and transmission of information

Given this result, would non-colluding duopolists wish to acquire more information and be interested in pooling the available information? The answer is: if they know the joint distribution of their signals and the residual intercepts, they will want more information but will not want to pool it unilaterally and be indifferent with respect to multilateral pooling.

To show this, Novshek and Sonnenschein (1982) specify their model a bit further. Each signal is defined as the simple average of a number of observations, drawn from a sample $t_1, t_2, \ldots, t_n$, on the intercept α. The total sample is generated and owned by an independent information agency. Each observation is defined as

$$t_k = \alpha + \varepsilon_k \tag{5.2}$$

with $E(\varepsilon_k)=0$, $E(\alpha\varepsilon_k)=0$, $E(\varepsilon_k,\varepsilon_{k'})=0$ and $E(\varepsilon_k^2)=v$. This amounts to supposing that t_k is unbiased, because $E(t_k)=\alpha$ if $E(\varepsilon_k)=0$, that α is uncorrelated with the error and that the errors are uncorrelated. Each error also has the same variance v.

Suppose each duopolist signs a contract with the information agency. Firm 1 agrees to buy n_1 observations, of which it transmits m_1 to a common pool that is available to both. It thus keeps $n_1 - m_1$ observations as private information. Firm 2 makes a similar arrangement.

Suppose also that the agency labels these observations in the following order: first come the $n_1 - m_1$ private observations of firm 1; then come the $m_1 + m_2$ pooled observations; finally, there are the $n_2 - m_2$ private observations of firm 2.

Under these arrangements, signal s^1 is the simple average of the observations bought by firm 1, plus those transmitted to the pool by firm 2, and vice versa. Since the optimal strategies are functions of these signals, and the latter are functions of the error terms ε_k, the expected equilibrium profits can be expressed in terms of the ε_k's and their variances and covariances. The properties of these variances and covariances can thus be used to simplify the results and to crank out precise results. Formally

$$s^1 = \frac{\sum_{k=1}^{n_1+m_2} t_k}{n_1+m_2} = \alpha + \frac{\sum_{k=1}^{n_1+m_2} \varepsilon_k}{n_1+m_2} \tag{5.3}$$

---

[3] See Novshek and Sonnenschein (1982) for the proof that the equilibrium pair $\sigma^i = s^i/3$ is unique.

and

$$s^2 = \alpha + \frac{\sum_{m_1+1}^{n_1+n_2} \varepsilon_k}{n_2 + m_1}. \tag{5.4}$$

At the Cournot–Nash equilibrium computed earlier, the expected profit for firm 1 is

$$E(\Pi_1) = E\frac{s^1}{3}\left[\alpha - \left(\frac{s^1}{3} + \frac{s^2}{3}\right)\right]. \tag{5.5}$$

Insert results (5.3) and (5.4) into (5.5) and use the assumptions made about the error terms ε_k. You end up with

$$E(\Pi_1) = \frac{1}{9}\left[E(\alpha^2) - \frac{v}{n_1 + m_2} - \frac{(m_1 + m_2)v}{(n_1 + m_2)(n_2 + m_1)}\right] \tag{5.6}$$

for firm 1. By a similar procedure firm 2 is seen to have an expected profit that is structured in the same way. These profits can be differentiated with respect to n_1 or n_2 (a positive direct derivative indicates that the firm wishes to acquire information; a zero cross derivative indicates that the firm is indifferent to its competitor acquiring information) or with respect to m_1 or m_2 (to see whether it is profitable to transfer information to a pool).

It is clear that the expected profit of firm i increases in n_i, so that firms find information acquisition profitable. This doesn't imply, of course, that they wish to share this information totally or partially. Looking at the signs of the derivatives, one finds *inter alia* that the expected profit of firm i decreases in m_i as long as the other firm does not pool all information[4] ($m_2 = n_2$), in which case firm i has no interest in transmitting its own information to the pool. So it is not profitable for non-colluding duopolists to transmit information to the pool unilaterally.

As for contractual arrangements between the firms jointly to transfer information to the common pool, one finds that the duopolists are indifferent between pooling all information ($m_1 = n_1$ and $m_2 = n_2$) and no pooling at all ($m_1 = m_2 = 0$), because in both cases expected profits are the same when $n_1 = n_2$.

With a linear market demand curve such as (5.1), expected consumer's surplus is easy to compute. It is the triangle under the demand curve above p; that is

$$\frac{1}{2}E(\alpha - p)q = \frac{1}{2}E(\alpha - \alpha + q)q = \frac{1}{2}E\left(\frac{s^1 + s^2}{3}\right)^2.$$

[4] The result reported by Novshek and Sonnenschein (1982, p. 217) on this point is not correct. I am grateful to Andrzej Baniak for drawing my attention to this.

Insertion of (5.3) and (5.4) shows that expected consumer's surplus

is lower the higher the value of n_1 and n_2. This is consistent with a familiar theme in the economics of uncertainty: in markets with uncertain demand, decreases in variance reduce expected consumer's surplus. Also, expected consumer's surplus is lower the higher the value of m_i when $m_j > (2n_j - n_i)/3$. (Novshek and Sonnenschein 1982, p. 218)

However, the total expected surplus in equilibrium (the sum of the expected profits and the expected consumer's surplus) turns out to be equal to $\frac{2}{3} E(\alpha^2) - \{$expected consumer's surplus$\}$ so that the effects of information acquisition and pooling on total surplus are exactly the opposite (of their effects on consumer's surplus).

The results are strengthened by Clarke (1983a, b),[5] who replaces the fulfilled expectations assumption by a 'Bayes–Cournot' assumption, implying that firms must make their quantity decisions based on their best Bayes estimates of their opponents' information. Using results obtained by Basar and Ho (1974), Clarke finds that in all cases where expectations are not actually fulfilled, firms would prefer not to share information,[6] even if they have less accurate information than their rivals, unless they may cooperate once information has been shared. We can summarise by quoting Clarke (1983b, p. 383): 'This situation is unfortunate as society's welfare is maximised only when firms share information, but act competitively. Thus society faces a dilemma. Information pooling is good if firms behave competitively, but shared information makes anticompetitive agreements easier to construct.'

5.3 Differentiated goods

Vives (1984) reconsiders the problem using a duopoly model with demand uncertainty but with duopolists who produce a differentiated good. The signals about the demand intercept α are defined in the same way as in Novshek and Sonnenschein. Bertrand price strategies are introduced and compared to the Cournot strategies postulated in the previous sections. This allows Vives to consider combinations of substitutability and Cournot or Bertrand strategies, on the one hand, and of complementarity and Cournot or Bertrand strategies, on the other hand.

When the commodities produced are substitutes and the duopolists are playing Cournot, then our previous conclusion is confirmed: *not* to share

---

[5] See also Gal-Or (1985b).
[6] See also Crawford and Sobel (1982) and Palfrey (1982). Empirical evidence on the exchange of information and collusion can be found in Eisenberg (1980).

information turns out to be a dominant strategy for each duopolist. The argument goes roughly like this. Expected profits are reduced by the pooling of information. Indeed, if I get a high signal on α and there is pooling, (a) my rival has more precise information and will produce more, and (b) the signals are more correlated, so that the probability that my rival increases his production is increased. As a consequence, I have to produce less. When the goods are substitutes but the producers play Bertrand, then the opposite holds: it is now a dominant strategy to share information. When the goods are complements, then the two previous results are reversed.

I do not see the immediate interest of analysing the case of complementary goods from the point of view of competition policy, *stricto sensu*, since complementary goods are in different markets. In a broader framework, in which market structure may change, complementarity may be linked to mergers for diversification purposes, but these possible links are outside the scope of this book. The result on Bertrand strategies suggests that information sharing should be looked at with less suspicion when the competitors are using price strategies, the difficulty being that it is not clear in which real-life situation the Bertrand model is the appropriate one. As far as I know, no convincing evidence is available on this preliminary rather fundamental question.

Vives (1984) also presents welfare results, among which I pinpoint the following. First, pooling dominates no pooling in terms of expected total surplus, when the goods are substitutes and a Cournot game is played. Second, the private value (to the firms) of information received is always positive. Third, the social value of information (that is, the change in total surplus due to information received) is positive in a Cournot game (and negative in a Bertrand game). Clarke's dilemma is thus confirmed. Vives concludes that, when the goods are substitutes and Cournot competition prevails, public policy should encourage information sharing.[7] From what was said in the previous sections, it should be clear that I cannot accept such a policy conclusion in the framework of competition policy.

5.4 Uncertainty about costs

When the information to be shared relates to the costs of production, a distinction is to be made between costs that are 'common' and costs that are 'private'. Indeed, the distinction leads to opposite policy conclusions. When the uncertainty is about a common value, such as the evolution of

---

[7] A survey of the welfare implications of information sharing in oligopoly can be found in Sakai (1990, 1991).

industry-wide wage costs or the cost of fuel, *not* to share information is an equilibrium Cournot strategy (Clarke 1983b). This is intuitively plausible, by analogy with the uncertainty about the demand case, since (the intercept of) market demand is also a common value. However, when uncertainty is about firm-specific costs (and the game is non-cooperative), then to share information is an equilibrium Cournot outcome (Okada 1982 and 1983, Fried 1984 and Gal-Or 1986). In addition, the exchange of cost information can be shown to increase efficiency by raising the market shares of lower-cost firms and reducing the variance of industry output (Shapiro 1986).

The policy conclusion is therefore that information sharing is likely to facilitate collusion only when it is about a common value of demand or costs. No such conclusion can be drawn when private cost information is being pooled in the absence of a formal cartel agreement!

5.5 Facilitating practices

It is easy to establish a list of explicitly collusive types of behaviour that are illegal. Nobody disputes the fact that signing a cartel agreement is illegal. The question really is which types of behaviour are tacitly collusive and therefore also illegal. In our discussion one such type was identified – a scheme for the systematic pooling of current information with the purpose of creating perfect information – by comparing the incentives for information transmission in a non-cooperative Nash equilibrium with the incentive properties of a collusive outcome. Can we identify other such practices by the same method?

Tying clauses

Non-systematic transmission of current information (i.e., sporadic transmission by a particular firm to another) by direct or indirect ways has been seen to be compatible with the search for a non-cooperative equilibrium in section 5.2. The same must be true for non-systematic acquisition of current information.

An example that comes to mind is a provision that requires buyers of Northern Pacific's land to ship timber produced on this land via the Northern Pacific Railway Lines unless lower rates or better services were available from competing railway lines. As argued by Cummings and Ruther (1979), the main purpose of such clauses is not to tie the shipping with the purchase of land, but to compel buyers to disclose the lower rate or better service offered by competing carriers. (The tying arrangement simply provided protection against non-reporting.) Such contracts imply no obligation for the seller to meet lower prices, so there is no automatic deterrence of cheating (in contrast with 'meet competition' clauses). As such, they are competitive rather than collusive.

Another classic example is the International Salt case. Following Peterman (1979), the tying clause used by the International Salt Company can be interpreted as a device to ensure good reporting by the lessees (of a machine that dissolves rock salt) of the competitors' prices of salt, because lessees were free to buy on the open market whenever International Salt failed to meet these prices.

'Meet competition' clauses

A 'meet competition' clause entitles a buyer who finds another seller offering a lower price to this same lower price. If the clause also contains a 'release' option, so that the buyer can choose to be released from his contractual obligation, I am ready to argue that this is again an innocent information acquisition device: it is only by informing the original supplier that the buyer can escape from an obligation to purchase. But the buyer can escape from this obligation, and this freedom gives the buyer an incentive to enter long-term arrangements that it might otherwise be hesitant to sign.

Deletion of the release option, however, transforms the clause into a powerful deterrent to cheating. Now the competitors know that this firm will retaliate to any detected price reduction and that customers will report any price reduction immediately to it. The deterrence effect is maximised. And because deterrence is a problem only in a collusive arrangement, the clause (without release) must be collusive.[8]

Salop (1986) has illustrated the deterrence effect with respect to the prisoner's dilemma in a game with two players (Ethyl and DuPont, say). First, the achievement of a collusive equilibrium is facilitated, because one firm can raise its price to the collusive level without losing any sales to a lower-priced rival in the transition period during which the rival sticks to the lower price. In addition, the rival is encouraged not to delay a matching price increase, because the transitional gains that could result from his lower price are eliminated by the clause. Second, once the collusive outcome is reached, it is stabilised. Indeed, with no-release meeting competition clauses on both sides, it becomes impossible for one player to undercut the other. The only possibilities are to stick to the collusive equilibrium or to shift to a non-collusive Nash equilibrium. The threat of such a shift is very credible and therefore effective. It can be reinforced by a 'most-favoured-customer' (MFC) clause.

---

[8] Logan and Lutter (1989) qualify this conclusion. See also Holt and Scheffman (1987).

'Most-favoured-customer' clauses

A MFC clause guarantees the buyer any discount offered to another buyer by the (same) seller under the terms of the contract. The clause can be contemporaneous or retroactive.

A *contemporaneous* MFC clause penalises and deters only price cuts that are restricted to a limited number of customers. Indeed, if one firm unilaterally institutes a contemporaneous MFC, it commits itself to retaliating to discounts offered by a competitor with a general price cut to all its customers (a price war, in fact). Its rivals will conclude that, because a general price cut is costly and easily detected, there will be no retaliation if they offer a discount only to a limited number of customers of the firm that instituted the MFC. Collusion is thus reinforced. If all competitors institute an MFC, selective discounts will, again, not be matched (because this would imply a general price cut) if they are restricted to a limited number of the rivals' customers. On the one hand, price undercutting is restricted in scope. On the other hand, the threat of a shift to a non-cooperative Nash equilibrium is made more credible. When an MFC clause is combined with a meeting competition clause, the threat is reinforced and the need to actually carry it out may be reduced (Salop 1986).

A *retroactive* MFC clause is more powerful. It offers a guarantee to current customers that becomes effective if the firm that institutes it offers a lower price during some specified *future* period. 'In that event the firm will pay past customers the difference between the price they paid and the lowest price offered during the prescribed period. If firms institute this policy and offer a collusive price in one period, the rebate provision penalises later attempts to shade the price' (Cooper 1986, p. 378). In particular, retroactive MFC clauses tend to prevent price reductions in case the market deteriorates, because later price reductions must be applied to some past sales. Their objective is thus to make prices stickier over time and to keep them at the collusive level. Salop (1986, table 3) again illustrates the mechanism with respect to the prisoner's dilemma by showing that, with a retroactive MFC clause, gains from retaliating are relatively smaller than in the absence of such clauses. Adjustments to changing market conditions (typical for non-collusive Nash equilibria) are prevented. In particular, a shift to the non-collusive Nash equilibrium is made relatively more unprofitable. The effect of a meeting competition clause is thus reinforced.

A well-documented duopoly case[9] illustrates how a retroactive MFC

---

[9] In his presentation of this case, Cooper (1986) uses information in Hay (1982), Sultan (1974) and the Department of Justice's memorandum concerning the proposed modification of the final judgement in *United States v. General Electric Co.*, *Federal Register*, 42 (March 1977), pp. 17005–10.

policy can be implemented in practice. Two firms, General Electric and Westinghouse, manufactured turbine generators for the US electrical public utilities in the 1960s and 1970s. Both used retroactive MFC clauses applicable during six months following a sale (from the early 1960s to the mid 1970s). To inform potential buyers, this pricing policy was publicly announced, also through the trade associations of the public utilities. Buyers were allowed to check the record for any relevant price cuts, which was easy and inexpensive, since only a few purchases were made during any six-month period.

The only difficulty in implementing the clause lay in the fact that most generators were custom-built.

Unless a firm happened to sell two identical generators in a six-month period, the most-favored-customer policy would not constrain pricing. The firms overcame this problem by publishing price books that contained relative prices for all components and the information needed to determine the price of any generator. Since each firm announced that it would change prices only by adjusting the multiplier used to convert relative prices into actual prices, reductions in the price of one generator would trigger the rebate provision for all sales in the previous six months. As a result, the publication of the price book made the most-favored-customer policy constraining despite product heterogeneity. (Cooper 1986, pp. 385–6)

Retroactive MFC clauses are very rarely used, compared to contemporaneous MFCs. The electricity generators case suggests why this is so: a number of circumstances have to be given for this policy to be effective. First, the cost of transmitting the information to competitors and buyers should not be high, which in turn requires that there should not be too many potential buyers. Second, detailed records of all sales must be kept to make identification of past customers possible not only for the producers but also for their clients. In most industries, these administrative costs are prohibitive. Third, the number of producers must be small: otherwise a subset of competitors may continue to compete among themselves. Fourth, entry barriers into the industry should be high to avoid limit pricing. Fifth, market demand and costs should not fluctuate too much over the business cycle: otherwise it may not be profitable to reduce price flexibility. Finally, for the publication of price books to have the desired effect, it should be impossible to hide a price reduction behind a change in the design of the product.

Cooper (1986) demonstrates that a duopolist has an incentive to adopt the retroactive MFC clause unilaterally. He defines a two-period duopoly game with perfect information and differentiated products. Both firms maximise the sum of their profits over the two periods. At time zero, each firm decides whether to offer an MFC policy. At the beginning of the first period, each firm sets its prices as a function of these decisions. At the beginning of the second period, each firm sets its price as a function of the period zero decisions and the price set in period 1. In equilibrium, at least one firm offers price protection and a price above the single-period Bertrand–Nash equilibrium price, the other firm raises its price and both firms earn higher profits. Initiating a retroactive MFC policy facilitates tacit collusion by generating increased industry profits without formal coordination.

Trade associations

Most industries, trades and professions have 'trade associations'. Such central organisations may function fairly innocuously, as noted by Rees (1993a). They handle public relations at the industry-wide level, organise conventions and trade fairs. Indirectly, of course, such meetings create opportunities for the transmission of information to competitors or buyers. What is of interest here is the case where they collect individual company data, compile industry-wide totals[10] and distribute aggregate totals to members or others.

We saw, in section 4.1, that such aggregate data may be of some use in the policing of an agreement between oligopolists. Often, however, the membership of such associations is large. Vives (1990) studied such a situation of monopolistic competition (Chamberlin's 'large group') in which there is no strategic interaction. He found that this sort of information sharing is not a self-enforcing agreement when the aggregate data are distributed to others than the association's members: it is always interesting to deviate since information can be obtained at no cost (with the implication that the totals are not reliable). When the distribution is limited to members only, however, the agreement is self-enforcing.

---

[10] When trade associations disseminate private data from competing firms, we are of course back in the standard information sharing case studied in sections 5.2 to 5.4. On this, see Hay and Kelley (1974) and Fraas and Greer (1977) who provide some empirical evidence on the effectiveness of trade associations as agents of collusion.

6   Repeated games with collusive outcomes

Explicit collusion aims at putting the members of an agreement at the point on the profit frontier at which joint profit is maximised. Tacit collusion aims at increasing the profits of the colluders above the level implied in the non-cooperative Cournot–Nash equilibrium until hopefully the same joint profit-maximising point is reached. The objectives are thus basically the same. But with tacit collusion the task is complicated by the fact that no explicit agreement in the form of a legally enforceable contract is possible, typically because such contracts are illegal. This chapter will show that, from an economic point of view, explicit collusion and tacit collusion are not fundamentally different. Section 4.1 made it clear that contracts, however enforceable legally, will not be carried out if there is no mechanism that deters cheating and that it is this mechanism that makes the agreement binding. If the mechanism is a set of strategies (such as Osborne's rule) which together constitute a non-cooperative Nash equilibrium, then the results of section 4.1 suggest that the outcome associated with collusion can be obtained in a non-collusive way. That is exactly the message of the present chapter, with the important proviso that the dynamics of the problem should be carefully spelt out. In particular, oligopolists should be seen as meeting over and over again in the marketplace, so that the time sequence of the deterring mechanism can be made clear to all.

6.1 Friedman's balanced temptation equilibrium

J. Friedman was one of the first[1] to work out such a solution. Time now explicitly enters the picture. Players are supposed to play the same game

---

[1] It was first presented by Friedman (1971) following an idea by Aumann (1960) and then included in Friedman's 1977 textbook (chapter 8). A short summary is given in Friedman and Hoggatt (1980, chapter 1). A very readable and reasonably complete version can be found in Friedman (1972), and some further discussion is contained in Rees (1985). See Friedman (1983, pp. 123–35) for a numerical illustration with price strategies.

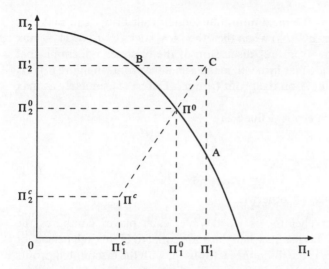

Figure 6.1 Tacit collusion: a balanced temptation equilibrium

repeatedly (they are said to play a stationary repeated game) and to have an infinite horizon. The strategic variables are either quantities (when the products are homogeneous) or prices (when the products are differentiated). This presentation concentrates on quantity (or 'Cournot') strategies. An infinite time horizon is chosen because this assumption describes best a situation where there is a high probability that the players will meet again in the next period and the end of the game is not known. The basic idea is, indeed, that firms meet over and over again in the marketplace.

Instead of using an instantaneous deterring mechanism such as Osborne's rule (4.8), Friedman postulates the following intertemporal strategy. In the first period of the game, all players choose the collusive Pareto-optimal quantities q_i^0. In any subsequent period, they continue to do so if, in all past periods, all players were loyal. If, however, this is not the case, then all players shift to the Cournot–Nash quantities q_i^c. The profit possibilities for a single period are represented in figure 6.1, reprinted by permission from Friedman (1983, figure 5.3).

Let $\Pi^0 = (\Pi_1^0, \Pi_2^0)$ be the profits realised in each period with the quantities (q_1^0, q_2^0) so that $\Pi_i^0 = F_i(q_1^0, q_2^0)$. These profits are somewhere on the profit frontier, possibly on the point that maximises joint profits. The stationarity assumption implies that the elements of the game are the same in each period, so that the profit frontier remains unchanged through time, and that each period is treated as completely independent of every other one. In a similar way, let $\Pi^c = (\Pi_1^c, \Pi_2^c)$ be the profits realised in each period with the equilibrium Cournot–Nash quantities (q_1^c, q_2^c) so that $\Pi_i^c = F_i(q_1^c, q_2^c)$.

Next define Π_1' as the maximum immediate profit firm 1 can make by cheating (producing $q_1' > q_1^0$) when the other firm sticks to q_2^0, or $\Pi_1' = \max F_1(q_1', q_1^0)$. We know from our discussion of the prisoner's dilemma that $\Pi_1' > \Pi_1^0$ and that the other firm will make a smaller profit. In figure 6.1, Π_1' corresponds to point A on the profit frontier. Define Π_2' similarly as max $F_2(q_1^0, q_2')$.

Each player's strategy is defined as

$$\sigma^i = \begin{cases} q_{i1} = q_i^0 & \\ q_{it} = q_i^0 & \text{if } q_{j\tau} = q_j^0 \, (j \neq i) \\ & \text{for } \tau = 1, \dots, t-1 \\ q_{it} = q_i^c & \text{otherwise.} \end{cases} \tag{6.1}$$

To decide whether cheating is worthwhile, each player compares the discounted value of his profits when these are equal to Π_i^0 in each period, or $\Pi_i^0/(1 - \delta_i)$ where δ_i is the discount factor used, with the discounted profits he would get if he were to choose q_i^0 for the first t periods and q_i' in period $t+1$. Because this deviation would be followed by a move to q_j^c, by his competitor in period $t+2$ and all subsequent periods, he would himself end up in q_i^c as of period $t+2$ because that is his best reply, so his discounted profits would be

$$\Pi_i^0 + \delta_i \Pi_i^0 + \cdots + \delta_i^{t-1} \Pi_i^0 + \delta_i^t \Pi_i' + \delta_i^{t+1} \Pi_i^c + \delta_i^{t+2} \Pi_i^c + \cdots$$

or

$$\frac{1 - \delta_i^t}{1 - \delta_i} \Pi_i^0 + \delta_i^t \Pi_i' + \delta_i^{t+1} \frac{1}{1 - \delta_i} \Pi_i^c.$$

Nobody will want to cheat – there is tacit collusion, that is, a non-cooperative collusive equilibrium – if, for all players

$$\frac{\Pi_i^0}{1 - \delta_i} > \frac{1 - \delta_i^t}{1 - \delta_i} \Pi_i^0 + \delta_i^t \Pi_i' + \delta_i^{t+1} \frac{1}{1 - \delta_i} \Pi_i^c$$

or

$$\Pi_i^0 > (1 - \delta_i)\Pi_i' + \delta_i \Pi_i^c,$$
$$\delta_i(\Pi_i' - \Pi_i^c) > \Pi_i' - \Pi_i^0, \tag{6.2}$$
$$\delta_i > \frac{\Pi_i' - \Pi_i^0}{\Pi_i' - \Pi_i^c}.$$

This is a particularly interesting result. The numerator $\Pi_i' - \Pi_i^0$ is the immediate extra gain from cheating. The denominator $\Pi_i' - \Pi_i^c$ is the per period decrease in profit in each succeeding period. Their ratio is compared with the discount factor. If the latter is sufficiently high, which means that a big enough weight is placed on the future (firms do not discount the future heavily), then cheating is not worthwhile. Firms that are not short-sighted but look far enough into the future will prefer tacit collusion to reaping immediate profits Π_i', and the vector q^0 repeated in each time period is a non-cooperative Nash equilibrium.[2] With $\delta_i = 1/(1+r)$, where r is the market rate of interest, it is clear that condition (6.2) is more likely to be satisfied in periods where the rate of interest is low. If the rate of interest is too high, it is optimal to set $t = 1$ and to cheat (choose q_i') in the first period, with the result that the industry is in a Cournot–Nash equilibrium as of period $t + 1$ and remains there.

When, in addition to (6.2)

$$\frac{\Pi_i' - \Pi_i^0}{\Pi_i' - \Pi_i^c} = \frac{\Pi_j' - \Pi_j^0}{\Pi_j' - \Pi_j^c} \ (i \neq j; \ i,j = 1,\ldots,n) \tag{6.3}$$

there is what may be called a 'balanced temptation equilibrium': each player has the same temptation to behave in a myopic way. Such an equilibrium is depicted in figure 6.1. (In that figure, point C does *not* represent the profits when both are cheating; there can be no profits outside the profit frontier! Point C is useful only to show that condition (6.3) is satisfied.)

We can now further elaborate Osborne's remark (see section 4.1) that collusion is difficult when the oligopolists have different time horizons. If, in the present context, some firms use a smaller discount factor than their competitors, so that their time horizon is in fact shorter, condition (6.2) may be satisfied for some and not for others. Tacit collusion is then not workable: Before you conclude that cheating is not profitable in the long run, you better check that all your competitors come to the same conclusion.

In fact, tacit collusion requires complete information exactly like in the case of explicit collusion. The equilibria described 'depend on each firm knowing the cost functions, demand functions, and discount parameters of all other firms for the present and all future periods. They depend also on the time lag during which a firm gains from deviation being of a known and fixed duration ...' (Friedman 1983, p. 133). It is a difficult empirical question to ascertain under which conditions real-life firms have information that is sufficiently complete for this model to have a descriptive value. Tacit collusion is likely to occur only in certain types of markets such as geographically segmented markets or markets with no rapid growth or

---

[2] An experiment conducted by Feinberg and Husted (1993) indicates that collusive duopoly equilibria are less likely to occur with lower discount factors.

slow technical progress, in which Friedman's inequality (6.2) is easy to compute.

Because of its reliance on complete information, Friedman's repeated game approach makes price wars appear as disequilibria. Although his approach has the advantage of giving a precise meaning to the concept of tacit collusion, it has the drawback that his non-cooperative equilibrium solves the prisoner's dilemma too well: No firm ever has an incentive to cheat in this equilibrium! One might want to treat price wars as part of an intertemporal equilibrium.

This is what Porter (1983a, b) and Green and Porter (1984) do, by introducing an extra incentive to cheat, based on incomplete information. They allow for random shocks in demand so that firms have incomplete information about their rivals' output. An observed price decrease may then be blamed on the demand shock rather than on cheating, so the intertemporal strategy (go to q_i^c if somebody cheats) is redefined in terms of a trigger price: Switch to the Cournot–Nash equilibrium as soon as the observed price is less than this trigger price. The equilibrium quantities are found to be above their joint profit-maximising level and to tend towards this level as the variance of the unobserved disturbance term (of demand) goes to zero. Interestingly, price wars now occur with positive probability as the result of unusual demand shocks. But individual deviations due to the availability of new information and the corresponding revision of beliefs about rivals' behaviour are not handled explicitly. Further work in this area will probably be devoted to the dynamic effects on cheating of the occurrence of new private information.[3]

This is not to suggest that price wars, treated as part of the intertemporal equilibrium, necessarily imply incomplete information. They can occur as well under complete (and perfect) information as part of non-cooperative intertemporal equilibrium price strategies. Selten (1965) showed this to be the case in a dynamic oligopoly game in which demand inertia dynamises consumer behaviour.[4] When oligopolists know that market demand will jump upward in the near future, they will conclude that the time has come to try to improve their market shares by engaging in active competition, because the foreseen improvement in market demand will allow all of them to recoup today's reduced profits (or losses). Launching a price war now can be in everybody's individual interest!

---

[3] As suggested by Fudenberg and Tirole (1986a). Slade (1987) analyses price wars as information-seeking devices used after shifts in demand occurred.

[4] The same result obtains when, in addition, the supply side of the market is dynamised by allowing producers to carry inventories, as in the generalised Selten model set up by Phlips and Richard (1989).

6.2 The 'Folk Theorem'

In Friedman's repeated game, the vector of collusive quantities q^0 of the one-period game turned out to be sustainable as a Nash equilibrium of the overall non-cooperative game. These quantities can be joint profit-max-imising ones. It is easily seen that they could as well be any quantities that give higher profits than the vector q^c of Cournot quantities. This is the basic intuition behind the different versions of the 'Folk Theorem', which implies that any vector to the North-East of the Cournot–Nash point in figure 4.1 can be sustained as Nash equilibria of the repeated game if the discount factor δ is large enough, that is, if sufficient weight is put on the future. In this sense, Friedman's balanced temptation equilibrium is an early version of the Folk Theorem.

The punishments envisaged by Friedman implied that a deviation be followed by a move of all competitors to the Cournot quantities q^c in *all* subsequent periods, that is, *forever*. By changing the nature of the punish-ments (also called 'trigger strategies'), different versions of the Folk Theorem emerge. One can make the punishments harsher. One can also make the punishment period shorter. On combining harsher punishments with a return to cooperation after some period of time, one gets a so-called 'stick and carrot' strategy, as suggested by Abreu (1986). Theorem 1 of Fudenberg and Maskin (1986) is based on such punishments. This is the version of the Folk Theorem considered in what follows and illustrated empirically in the next section.

The classical folk theorem asserts that any outcome that Pareto domi-nates the 'minimax point' can arise as a Nash equilibrium in infinitely repeated games when the discount factor is high enough. Fudenberg and Maskin's Theorem 1 refers to two-player games in which future outcomes are discounted. It states that if after any deviation *both* players would switch *for a specified number of periods* to strategies that minimise their opponent's maximum payoff (that is, there is a threat of mutual minimax-ing), then there exists a subgame perfect equilibrium for any pair of payoffs that Pareto dominates the minimax point when the duopolists have a discount factor that is above some minimum value.

Minimax strategies can be defined as follows. Let a_1, a_2 denote the best responses (choice of output or price) of duopolists 1 and 2, so that $a_i = r_i(a_j)$ is i's reaction function $(i, j = 1, 2, i \neq j)$ in a one-shot game. Then j minimaxes i by choosing the quantity or price $\hat{a}_j$ which minimises i's profit $\Pi_i(r_i(a_j), a_j)$. As a result of this choice, the best payoff i can get is $\Pi_i^* = \Pi_i(r_i(\hat{a}_j), \hat{a}_j)$ which is called i's minimax profit. It is the smallest payoff i can guarantee itself and results from i's best reply to being minimaxed by j.

The theorem supposes the following strategies. The duopolists choose prices or quantities, that give profits Π_1^0 and Π_2^0 which Pareto dominate the pair (Π_1^*, Π_2^*), as long as these prices or quantities were chosen last period. If one of the duopolists deviates, then each minimaxes the other during the next $v(\delta)$ periods. (The notation $v(\delta)$ indicates that the length of this period depends on the discount factor δ.) Following this punishment phase, the duopolists revert to the original prices or quantities. If either firm does not minimax the other during the punishment phase (thus deviating from the punishment path) the punishment phase is begun again.

The theorem shows that there exist discount rates between δ and 1 such that a positive punishment period v can be found for which the inequality

$$\Pi_i' - \Pi_i^0 < \frac{\delta \Pi_i^0}{1-\delta} - \left[\frac{(1-\delta^v)\delta}{1-\delta} \Pi_i^{**} + \frac{\delta^{v+1}}{1-\delta} \Pi_i^0 \right] \qquad (6.4)$$

is satisfied. As before, Π_i' is the maximum immediate profit firm i can make by deviating, while Π_i^{**} is the profit resulting from mutual minimaxing. Π_i^0 is any collusive payoff that Pareto dominates Π_i^{**}. The left-hand side of the inequality (6.4) therefore measures the gain from deviating this period. The right-hand side gives the difference between the present value of receiving Π_i^0 forever, *starting next period*,[5] and that of a profit stream consisting of the profit with mutual minimaxing during the next v periods, followed by reversion to Π_i^0 forever. When the inequality is satisfied, each duopolist prefers not to deviate since the one-period gain from deviating is smaller than the loss of profit from being minimaxed.

Would a firm be willing to minimax the other under these conditions? The answer is: yes. And the implication is that the threat to punish by mutual minimaxing is credible, so that the collusive outcomes Π_i^0 correspond to a subgame perfect equilibrium, that is, a Nash equilibrium in *all* subgames (periods). Indeed, it is possible to choose the length of the punishment period in such a way that

$$\Pi_i^* - \Pi_i^{**} < \delta^v (\Pi_i^0 - \Pi_i^{**}). \qquad (6.5)$$

The expression $(\Pi_i^* - \Pi_i^{**})$ measures the gain for firm i from not minimaxing its competitor. The right-hand side of the inequality is the present value of the loss of profits due to the postponement of the reversion to Π_i^0 by v periods. (Remember that if either firm does not minimax the other during the punishment phase, the punishment phase is begun again.)

In the next section, this theory of tacit collusion in a repeated game with minimax punishments is used to explain why no deviations from suppo-

---

[5] Remember that the present value of a constant stream of profits Π^0, starting today, is $\Pi^0/(1-\delta)$, while it is $\delta\Pi^0/(1-\delta) = \Pi^0/r$ when the discounting starts next period.

sedly collusive prices were observed in the UK market for salt during the years for which data are available.

6.3 The great salt duopoly

After a period of price wars in the 1930s, the British producers of white salt made an explicit agreement to fix common prices. This agreement was discontinued in 1956 after the passing of the Restrictive Practices Act in the UK. Was explicit collusion replaced by tacit collusion? If so, are the facts compatible with the assumptions of the Folk Theorem? Rees (1991) answers this question affirmatively with the help of Fudenberg and Maskin's 1986 version[6] of the Folk Theorem discussed in section 6.2, using yearly data on the period 1980–4 provided in a report by the UK Monopolies and Mergers Commission.[7]

During the period of investigation the market structure is as follows. There are two producers, British Salt (BS) with more or less 55 per cent of the UK market, and ICI Weston Point (WP). Each duopolist has an exogenously fixed capacity. Although BS has the larger market share, it has the smaller capacity. Both duopolists have excess capacity. Imports are negligible and there is no threat of new entry, so that their market is geographically separated (a circumstance which facilitates tacit collusion, as suggested in section 6.1). Note also that BS has a cost advantage. The products are perfectly homogeneous.

The observed time shape of the prices is one of 'parallel pricing'. For all observed price changes (increases), one firm announced the change and the other firm followed it within a month (usually two weeks) with an identical change. BS led eight times and WP five times between 1974 and 1980. WP was the leader in each of the years 1981–4. There was price leadership, but the bigger firm (WP) was not always the leader. Whoever took the initiative of a price change informed the follower a month in advance and the follower informed the leader of a proposed identical change within that period. In the next chapter (sections 7.3 and especially 7.4) it will be shown that this type of price leadership, modelled as a repeated game, leads to collusive profits that are between those of the one-period Nash equilibrium and the full maximisation of joint profits. Here we wish – following Rees

---

[6] In the published version of his paper, Rees (1993b) uses the simple penal code defined by Lambson (1987) for price-setting repeated games with capacity constraints.

[7] 'White salt: A report on the supply of white salt in the United Kingdom by producers of such salt', HMSO, London, 1986.

(1991) – to quantify[8] the potential gains and losses from deviations followed by punishments in order to see whether the Fudenberg–Maskin (1986) minimax punishments give a satisfactory explanation of why no deviations actually occurred during the observation period.

To compute minimax strategies, one has to know the cost structure of the firms involved. While BS has a constant average variable cost of production (AVC), WP's AVC rises in a stepwise way when output is reduced below capacity. Marginal cost (MC) is the sum of AVC and average distribution cost (mainly transport costs). Rees defines average avoidable cost (AAC) as a firm's MC plus average 'fixed' production costs (mainly labour, management and maintenance costs that do not vary with output but are incurred only if the plant is operating). Whenever AAC is above any feasible price it is rational to shut down the plant.

Let BS be player 1 and WP player 2. Then $\overline{AAC}_1$ denotes BS's AAC at its capacity output (824 kilotonnes) and $\overline{AAC}_2$ is WP's AAC at capacity (1095 kilotonnes). Suppose both players use price strategies. To minimax player 1, player 2 sets a price p_2 equal to $\overline{AAC}_1$, so that player 1 cannot undercut it. This price minimises player 1's profit. This 'minimax' profit is zero if there is no higher price player 1 could set that is above its AAC curve. It is positive if there exists such a higher price because player 1's residual demand curve lies above its AAC curve. This residual demand curve represents any demand in excess of player 2's capacity output (which player 2 will supply since p_2 is then lower than the price of player 1). Player 1's (positive) profit is maximised, given $p_2 = \overline{AAC}_1$, by choosing the appropriate p_1 on the residual demand curve.

The minimaxing prices of WP and BS can be computed from the data given in table 6.1 for any year. In 1984, for example, BS's total production cost function can be seen to be

$$C_1 = 3{,}004 + 9.07\,q_1.$$

WP's total production cost function, in the same year, is

$$C_2 = \begin{matrix} 3{,}376 + 14.66\,q_2 & \text{for} & 0 < q_2 \leq 300 \\ 3{,}376 + 11.47\,q_2 & \text{for} & 300 < q_2 \leq 800 \\ 3{,}376 + \ \ 9.97\,q_2 & \text{for} & 800 < q_2 \leq 1{,}095. \end{matrix}$$

Since WP's output was 450 kilotonnes, its actual AVC was £11.47. $\overline{AAC}_1$ is equal to 9.07 (AVC) plus 4.29 (average distribution cost) plus 3.65 (BS's

[8] Rees presumes that the data given in the report of the Monopolies and Mergers Commission are correct. Data reporting by firms that have an informational advantage relative to the antitrust authority and can thus make the detection of tacit collusion difficult (if not impossible) is discussed in chapter 8.

Table 6.1. *Costs and profits of UK salt producers (1980–4)*

	1980	1981	1982	1983	1984
Outputs (kilotonnes)					
BS	702	587	649	570	553
WP (UK only)	592	512	476	437	450
WP (exports)	232	158	246	199	257
Average variable costs (£)					
BS	6.30	8.07	8.12	9.21	9.07
WP for $0 < q_2 \leq 300$	7.70	9.45	12.13	13.83	14.66
$300 < q_2 \leq 800$	6.02	7.39	9.49	10.82	11.47
$800 < q_2 \leq 1,095$	5.24	6.23	8.25	9.41	9.97
Average distribution costs (£)					
BS	3.51	4.04	3.91	4.46	4.29
WP	6.75	6.83	5.25	5.95	4.67
Fixed production costs (£000)					
BS	2,307	2,439	2,218	2,800	3,004
WP	2,702	2,651	3,032	3,432	3,376
Average avoidable cost at capacity					
BS ($\overline{AAC_1}$)	12.61	15.07	14.72	17.07	17.01
WP ($\overline{AAC_2}$)	14.46	15.68	16.28	18.49	17.72
Net sales value (average revenue minus distribution cost)					
BS	19.65	25.21	27.70	31.93	34.18
WP (UK sales)	20.80	25.60	29.40	32.00	32.00
WP (exports)	11.30	12.80	11.10	13.20	12.80
Profits (£000)					
BS	7,065	7,622	10,489	10,150	10,882
WP (in UK only)	6,048	6,673	6,445	5,824	5,863

Source: Rees (1991), table 1 and appendix.

fixed production cost divided by its capacity output), that is, £17.01. $\overline{AAC_2}$ is obtained by adding 9.97 (AVC at capacity) plus 4.67 (average distribution cost) plus 3.08 (WP's fixed production cost divided by its capacity output), that is, £17.72.

If WP were to set $p_2 = 17.01$ and produce 1,095 kilotonnes, BS's residual demand $(q_1 + q_2 - 1,095)$ would be negative in 1984 and its minimax profit zero. Its optimal action would have been to shut down. This is in fact true for every year. If BS were to deviate from the announced prices, WP could punish it very severely indeed. The converse is not true. If BS were to minimax WP, setting $p_1 = 17.72$, the latter could still make a positive minimax profit since its residual demand is positive. While WP's retaliation makes BS lose its entire profit, BS's retaliation would be much less harmful for WP. BS has to stick to the agreement, although it is the lower cost producer, while WP might hesitate, depending on the profit gain from deviating.

However, during the punishment phase, envisaged by the Fudenberg–Maskin theorem, there is *mutual* minimaxing. Mutual minimaxing means that, instead of choosing its best response to the minimax price of the other, each firm now chooses its minimax price. There is mutual retaliation. If BS were to set $p_1 = \overline{AAC_2}$ in a particular year (it is supposed that deviations last one year and that retaliations last one year during the following year, since only yearly data are available), then WP would set $p_2 = \overline{AAC_1}$ during the same year. The values for $\overline{AAC_1}$ and $\overline{AAC_2}$ are given in table 6.1 and imply that WP would set the lower price in each year in case of mutual punishment. Since the product is homogeneous, WP would produce at capacity while BS would still produce nothing. BP's loss would be the entire profit made at the agreed price. But since WP is now selling at a price $(\overline{AAC_1})$ which is below its own average avoidable cost at capacity, it would produce at a loss. Its total loss due to the punishment would be this loss plus the profit it makes at the agreed price.

Table 6.2 gives the profit gains due to a deviation in a particular year and the losses in the next year due to (a) a minimax punishment by the other firm and (b) mutual minimaxing.[9] With mutual minimaxing, BS's losses are the same while WP's losses are much higher. Why would WP then resort to mutual minimaxing? In the logic of the Fudenberg–Maskin theorem, it would do this to avoid an extension of the punishment period so that both firms revert sooner to the agreed prices and higher profits. So this type of

---

[9] To understand how the numbers appearing in table 6.2 are computed, consider year 1984. Deviations are supposed to consist of undercutting the announced price in such a way that net sales value (average revenue minus distribution cost per unit) fall by 1 per cent, enabling the deviator to increase its output to capacity. BS's profit gain from deviating in 1984 is the difference between the profit it made in that year (10,882) and the profit it would make at the lower net sales value. Profits are calculated as (net sales value − average variable cost) output − fixed production cost. The deviation implies a net sales value of $34.18 - 0.3418 = 33.84$. It would give a profit of

$$(33.84 - 9.07)\,824 - 3{,}004 = 17{,}405.$$

BS's profit gain is $17{,}405 - 10{,}882 = 6{,}523$.

In 1984, the profit of WP is 5,863. With mutual minimaxing, selling at full capacity implies a loss of $(17.72 - 17.01)\,1{,}095 = 777$. Its total loss from punishment is $5{,}863 + 777 = 6{,}640$.

Table 6.2. *Gains and losses from deviating of UK salt producers (£000)*

Year	Profit gain from deviating	Loss from mini-maxing by competition	Loss from mutual minimaxing
BS			
1980	1,466	—	—
1981	3,855	7,622	7,622
1982	3,199	10,489	10,489
1983	5,508	10,150	10,150
1984	6,523	10,882	10,882
WP			
1980	8,050	—	—
1981	11,387	3,915	7,341
1982	13,360	2,914	8,109
1983	11,976	4,142	7,379
1984	11,380	4,145	6,640

Source: Rees (1991, tables 2 and 3).

mutual punishment is a credible threat and WP also wants to stick to the agreement. Further evidence suggesting that the profits reported in table 6.1 are indeed collusive will be given in section 9.6 on the basis of the semicollusive model discussed in chapter 9.

7   Price leadership and conscious parallelism

The invasion of economic theory by game theory does not seem to have spared any part of microeconomic theory. In this chapter, I intend to give an account of the beneficial contributions of this invasion for a better understanding of parallel behaviour and its more or less collusive nature. Inevitably, attention will be focused on price leadership[1] which is frequently observed in oligopolistic markets.[2]

When leadership is mentioned the Stackelberg model comes to mind. Two firms have quantity strategies and the leader increases his market share (and his profit) by anticipating the follower's behaviour (who takes the leader's output as given). Unfortunately, this model does not adequately explain parallel behaviour such that the announcement by a firm of a new price is very quickly adopted by its competitors. On the one hand, the sequential character of these announcements is neither modelled nor

---

[1] I limit myself to the case where a *single* firm announces a price, followed quickly by the other competitors. Therefore, I do not consider the situations of collusive price leadership where a *group* of dominant firms is followed by a competitive fringe. The conditions in which such groups can be formed and can be maintained are examined, for example, by Markham (1951), Oxenfeldt (1952), Lanzillotti (1957), d'Aspremont *et al.* (1983) and Sleuwaegen (1986). Shaw (1974) discusses the difficulties of leaders, faced with new entry, in the UK petrol industry. The welfare losses associated with these situations are empirically evaluated by Gisser (1984 and 1986), Dickson (1988), Gisser (1988), Willner (1989) and Gisser (1989) for the US. The legal concept of 'collective dominance' used recently by the European Commission with reference to Article 86 of the Treaty of Rome, seems to correspond to the concept of collusive leadership of the above-mentioned economists (see 'Re Italian flat glass', *Common Market Law Report* 1990, 4, 535). Naturally, I will discuss non-cooperative equilibria of the leader–follower type which imply collusive profits.

[2] Several cases of price leadership in the US are well documented in Scherer (1980, chapter 6). On Europe, see Bourdet (1988, pp. 177–88) and Kirman and Schueller (1990) on the automobile industry and Phlips (1962, chapter 8) on photographic products. Fog (1960) analyses a great number of Danish industries. The newspaper industry in Sidney is analysed by Merrilees (1983). See also section 6.3 on the white salt industry in the UK, which is based on Rees (1991 and 1993b).

explained. On the other hand, the identity of the leader remains undetermined: the two Stackelberg firms both want to be the leader.

Can one define a non-cooperative equilibrium which incorporates sequential decisions and in which the identity of the leader is endogenous? In the following, I shall describe the progress made, step by step, in order to answer this question. Quite naturally, the first analytical efforts used static games (with or without uncertainty). More recently, the problem has been re-examined in a repeated game framework.

This dynamic approach illustrates the role played by pre-play conventions on the policy to be followed during the game. It will be shown that price parallelism *over time* which characterises price leadership is facilitated by an implicit convention between the players, according to which they agree to adopt the same rule of behaviour. This rule says that each one will align to the other as soon as a price rise is announced by one of the players. An important distinction is thus made between a 'pricing policy' agreed upon before the beginning of the game and the fixing of a particular price in the course of the game. (In legal terminology, this convention is what one calls a 'concerted practice' facilitating collusion.) *Spatially*, the adoption of a rule of alignment on prices calculated from multiple basing points plays the same role. I could not resist the temptation to devote a final section to this spatial pricing policy. Particular attention will be given to the implications for competition policy, as pursued by the European Commission, the more so as the convention on spatial alignment is rendered obligatory (sic!) by the Treaty of the European Coal and Steel Community (ECSC) in the coal and steel industry.

7.1 Static games without uncertainty

Let us, to begin with, confine ourselves to a world without uncertainty and pinpoint some studies that have deepened Stackelberg's contribution while remaining faithful to the assumption that the players use either quantity strategies or price strategies. Under what conditions would a duopolist have an interest in being the first to move given this assumption? Gal-Or (1985a) shows that this depends on the slope of the reaction functions. If these functions are both decreasing, as in the case of quantity competition between homogeneous products where the strategies are negatively correlated, the leader makes more profit than the follower. If these functions are both increasing, as in the case of price competition between differentiated substitutes where the strategies are positively correlated, it is the follower who makes the largest profits. In the first situation, each firm prefers to be the leader. In the second situation, each firm prefers the other to be the leader, *if* both firms have similar profit functions. This is Dowrick's (1986) point. In other words, if both firms have positively sloped reaction functions, the Stackelberg game has a reasonable solution only if the firms are sufficiently asymmetric in terms of costs and demand, such that one will prefer to lead. With decreasing reaction functions, they will fight to be the leader.

Clearly, the preceding analysis does not entirely answer the question of who will be the leader. Just because one firm wishes to be the leader, that does not imply that the other firm will agree to be the follower. If the two firms prefer to lead (or follow), neither can claim the preferred role. And even if the two firms agree that one of them should lead, it remains to be shown that this solution is the relevant non-cooperative equilibrium rather than a non-cooperative equilibrium with simultaneous actions. This is why Hamilton and Slutsky (1990) analyse an extended game where the players must choose both an action and the date of this action. If the firms have to carry out the action for which they have chosen a date, sequential results are obtained for non-dominated strategies. However, if the firms choose the date but need not specify the action they will take when they choose to lead, the equilibrium will result in simultaneous actions unless the resulting profits from the sequential actions Pareto dominate, that is to say, unless the two prefer the same sequential action to a simultaneous action. The existence of leader–follower type equilibria is thus well established. The equilibria typically arise in asymmetric cases where the firms are different and where they use price strategies.

I do not wish to explore these generalities any further, but rather specify, in more detail, the asymmetries and further enlarge the set of feasible strategies, for example[3] by combining price and quantity strategies. In this respect, Ono's approach (1978) appears exemplary: it uses more realistic assumptions and leads to precise results (at the cost of a loss in generality).

Ono assumes that the follower fixes a price infinitesimally smaller than that of its competitor and determines his output under the assumption that he is facing the entire demand of the market at this price (the products being homogeneous). The leader knows that the follower acts in this way and determines his price and output with respect to his individual demand curve. The latter is obtained by subtracting the rival output from the market demand curve.

We can represent the (downward-sloping) market demand curve by $x = D(p)$. If the leader (firm 1) fixes a price p, then the follower (firm 2) determines its output such that $p = C_2'(x_2)$ where $C_2'(x_2)$ is the (convex) marginal cost. The output of the follower is therefore

---

[3] Anderson (1987) shows, in the framework of the Hotelling model, that the introduction of the spatial dimension makes it possible to endogenise the Stackelberg leader.

$$x_2 = C_2'^{-1}(p) \qquad \text{if } C_2'(0) < p \le C_2'\{D(p)\}. \tag{7.1}$$

The follower monopolises the market if $p > C_2'\{D(p)\}$. The individual demand curve of the leader is thus

$$
\begin{aligned}
x_1 &= D(p) && \text{if} \quad p \le C_2'(0) \\
x_1 &= D(p) - C_2'^{-1}(p) && \text{if} \quad C_2'(0) < p \le C_2'\{D(p)\} \\
x_1 &= 0 && \text{if} \quad p > C_2'\{D(p)\}.
\end{aligned}
\tag{7.2}
$$

From these assumptions, Ono (1978 and 1982) obtains the following results for homogeneous products:[4]

1 If one of the firms has sufficiently low marginal costs such that the optimal output of any other firm choosing to be leader is sufficiently small, it is more profitable for this firm to be the leader. Moreover, when a firm makes more profit as leader than as follower, all other firms prefer to follow. Put more simply, 'sufficiently inefficient' firms prefer to follow whilst the 'sufficiently efficient' firm prefers to lead. This implies that a Stackelberg war is impossible in equilibrium.

2 When each firm has the same marginal cost, they all prefer to follow.

3 All firms which accept to lead can obtain a greater profit than in the Nash equilibrium. Thus there is a common disadvantage when all firms try to act as a follower *vis-à-vis* the others.

Ono (1982) notes that the firm which leads voluntarily is not necessarily the one which has the largest market share. Figure 7.1 illustrates this possibility. Firm 1 has the lowest marginal cost and will therefore be the leader. MN is the market demand curve. The residual demand curve of the leader is ST, obtained by horizontal subtraction of the marginal cost of the follower MC_2. The point where marginal revenue (MR_1^1) equals marginal cost (MC_1) gives the price B, for which firm 1 receives the profit ABDE (whilst the follower makes the profit ACF). At the leader's price, B, the leader's market share, AB, is smaller than the follower's, AC. When examining the profits that firm 2 could make as the leader, it can be seen that it is in the interest of firm 1 to be the leader and of firm 2 to be the follower. Firm 2's residual demand curve would be QR and its marginal revenue would be MR_2^1, so that it would fix price H and would gain profit GHKF, which is smaller than ACF. In this case, firm 1 would only obtain GLE < ABDE.

Like Ono, Boyer and Moreaux (1986, 1987) endow firms with price *and* quantity strategies. However, they do this for both duopolists, while only the follower is allowed two strategies in Ono's approach, the leader having to be satisfied with fixing the price. Boyer and Moreaux (1987, note 4)

---

[4] He obtains analogous results for differentiated products.

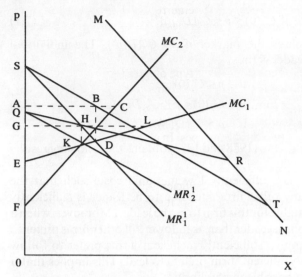

Figure 7.1 The leader has the smaller market share
Source: Ono (1982)

criticise this assumption in the following words: 'Why would the leader give the follower the possibility of acquiring the market share that the latter prefers? This is a privilege that the leader gives to the follower and is contrary to the interests of the leader. No valid justification of such a philanthropic behaviour is given by Ono.' I do not understand this criticism. The possibility of appropriating the market share that is optimal for the follower (including the whole of the market) with an infinitesimal price decrease, results from the homogeneity of the product and has nothing philanthropic about it. Given this homogeneity, the interest of the leader is to put itself on its residual demand.

In the models of Boyer and Moreaux, each firm fixes a price and decides to 'offer' a certain quantity, in the sense that at this price it is willing to sell this quantity or less (but not more). There is, therefore, a possibility of rationing, each firm being able to put itself below its demand function. This assumption is supposed to correspond to observed business behaviour. 'Rare, indeed, are firms who would accept to sell a certain quantity whatever the market price, which is what an output strategy ultimately implies ...' (Boyer and Moreaux 1986, p. 57). Here again it is difficult to understand. What I do understand is the remark made by Friedman (1983, pp. 47–8) that car manufacturers are obliged to plan their production in advance and subsequently to fix a price that the market will accept. It is in this way that output strategies can be interpreted in business practice. I also note that the choice of the rationing scheme remains entirely arbitrary: random rationing is postulated for the sole reason that it is simple! I finally note that, in practice, firms try to avoid having to ration their customers, because a rejected customer is a lost customer.[5]

Whatever the case, let us consider what type of equilibrium the assumption of demand rationing leads to. As in the Ono model, when the costs of production are identical or similar, both firms prefer to be the follower. If, to the contrary, there is a substantial cost difference, the non-cooperative equilibrium can only be of two different types. In one case, the *least* efficient firm behaves as leader and sells a *limited* quantity at a *low* price, whilst the most efficient firm behaves as a follower and sells to the residual demand at a higher price. In the other case, the most efficient firm eliminates the other by adopting a limit-price strategy. In doing so, it receives a lower profit than if it had behaved as a follower. To sum up, this is the world upside down, the intuition being that the poor buyers who are not served by the leader will be exploited by the follower.

7.2 Static games with uncertainty

The results obtained by Ono in a static world without uncertainty (and where the players are perfectly informed) are already very satisfying. Let us nevertheless see how the analysis can be refined by confronting the players with imperfect information. I will first introduce demand uncertainty. Secondly, I will examine how the Stackelberg leader emerges when production costs are uncertain. Finally, I will examine the role a group of loyal customers, who cannot be distinguished from price sensitive consumers, may play.

Let us assume that the firms are confronted with both a random market demand and an uncertain market share. When an economic shock (for example, a recession) occurs, it is immediately reflected in their sales and in their stocks. For the individual firm, the reason for this is not clear: is the unexpected fall in sales due to a shift in the market demand function or is it due to a random variation around an unchanged function? In order to detect the shock, the firm must estimate market demand. But for this, its own sales are the most immediate source of information.

Eckard (1982) thinks that the smaller the market share of the firm, the greater the variance of its estimate will be, in view of the uncertainty about the evolution of its rivals' sales (and, therefore, about its own market share). In fact, rival competition generates statistical 'noise' which reduces the

---

[5] Delivery delays which are typical for certain makes of car (Mercedes!) can be interpreted as a marketing device to maintain the car's image.

precision of its estimate. The probability of detecting the shock (and of a suitable reaction in price) is therefore greater for the firms who have the relatively larger market shares.

From here, the transition towards a leader–follower model is immediate: on the one hand, the largest firm is the most likely to be the first to detect the shift in market demand; on the other hand, the smaller firms observe the price reactions of the large firm, in order to get valuable information for their own market analyses. The small firms profit from the largest firm's ability to generate the most efficient information.

This information is a public good which the leader provides to the whole industry. It remains to be seen whether the leader has an interest in obtaining this information, given that the gathering of information has a cost. Higgins *et al.* (1989) show that this is indeed the case. They assume that the industry is composed of r factories of equal size and that the dominant firm controls t of these. As in the Ono model, the small firms adopt the price fixed by the dominant firm and determine their sales by equalising their marginal cost with this price. Hence their global offer O^f is $(r-t)p/c$. The cost function of the dominant firm is $(c/2t)(D-O^f)^2$, where $D = A + bp$ is the market demand. Given O^f (known) the leader's residual demand is $D - O^f = A + [bc - (r-t)]p/c \equiv A + Bp$. Higgins *et al.* assume that intercept A is uncertain and equal to the sum $X_1 + \ldots + X_n$. The X_i are random, identically and independently distributed variables with mean μ/n and variance σ^2. The dominant firm can know m among the X_i at a search cost of $(d/2)m^2$. Hence its profit function is

$$\Pi = (D - O^f)p - (c/2t)(D - O^f)^2 - (d/2)m^2$$
$$= A(1/t)(t - cB)p + (1/2t)(2t - cB)Bp^2 - (c/2t)A^2 - (d/2)m^2. \tag{7.3}$$

In a first stage, the expectation (conditional on the information obtained) is maximised to determine the optimal price p^*. Using this result, the unconditional expected profit

$$E^*(\Pi) = \gamma(\mu^2 + m\sigma^2) - (c/2t)\eta\sigma^2 - (d/2)m^2 \tag{7.4}$$

is maximised, in a second stage, to determine the optimal size of the sample m.

One obtains

$$m^* = \gamma\sigma^2/d,$$
$$\text{where } \gamma = -(1/2tB)(t - cB)^2/(2t - cB). \tag{7.5}$$

A similar calculation is made for the small firms. Their expected profit turns out to be an increasing function of m. The more precise the pricing policy of the dominant firm, the more profits they will make. Consequently, as Eckard (1982) had already noted, the variability of prices increases with the market share of the leader.[6]

Note that in the Stackelberg game (using quantity strategies) where the leader has private information about the state of market demand, this information is also revealed to the follower through the leader's output. Gal-Or (1987) shows that, in a linear world, the inferences made by the follower increase the slope of its reaction function. This slope can even become positive if, at the time the follower revises its a priori beliefs, it gives sufficient weight to the quantity produced by the leader. Consequently, it is not necessarily true that the leader makes more profit than the follower, as was the case when there was perfect information (see above).

Consider uncertainty about the costs of production in a static non-cooperative duopoly game. Assume that the two firms neither know their own marginal cost nor their rival's. However, they both know the parameters of the distributions from which these costs are drawn at the time when they agree on the distribution of roles (leader or follower). (In case of a disagreement, they will play the relevant Nash game.) When they then decide on their output, they know their own but not their rival's marginal cost.

It is with this information structure that Albaek (1990) proves the existence of a 'Natural Stackelberg Situation' (NSS). Since it implies an agreement, there is a cooperative aspect to it. But, this is only apparent: true cooperation – in particular an exchange of information – is excluded. The idea is to calculate the expected profits for the three possible outcomes: leader, follower or Nash, *before* the firms know their marginal cost. A NSS exists when one of the firms has the greatest expected profit as leader and the other as follower. A NSS does not exist when pricing strategies are used. Albaek emphasises that the solution does not depend on the substitutability or the complementarity of the products. Even when there is complementarity, a firm can still wish to be leader, because the strategic disadvantage of the leader can be compensated by better coordinated responses to cost variations. In the case of substitutability, it is the strategic disadvantage of the follower which can be compensated by the information it obtains on the costs of the rival.

It remains to introduce the role that customer loyalty can play in determining the identity of the leader. Deneckere, Kovenock and Lee (1992) assume that two firms produce a non-durable differentiated product at zero cost. The consumers, who buy at the most one unit from one of the firms, are partitioned into three groups. In the first group, firm 1 has n_1 loyal consumers, in the sense that they buy one unit of its product if its price is

---

[6] According to Holthausen (1979), price variation is greater when the firm is less risk averse.

$p_1 < r$, the common reservation price. The second group consists of n_2 consumers who are loyal to firm 2, and are defined in a similar way. The third group is composed of m consumers who buy at the lowest price (as long as it is less than r). The two firms know the value of n_1, n_2 and m but do not know which group a consumer belongs to (so that they cannot price discriminate).

The profit of firm i ($i = 1,2$) is therefore

$$\Pi_i(p_i, p_j) = \begin{cases} L_i(p_i) = (n_i + m)p_i & \text{if } p_i < p_j \\ T_i(p_i) = (n_i + D_f^i m)p_i & \text{if } p_i = p_j \\ H_i(p_i) = n_i p_i & \text{if } p_i > p_j \end{cases} \tag{7.6}$$

on the assumption that the third group buys from the follower when prices are equal, so that $D_f^i = 1$ if i is the follower and $D_f^i = 0$ if i is the leader. If $n_1 > n_2$, firm 1 is shown to have equilibrium profits $\Pi_1 = n_1 r$ if it acts as either leader or follower or as a result of playing a simultaneous game (so that $\Pi_1^L = \Pi_1^F = n_1 r$). This firm is therefore indifferent between the three situations. To the contrary, firm 2 (which has the smallest segment of loyal clients) prefers to follow (so $\Pi_2^F = (n_2 + m)r$) and is indifferent between leading and playing simultaneously (its profit then being $\Pi_2^L = ((n_2 + m)/(n_1 + m))n_1 r < \Pi_2^F$). In equilibrium, $p_1 = p_2 = r$ when firm 1 is the leader. If firm 2 leads, it attracts the third group at the cost of a lower price $p_2 = n_1 r/(n_1 + m)$ but firm 1 keeps the price $p_1 = r$ and therefore continues to sell only to its own customers.

In order to show that firm 1 is the endogenous leader, Deneckere *et al.* construct a game in which the optimal date of the price announcements is determined. The time period considered is the unit interval $[0,1]$, divided into T (T even) periods of length $\tau = 1/T$, where $t = 0, \cdots, T-1$. Firm 2 may announce its price at the beginning of intervals with an even index and firm 1 may announce at the beginning of intervals with an odd index.[7] There is a cost of waiting, so that profits are discounted using a discount factor $\delta = e^{-\rho t}$.

Proceeding backwards, firm 2 announces its leader price, p_2, at time $T-2$ since that is the last date at which it can fix a price. No price is announced previously. Firm 1 follows at $T-1$ by announcing its follower price p_1. The discounted equilibrium profits will be $\delta^{T-1}\Pi_2^L$ and $\delta^{T-1}\Pi_1^F$ respectively. At any period t (for $t = 1,3,\cdots.T-3$) no price having previously been announced, firm 1 must compare $\delta^{t+1}\Pi_1^L$ to $\delta^{t+j+1}\Pi_1^L$ (if it leads at $t+j$,

---

[7] The prices are fixed only once and remain in force for the duration of the unit interval rather than for a particular period. Profits only materialise after the moment when the *two* firms will have made their announcements. These restrictions can be relaxed: see Deneckere *et al.* (1992, p. 154).

except when $t = T - 3$, since then the profit of the leader is zero at $t + 2$) or to $\delta^{t+j}\Pi_1^F$ in case it follows at $t + j$ ($j > 2$, even). However, we know that $\Pi_1^L = \Pi_1^F$. Firm 1 will therefore always announce its leader price at the first opportunity (so long as no price has been previously set). As for firm 2, it must therefore, at $t = 0,2,4,\cdots,T-4$ compare $\delta^{t+1}\Pi_2^L$ to the profit it would have earned after having waited for the announcement of firm 1, that is $\delta^{t+2}\Pi_2^F$. If $(\Pi_2^L/\Pi_2^F) < \delta$ it prefers to wait. However, $(\Pi_2^L/\Pi_2^F) < 1$. For a sufficiently large discount factor δ, firm 2 will always wait until firm 1 has fixed its leader price at $t = 1$, and fix its follower price at $t = 2$. Firm 1 is an endogenous leader.

It is clear that this model enables us to understand why, in an international context (for example within the Common Market), national firms emerge as leaders in their respective national markets to the extent that patriotic feelings ensure them more loyal customers.

The chronological order of the events is explicitly taken into account in the preceding paragraphs but the equilibrium prices announced at a certain date are the result of an instantaneous game. The time has come for us to turn towards a dynamic approach in which the time shape is incorporated in the basic model. A repeated game appears to be the simplest approach to take.

7.3 A repeated game

The pricing policy examined here is often observed in oligopolistic markets. Often, there is one firm which announces a price change some time before the date at which the new price will be valid. This date, as well as the new price, are adopted after a brief delay by the other firms. The new price is often accepted as such, even when the products are differentiated, so that all the rival firms make the same announcement within a short time period.[8] The question to answer is whether collective behaviour of this type can lead to collusive results in the absence of explicit collusion. The answer of Rotemberg and Saloner (1990) is affirmative.

The model has two firms producing good 1 and good 2 respectively at a constant marginal cost c. The demand curves of these firms are

$$q_1 = x - bp_1 + d(p_2 - p_1)$$
$$q_2 = y - bp_2 + d(p_1 - p_2). \tag{7.7}$$

---

[8] Often as well, a considerable time period separates the dates at which the prices change. This price 'rigidity' should not be confused with a small variability (which depends on the size of the price variation). Rotemberg and Saloner (1990, pp. 100–4) show that such a rigidity can reduce the difference between the profit of the leader and that of the follower (which occurs when the leader changes price too often).

They are symmetric, apart from the intercepts x and y. These parameters fluctuate over time. Define $a \equiv (x+y)/2$ and $e \equiv (x-y)/2$. Hence, equations (7.7) become

$$q_1 = a + e - bp_1 + d(p_2 - p_1)$$
$$q_2 = a - e - bp_2 + d(p_1 - p_2). \tag{7.8}$$

The change in variables gives a common component, a, which affects the level of the two demands in the same way, and an idiosyncratic component, e, which increases q_1 by the same amount as it decreases q_2.

The information structure is the following. Firm 1 knows the values of a and e whereas firm 2 knows only their distribution, as well as the history of the prices and the quantities. When a and e are distributed independently, this history does not give any information about the current value of a and e. As a consequence, firm 2 only knows the unconditional means, which are a' and zero. Firm 1 is unable to communicate its information in a credible way.

If the information had been perfect, the firms would have been able to maximise joint profit, that is $[q_1(p_1 - c) + q_2(p_2 - c)]$, which would have led them to announce two different prices

$$p_1 = [a/b + c + e/(b + 2d)]/2$$
$$p_2 = [a/b + c - e/(b + 2d)]/2 \tag{7.9}$$

and to obtain a global profit of

$$R = (a - bc)^2/2b + e^2/(2b + 4d). \tag{7.10}$$

In reality, they play a non-cooperative repeated game whose collusive result can be sustained at equilibrium by the credible threat of a price war if one of them deviates from the agreed pricing policy. The collusive outcome results from an implicit *preliminary* agreement on the following pricing policy: at the beginning of each period, firm 1 announces its price for this period, to the extent that firm 2 has not previously deviated; firm 2 next announces the same price that period; if firm 2 should announce another price, an infinite price war would ensue, in the sense that in all following periods the announced prices would be the equilibrium prices of the corresponding static (single period) price leadership game.

At the equilibrium of the repeated game, firm 1 is certain its price is also that of the other ($p_1 = p_2 = p$). Its profit for each period is therefore

$$R_1 = (p - c)(a + e - bp) \tag{7.11}$$

and in equilibrium

$$p^* = c/2 + (a + e)/2b \tag{7.12}$$

$$R_1^* = (a + e - bc)^2/4b. \tag{7.13}$$

For the follower

$$R_2 = (p - c)(a - e - bp) \tag{7.14}$$

and in equilibrium

$$R_2^* = (a + e - bc)^2/4b - (a + e - bc)e/b \tag{7.15}$$

so that the global profit is

$$R^* = R_1^* + R_2^* = (a - bc)^2/2b - e^2/2b \tag{7.16}$$

which is less than the maximised joint profit R in (7.10) for e non-zero. Note that if e is always equal to zero (the unknown level of demand is the same for the two firms), then $R^* = R$ and $R_1^* = R_2^*$: the two firms make the same profit and firm 1 chooses the price which maximises the joint profit.

When e is different from zero, firm 1 fixes a price which raises its profit at the expense of overall industry profits. Then the average values of (7.15) and (7.16) decline as the variance of e rises: the expected profits of firm 2 and of the industry are decreasing in the variance of e. This gives firm 2 a specific motive to deviate from the agreed policy by announcing a lower price. It can be shown that, in fact, it will not deviate when orthodox behaviour ensures a higher profit than the expected profit from a deviation followed by eternal punishment.

Price leadership by firm 1 is endogenous when the variance of e is sufficiently small with respect to the common variance of market demand. Indeed, the difference between the expected profit of firm 2 when firm 1 acts as leader and its expected profits when it acts itself in this capacity is

$$[E(a - a')^2 - 3Ee^2]/4b. \tag{7.17}$$

The variance of a must be at least three times that of e.

7.4 Price parallelism and collusive practices

In terms of observed behaviour, the pricing policy analysed above leads to parallel price variations. MacLeod (1985) shows that it is possible to generalise this result for a market composed of n firms on certain conditions. Proof is thus given that a social convention to adopt a policy of parallel price variations leads towards collusive profits that are between those of a static Nash equilibrium and those resulting from the full maximisation of joint profits, given non-cooperative behaviour.

Let $\underline{P} = (p_1, p_2, \cdots, p_n)$ be the vector of prices charged by the industry. Suppose also that the firms can announce the prices that will be applicable in the following period in advance and that firm i announces a variation Δp_i. Firm i can be any firm.

The firms do not know the profit functions of their rivals, but they can observe the prices of the previous periods as well as the announced price change. They tacitly adopt the convention to react to the announcement according to an alignment rule, independent of the profit functions, which is written as

$$\Delta p_j = r_j^i(\underline{P}, \Delta p_i), \quad j \neq i. \tag{7.18}$$

MacLeod demonstrates that the agreed alignment is defined by

$$r_j^i(\underline{P}, \Delta p_i) = \Delta p_i, \tag{7.19}$$

that is to say by price changes equal to those announced by i, when three conditions are satisfied. The alignment rule must
1 be continuously differentiable;
2 be independent of scale changes (for example inflation), that is $r_j^i(\alpha \underline{P}, \alpha \Delta p_i) = \alpha r_j^i(\underline{P}, \Delta p_i)$ for all i, j and $\alpha > 0$;
3 be independent of the order in which the firms are indexed.

Convention (7.19) is independent of profits and leads nevertheless to tacit collusion in a signalling game where the players adopt the following strategy: (1) When a price increase is announced, follow it if it is profitable to do so and if the others do the same; otherwise, do not change the price; (2) when a price decrease is announced, follow it as long as it does not lead to prices lower than the price $\underline{P}^0$ which would result in a static Nash equilibrium; (3) if any rival firm does not behave according to (1) and (2), announce the punishment price $\underline{P}^0$. If each firm adopts this strategy, there exists a non-cooperative equilibrium with prices $\underline{P}^*$ higher than $\underline{P}^0$ and lower than the prices which would maximise the joint profit on condition that the products are sufficiently close substitutes so that a unilateral price increase leads to a loss of profits. The price $\underline{P}^*$ results from parallel price increases thanks to convention (7.19), which ensures that the expectations about the rivals' reactions are correct.

Convention (7.19) is therefore a 'concerted practice'.[9] It makes 'tacit'

[9] Under the law of the Community, a concerted practice implies the existence of a common will that does not necessarily result from a legally binding agreement. See especially the judgements of the Court of Justice of the European Communities on 14 July 1972, ICI (48/69, *European Court Reports (ECR)*, p. 619), BASF (49/69, *ECR*, p. 713), Bayer (51/69, *ECR*, p. 745), Geigy (52/69, *ECR*, p. 787), Sandoz (53/69, *ECR*, p. 845), Francolor (54/69, *ECR*, p. 851), Cassella (55/69, *ECR*, p. 887), Hoechst (56/69, *ECR*, p. 927), ACNA (57/69, *ECR*, p. 933); judgement of the 16 December 1975, Suiker Unie e.a. (40 to 48, 50, 54 to 56, 111, 113 and 114/73, *ECR*, p. 1663); judgement of the 7 June 1983, Musique Diffusion Française (100 to 103/80, *ECR*, p. 1825); judgement of the 28 March 1984, CRAM and Rheinzink (29 and 30/83, *ECR*, p. 1679); judgement of the 14 July 1981, Züchner (172/80,

collusion possible, tacit collusion being nothing other than a collusive outcome obtained in a non-cooperative repeated game. The convention itself does not imply an explicit agreement. This explains the difficulty which the authorities in charge of competition policy (for example, in the enforcement of Articles 85 and 86 of the Treaty of Rome), have in proving its existence. Can these authorities deduce the existence of a concerted practice, forbidden by Article 85, paragraph 1 from the observation of parallel price variations? In other words, can they distinguish between the static Nash equilibrium P^0 and the collusive equilibrium P^*? The answer is no. In the framework of the MacLeod (1985) model, the answer is negative for two reasons. First, for parallel price changes to be sustainable, the products must be sufficiently close substitutes. For such products a price change by one firm immediately affects the profits of the rivals, regardless of the initial price level. Hence, we must expect all firms to respond at the same time to exogenous shocks, regardless of whether tacit collusion is present or not. The simultaneous nature of price changes, therefore, is not proof of collusion. Secondly, as long as the profit functions are not known, there are no systematic differences between the size of price responses at the non-cooperative and collusive equilibria. In particular, the identity of the price variations is not a proof in itself. It is therefore unfortunate that the European Commission uses price parallelism as a proof of tacit collusion, as in the 'Wood Pulp' decision of 19 December 1984. This decision is examined in detail in section 8.3.

The previous discussion focused on intertemporal alignments. It would have been possible to stop the discussion here, if there had not been a striking analogy with the spatial alignment rule which characterises the basing point price system.

7.5 The basing point system in the ECSC[10]

In this final section we move to the spatial domain and try to show why the multiple basing point price system imposed by the Treaty of the ECSC implies a concerted practice that facilitates tacit collusion, exactly as the intertemporal alignment rule (7.19) does.

First, a little history. Before 1951, the German and French steelmakers fixed their national prices according to a single basing point price system. Oberhausen was the only basing point for Germany. Thionville was the basing point for France. Consider Thionville: the biggest steel plants were

ECR, p. 2021), judgement of the 10 December 1985, Stichting Sigarettenindustrie (240, 241, 242, 261, 262, 268 and 269/82, ECR, p. 3831).
[10] This section reproduces part of my 1993 paper 'Basing point pricing, competition and market integration'.

located in and around that town. In all of France, the franco prices[11] were calculated by summing the base price at Thionville plus the transportation cost to a particular delivery point. This implies that the franco prices went up to the extent that steel was moved towards the South and the South-West. Note also that the franco price went down when steel was produced in the South and transported for delivery towards the North. In other words, the big Northern producers were able to sell anywhere in France, while the small Southern producers were constrained to sell in their local regional markets. But the South was compensated for this in terms of phantom freight collected in the vicinity of its plants. The system was meant to keep the Southern producers happy and small. In that sense, it was the equivalent of a national geographical market-sharing agreement.

When a common steel market between the Benelux countries, France, Germany and Italy was envisaged, the problem arose of how to define a common pricing policy, such that the prevailing allocation of geographical markets could be maintained. An agreement was reached after long discussions between the steelmakers. Far from being implicit, it was as explicit as possible, since it was written down in Article 60 of the ECSC Treaty and thus became obligatory for everyone! This is the more surprising as similar conventions were declared illegal by the American courts because contrary to antitrust legislation.

Different possibilities were discussed. Should a fob-mill[12] pricing policy be imposed? In those days, economic theory considered this the only system compatible with a Pareto optimum. The big production centres didn't like it, because they would have lost access to peripheral regional markets. In particular, the Belgian steelmakers (who had to export more than half of their production) would have lost many export markets inside the Common Market, given their location between Thionville and Oberhausen at a short distance from these centres. Second, it is very difficult to compute and compare delivered prices in any given location under a fob-mill system, because of the large number of steel plants in the European Common Market *and* because buyers can use different means of transportation (so that effective transportation costs vary from buyer to buyer). To enter a distant market, competitors would have had to grant secret price discounts. The end result would have been a series of regional price wars to avoid a loss of distant markets.

A single basing point system would have made it easier for the producers to compute the delivered price to be quoted in any location, given a

[11] The 'delivered' price is the price at the point of delivery. It is called the 'franco' price when it is directly fixed by the producers.
[12] This implies that the buyer must take care of the transportation from the factory and pay its full cost.

particular means of transportation. But where to locate such a single basing point? Not in France, since that would have limited the geographical extent of German sales west and southwards. Not in the Ruhr area, for symmetric reasons. Not in Benelux or Italy: that would have made all other countries unhappy.

The only way to maintain the existing trade patterns inside and between the six countries was to create a multiple basing point system, characterised by an alignment rule. The alignment rule ensures that, at any geographical location, the delivered price to be quoted by all the competitors is equal to the lowest combination of a base price plus freight (to that location) calculated from all basing points existing in the system. (Since base prices differ, the lowest delivered price does not necessarily correspond to the nearest basing point.) Thus at a given place of destination only a single delivered price is possible, identical and known with precision regardless of the seller and regardless of the actual distance covered in carriage to the place of destination. Indeed, the freight to be added to the base prices is worked out from a published tariff accepted by all concerned, such as a railway company's schedule of charges.

The analogy with the intertemporal alignment rule (7.19) is clear. The intertemporal rule and the spatial rule both ensure unicity of prices at any point in time or space. Each rule makes the reactions of the competitors perfectly predictable. Furthermore, spatial alignment simplifies the life of a possible leader: if a firm i wants to be the leader, it suffices to announce a sufficiently low base price so that the other producers are obliged (by the alignment rule) to adopt the delivered price of the leader at all their selling points; in a similar way, it suffices, for the follower, to announce a sufficiently high base price so that it is never applied.

The convention written down in Article 60 of the ECSC Treaty is clearly a concerted practice transformed into a binding legal agreement in full contradiction with Article 85 of the Treaty of Rome. It creates conditions which sustain a non-cooperative equilibrium whilst ensuring collusive profits. In more simple terms, Article 60 makes tacit collusion possible.

To see this, consider the functioning of the system. The obligation to align makes local price competition impossible. It is true that it guarantees a delivered price that is the lowest possible whatever the geographical location (the rules of the system, the base price and the transport tariff being given). Nevertheless, alignment has no competitive virtue. At first sight, the word alignment suggests aggressive behaviour. In reality, it is purely defensive, because it excludes the possibility of selling below the delivered price of the other firms. Given equal prices, the sellers can tie traditional pre-Common-Market customers to them wherever such customers may be located. The purpose is to freeze existing trade patterns and thus to leave

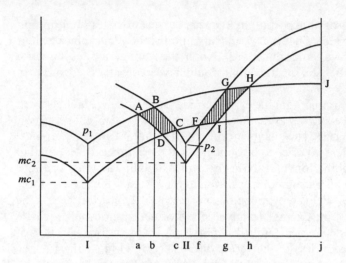

Figure 7.2 The multiple basing point system with alignment

market shares unchanged. Since alignment implies cross-hauls, the allocation of resources is less efficient than in the case of joint profit maximisation. The collusive profits made are therefore less than the profits resulting from explicit regional price agreements.

Figure 7.2 illustrates what has just been said and also shows that the alignment rule allows some interpenetration of markets without endangering the geographical price structure (that is to say, without provoking a price war). Space is represented on the horizontal axis. Points **I** and **II** represent basing points, where marginal costs are mc_1 and mc_2 respectively ($mc_1 < mc_2$). The figure shows marginal delivered costs (marginal production cost plus unit transport cost). The announced base prices are p_1 and p_2 from which the corresponding delivered prices increase in both directions. Firms located at **II** sell westwards until point a and eastwards until point h. Firms located at **I** sell eastwards until point c and then from f till j.

The firms align on the delivered price calculated from a base point which is not their own along the segments AB, BC, FG and GH. Along AB, firms located at **II** align on p_1 – plus delivered prices fixed by firms located at **I** (so that the delivered prices of firms **II** go *down* as they sell more towards **I**). Along BC, firms located at **I** align on p_2 – plus delivered prices fixed by firms located at **II** (so that their delivered prices go down as they sell more towards **II**).

These alignments ensure that (a) **I** can sell in the segment bc; (b) **II** can sell in the segment ab; and (c) there will be no price competition pushing the delivered prices down to ADC inside the area ABCD.

A similar argument applies to FG (where **I** aligns on p_2 – plus) and GH (where **II** aligns on p_1 – plus). Both centres enlarge their market area while avoiding price competition inside the area FGHI. Without the alignment rule, prices would have dropped to FIH along the segment fh.

Finally, cross-hauling occurs over the distance between a and c.

8   Collusion detection

8.1 Informational requirements of collusion detection[1]

A sensible economic interpretation of the European Communities' Directorate General (DG) IV's competition policy is as follows. Suppose a structural oligopoly is modelled as playing a repeated game. If the path of prices and quantities can be justified as the non-cooperative equilibrium of some stage game in every period, then the industry's behaviour is 'permitted'. On the other hand, if the path of prices and quantities can be justified only as an equilibrium of the repeated game in history-dependent strategies (e.g., 'trigger' or 'carrot-and-stick' strategies), the industry's behaviour is 'forbidden', and subject to antitrust redress. Stated differently, if the level of profits being attained can only be reached via threats to punish deviations from a tacitly collusive path (see chapter 6), then the behaviour is 'forbidden'. These concerns are also relevant to antitrust policy in the United States and other nations.[2]

Only this game-theoretic interpretation per se, rather than any issues of how closely this interpretation fits DG IV policy, is explored here. A welfare analysis of the merits of a policy which fits this interpretation is also outside our scope. Our concern is with the prior question of whether a policy so interpreted can be implemented given sensible models of the information available to antitrust authorities. The conclusions are not heartening.

Our analysis is presumably of interest only to those who share our

---

[1] Sections 8.1 to 8.3 reproduce my joint 1994 paper with R. Harstad (with minor modifications).

[2] Due to its dependence on case law and precedent, a particular economic interpretation of current US antitrust policy strikes us as more controversial and perhaps less amenable to analysis. See Martin (1993a, 1993b). It seems clear that current US antitrust precedent recognises that 'conscious parallelism' is not per se evidence of forbidden behaviour (Martin 1993b). However, there are serious difficulties reconciling economic reasoning and US legal doctrine. In any case, antitrust policy to limit tacit collusion faces precisely the questions raised here.

starting presumption that antitrust authorities are at an informational disadvantage relative to the firms in the industries they seek to control. In part, this presumption is based on the wide variety of circumstances with which the authorities are supposed concurrently to acquaint themselves, while the firms need concern themselves only with the smaller set of technical details relevant to their industry. Also in part, the firms should have some flexibility in decisions about experimentation, for example with cost-reducing techniques, or sales to help determine elasticities of demand for variety or rival aggressiveness and responsiveness; the authorities may be able to observe at least some of the data from such experimentation, but cannot affect its scope, scale, target parameters and timing.

We consider the following stylised model of an antitrust proceeding. The firms in the industry proceed in their business, creating a history of prices and sales quantities $h = \{(p_t, q_t)_{t=1,2,...}\}$ in periods $t = 1, 2, \ldots$. Based on some truncated history h^T through period T, the antitrust authority challenges the firms with a finding of forbidden behaviour that we are calling tentative. In essence, the authority claims that, based on the record and its knowledge of industry conditions, the firms must have been tacitly colluding. The firms then have the opportunity to respond as follows: they can fill in the gaps in the authority's information with reported data for key elasticity or other parameters that the authority does not know. If the reported data support the record as the unfolding over time of static non-cooperative Nash equilibria of a single-stage game, then the industry has successfully refuted the tentative finding, and is permitted to continue with no new antitrust constraints. If the industry is unable to provide such a defence, some judicial process determines appropriate redress.[3]

A simple oligopoly with a seasonal pattern of demands and costs is initially explored, in section 8.2. We make the strong assumption that the authority knows that products are undifferentiated, costs symmetric and linear, demands linear, and that behaviour is Cournot. Nonetheless, for three mild specifications of the authority's informational disadvantage, supposedly forbidden behaviour is completely indistinguishable from permitted behaviour. That is, the industry is able to fill in the authority's report with false but indisputable data that make even joint profit-maximising behaviour appear to be static Cournot behaviour. Of course,

---

[3] This stylisation is intended as applicable to the American judicial procedures as well as the European, though its expression is more in accord with the latter. Any judicial procedure in which the prosecution presents its case and the defence follows with its refutation should admit something akin to this stylisation. Issues of cross examination and introduction of new evidence, as well as impacts of out-of-court settlement opportunities would only divert attention from our basic points.

such indistinguishability renders implementation of antitrust policies that are dependent on detection of tacit collusion a farce.

The simple seasonal market has production and pricing decisions in one season unrelated to production and pricing decisions in the other season. The realistic complication of production smoothing across seasonal variations via holding stocks is therefore briefly discussed. To some extent, the implied relationships strengthen the inferences the authority can draw from the historical record. Nonetheless, mild specifications of its informational disadvantage yield an indistinguishability theorem.

Antitrust authorities can of course hire econometricians to estimate relevant unknown parameters. Essentially, collusion detection requires that the authority rely on econometric techniques whose inferential power was not anticipated by the colluding firms when their behaviour built up the record that was grist for the data mining. At best, understood econometric techniques have the potential to force collusion to stop short of attaining full monopoly profits, more so if the firms are more averse to the risk of redress.

Sections 8.3 and 8.4. review the record of two important antitrust proceedings in light of our findings. In 1981, DG IV claimed that the seasonal pattern of pricing in the European wood pulp industry constituted evidence of tacit collusion. A 1984 Commission decision against the industry was annulled in 1993 by the European Court of Justice. The annulment strikes us as indicating that the entire methodology of the wood pulp antitrust investigation fails because of indistinguishability problems. This is the message of section 8.3.

Section 8.4. applies the indistinguishability argument to the 1990 decision of the Commission in the ICI–Solvay case. The two main producers of soda-ash in Europe, ICI and Solvay, were accused of having engaged in a concerted practice from the early 1970s until the time of the decision. The Commission argued that the absence of trade between ICI's home markets (the UK and Ireland) and Solvay's home markets (continental Europe) gave proof of the existence of tacit collusion which had led to monopoly prices in these markets. We argue that the Commission did not have all the information necessary to exclude an alternative (competitive) interpretation. Price strategies are appropriate to analyse the ICI–Solvay case, while the wood pulp case is handled with reference to the model with quantity strategies presented in the next section.

8.2 A simple Cournot model with seasonal adjustments

Consider a structural oligopoly consisting of F firms protected from further entry, producing in periods $t = 1, 2, \ldots$. Each period is divided into two seasons, w (wet) and d (dry). Inverse demand follows the same seasonal pattern over time:

$$p_{wt} = a_w - b_w Q_{wt},$$
$$p_{dt} = a_d - b_d Q_{dt},$$

where $Q_{mt} = \sum_{f=1}^{F} q_{fmt}$, $m = w, d$ and q_{fmt} is output of firm f in season m of period t.

As all behaviour studied will be symmetric, we drop the f subscript, letting q refer to output of any one firm, and Q to aggregate industry output.

Prices are present values discounted to the beginning of period t, so it makes no difference whether season w precedes or follows season d. The F firms are assumed to produce homogeneous outputs at common marginal costs which may follow a seasonal pattern: c_w, c_d.

The joint profit-maximising outcome follows the time path

$$q_{wt} = \frac{a_w - c_w}{2b_w F}, \qquad q_{dt} = \frac{a_d - c_d}{2b_d F}, \qquad t = 1, 2, \ldots \tag{8.1}$$

$$p_{wt} = \frac{a_w + c_w}{2}, \qquad p_{dt} = \frac{a_d + c_d}{2}, \qquad t = 1, 2, \ldots \tag{8.2}$$

Let m be the season for which $(a_m - c_m)^2 / b_m$ is larger, with n the other season. Then a sufficient condition for the joint profit-maximising outcome to be sustainable as a repeated game subgame-perfect equilibrium is

$$\frac{(a_m - c_m)^2}{4F b_m} \le \left(\frac{\delta}{1-\delta}\right) \left(\frac{(a_m - c_m)^2}{b_m (F+1)^2} + \frac{(a_n - c_n)^2}{b_n (F+1)^2}\right)$$

where δ is the discount factor. This condition, derived in the standard way,[4] implies that it does not pay to defect in season m if m is the second season of the period, and retaliation (Cournot behaviour) would start in the next period. If it does not pay to defect then, it will not pay to defect in m if m is the first season, as the cost will include additionally retaliation in the following season n. The gain to defecting in n is always less than to defecting in m. We assume that δ is sufficiently close to 1 to allow this condition to hold.

The model has six parameters $z = (z_1, \ldots, z_6) = (a_w, b_w, c_w, a_d, b_d, c_d)$. For the history to appear to be in static Nash equilibrium, the firms must report parameters $\hat{z}$ satisfying

$$q_{wt} = \frac{\hat{a}_w - \hat{c}_w}{\hat{b}_w (F+1)}, \qquad q_{dt} = \frac{\hat{a}_d - \hat{c}_d}{\hat{b}_d (F+1)}, \qquad t = 1, 2, \ldots \tag{8.3}$$

[4] See, for example, Martin (1993a) and chapter 6. Weaker sufficient conditions are possible.

$$p_{wt} = \frac{\hat{a}_w + F\hat{c}_w}{(F+1)}, \qquad p_{dt} = \frac{\hat{a}_d + F\hat{c}_d}{(F+1)}, \qquad t = 1,2,\dots \qquad (8.4)$$

and satisfying $\hat{z}_k = z_k$ for all $k \in K$, where K is the set of parameters known to the authority.

Proposition 1: For each of the following specifications of the authority's information, joint profit maximisation and static Nash equilibrium are indistinguishable in the simple seasonal Cournot model:
 (i) The authority does not know the demand parameters.
 (ii) The authority does not know the cost parameters, or demand intercepts.
(iii) The authority knows that the cost parameter is common to both seasons, and knows that the seasonal character of demand is a parallel shift, but has no further information on costs or demands.

The proof consists of simple algebraic constructions of the firms' reports and will be illustrated in section 8.3.

A seasonal model with stocks

The principal features and notation of the previous model are maintained: F firms, *w*et and *d*ry months, linear demand unchanged. We still use q_m to denote quantity sold by an individual firm in season $m = w, d$. Let
 x_m denote an individual firm's production in season m,
 σ_m denote firm's inventory stock of finished product at the end of m, and
 $\bar{\sigma}$ denote the storage cost-minimising end-of-season stock level.
We will use $s = \sigma_w - \bar{\sigma}$, the excess of stocks over this storage cost-minimising level at the end of the wet season. Inventories are accumulated in this season, when demand is low, and sold in the dry season.
 Of course, constant marginal costs no longer allow an interesting model. Variable production costs in season m are

$$(c/2)x_m^2 + gx_m.$$

Variable storage costs for season w:

$$(v/2)s^2 + us.$$

The true value of u will be 0, but u is included as a parameter which the authority may not know. This is a convenient method for specifying whether the storage cost-minimising level of stocks is known to the authority.
 Cost-minimising behaviour sets $\sigma_d = \bar{\sigma}$, and equates marginal costs over the two seasons

$$cx_d = cx_w + u + vs. \tag{8.5}$$

The joint profit-maximising outcome path equates each season's industry aggregate marginal revenue with the common marginal cost

$$a_d - 2Fb_d(x_d + s) = cx_d + g \tag{8.6}$$

$$a_w - 2Fb_w(x_w - s) = cx_w + g. \tag{8.7}$$

The three equations (8.5)–(8.7) can be solved simultaneously to determine x_d, x_w, s. Sales are then: $q_d = x_d + s$, $q_w = x_w - s$. Finally, these sales formulas yield p_d, p_w via demand curves.

A Nash equilibrium path would be calculated from reported variables via the Cournot formulas equating an individual firm's marginal revenue to marginal cost

$$\hat{a}_d - (F+1)\hat{b}_d(x_d + s) = \hat{c}x_d + \hat{g},$$
$$\hat{a}_w - (F+1)\hat{b}_w(x_w + s) = \hat{c}x_w + \hat{g},$$
$$\hat{c}x_d = \hat{c}x_w + \hat{u} + \hat{v}s.$$

These three equations can be solved simultaneously to determine $\hat{x}_d, \hat{x}_w, \hat{s}$, as before. Similarly, sales are: $\hat{q}_d = \hat{x}_d + \hat{s}$, $\hat{q}_w = \hat{x}_w - \hat{s}$. Again, these sales formulas yield $\hat{p}_d, \hat{p}_w$ via demand curves.

Assume the authority observes only the history h^T of prices and sales quantities, and thus does not separately observe seasonal production data or levels of inventories. Then four equations, $\hat{p}_d = p_d, \hat{q}_d = q_d, \hat{p}_w = p_w, \hat{q}_w = q_w$, characterise acceptability of h^T as a static Nash equilibrium for the reported parameters. There are eight parameters

$$z = (z_1, \ldots, z_8) = (a_d, b_d, a_w, b_w, c, g, u, v),$$

intercept and slope parameters for each season's demand, production cost and storage cost. As before, an acceptable report $\hat{z} \in \mathscr{R}^8$ must satisfy $\hat{z}_k = z_k$ for all $k \in K$, the set of parameters assumed known to the antitrust authorities. Let $\#K$ stand for the cardinality of K, i.e., the number of known parameters.

Proposition 2: For any specification of the authority's information such that $\#K \leq 3$, joint profit maximisation and static Nash equilibrium are indistinguishable in the seasonal Cournot model with stocks.

Proposition 2 understates the scope for indistinguishability in this model. Many cases in which $\#K = 4$, i.e., four variables are unknown, also exhibit indistinguishability.

It bears repeating that this result survives despite having assumed that the authority knew that products were homogeneous, demands were seasonal and linear, production and storage costs were quadratic, and behaviour was Cournot. If the firms had an informational advantage over the authority in knowledge of functional forms of demands and costs, this would provide additional ammunition for the defence.

On detection possibilities via econometric inference

Relevant parameters which the authority does not know can be estimated econometrically. Realistically, the authority probably has to settle for a flexible functional-form simultaneous estimate of all parameters. Assuming that any parameter is known without allowance for residual error has simplified the two previous models, but is surely over strong.

Our key point is that virtually no parameter of interest can be estimated in isolation, let alone in context, without reference to the history h^T of prices and sales quantities in periods $1, \dots, T$. Thus, the firms are creating the fodder for the econometrician's cannon; with appropriate anticipation, they can have considerable flexibility for sustaining profits above a static Nash equilibrium level while still maintaining a high confidence that the cannon will misfire.

Though it is fictitious and overly simple, an example will help to make the implications concrete. Suppose that the key parameter to estimate is a_d, the intercept of the demand curve in the dry season.[5] Let the true value be 582, and suppose the firms in the industry are in fact earning profits in excess of Cournot levels, so that they must be able to defend a higher value of the intercept than the true value. For the sake of argument, imagine that the authority's econometrician correctly estimates the intercept at 582, but with a standard error of 509. Then a reported intercept $\hat{a}_d$ of 1,091 would be extremely conservative, only one standard error above the estimate. It is likely that a reported intercept as high as 1,447 would have no difficulty surviving a judicial process, as it is within 1.7 standard errors of the estimate.

To consider an extreme, suppose the joint profit-maximising outcome could only be justified as a static non-cooperative outcome by a claim that the intercept was 3,500. Then the availability of the econometric evidence just described has served to limit the firms to a fraction of the gain over Cournot profits via tacit collusion. In a more realistic, simultaneous-equations estimate of several parameters, it is not difficult to imagine that econometric evidence would have little power to enforce limits on undetectable collusion at profit levels notably below joint profit-maximising levels.

---

[5] Because the history h^T reveals one point on the demand curve, a higher intercept will correspond to a steeper slope; here we focus on the intercept.

This is particularly true if the firms are able to offer as a defense claims that the econometrician has not specified the functional forms of demands or costs correctly, or has misunderstood the nature and degree of product differentiation.

If the firms understand the range of econometric techniques available to the authority, they can calculate the limits of undetectable collusion. In line with the symmetry assumptions of the above models, suppose all firms are willing to accept a probability π of collusion detection and redress, and that they share a common perception of how confidence intervals in econometric evidence translate into judicial determinations. Then, at $t = 1$, firms can calculate the extent of collusion legally sustainable with probability $1 - \pi$, and behave with confidence that the history h^T they generate will not allow for distinguishing their behaviour from static Cournot.

The last point about econometric evidence is that, unlike most inferential problems, time is not on the econometrician's side. If the repeated-game model is taken literally, then waiting more time periods to collect more data will not reduce standard errors of estimates. Underlying fluctuations in demands and costs may produce a pattern of seasons longer than two periods; nonetheless, the data generated in another run through the pattern will be identical to the data last time, rather than improving the cannon's accuracy. If this is not literally a repeated game, in that the seasonal pattern changes over time, then the firms may be able to argue that only a short time horizon's data are relevant to estimates of these parameters.

8.3 The wood pulp case

Our analysis suggests an interpretation of the so-called Wood Pulp Decision in 1993 by the European Court of Justice. Let us first summarise the legal history of the case. In 1981, forty-three defendants (six Canadian wood pulp producers, ten American, eleven Finnish, ten Swedish, one Norwegian, one Portuguese and one Spanish producer, plus the US Pulp, Paper and Paperboard Export Association (K.E.A.), the Finnish Common Sales Agency (Finncell) and the Swedish Association of Wood Pulp Producers (Svenska Cellulosa)) were informed that the Commission of the EC had found evidence of collusive behaviour with regard to the prices of their exports to the EC, that is, their sales to the (more than 800) European paper producers.

The main evidence given is the fact that, from 1975 to 1981, these prices moved in a parallel way from quarter to quarter. Indeed, these firms were observed to match competitors' announced price changes within hours or days. Individual prices were announced to clients, agents and the press (verbally, by telephone, in writing or by telex) a few weeks in advance of the next quarter. All competitors were thus immediately informed of a future price change and were given the opportunity to match it by announcing an identical change. As a result, the announced prices were most often identical in the North-West of Europe. Transaction prices were most often identical with the announced prices. Price announcements were in US dollars rather than in the local European currencies.

On 19 December 1984, the Commission decided that all defendants, except one American, one Norwegian, and the Portuguese and the Spanish producer, had to pay (within three months) fines ranging between 50,000 and 500,000 ECU. The fines imposed on the Finnish and Swedish producers were reduced to take account of the fact that they pledged (in a written undertaking) to reduce the 'artificial transparency' of the market by quoting prices in local currencies and to refrain from making announcements on a quarterly basis, from exchanging information about prices or other confidential data and from colluding.

In April 1985, the firms that were fined lodged an appeal against this decision with the European Court of Justice. On 7 July 1992, the Advocate-General of the Court concluded that the Commission had not given proof of collusion and in particular that parallel prices do not imply tacit collusion. On 31 March 1993, the Court accepted this reasoning and annulled the decision and most of the fines.[6]

In game-theoretic terms, the Commission's task was to distinguish between two equilibria and decide which of these had actually been played between 1975 and 1981. The first repeated-game equilibrium is repetition of a non-cooperative equilibrium of a Cournot stage game, moving from one static Cournot equilibrium to another, quarter to quarter, as market demand shifts upwards or downwards depending on the season.[7] The second repeated-game equilibrium has producers moving from one joint profit-maximising outcome to another, quarter to quarter. In this particular case, these collusive profits could arise as a (non-cooperative) equilibrium outcome if the producers tacitly adopted the preplay convention that each will follow an alignment rule, implying that if any producer raises his price all others will follow. Any producer could thus act as a price leader for any quarter: there is not one price leader, but as many potential price

---

[6] The Commission's decision was published in the *Official Journal of the European Communities*, No. L851. The conclusions of the Advocate-General, Marc Darmon, and the judgement of 31 March 1993 can be found in the *Recueil de la Jurisprudence de la Cour de Justice et du Tribunal de Première Instance*, Part I, 1993, No. 3, pp. 1307 ff.

[7] Although prices are announced in this industry, rather than publicly setting quantities, we regard Cournot as a better simple model than Bertrand competition, in view of production scheduling needs and the difficulty in adjusting productive capacity over a time horizon as short as a quarter.

leaders as there are players. This is the type of game analysed by MacLeod (1985) (see section 7.4). He defines a strategy with three components: [α] When a price increase is announced by a competitor, follow if it is profitable to do so and if the others do the same; otherwise do not change your price. [β] When a price decrease is announced, follow it as long as it does not lead below the non-cooperative Nash equilibrium price. [γ] If any rival firm does not behave according to components α and β, forever announce the non-cooperative Nash equilibrium price. Component γ makes this an example of a 'trigger' strategy. MacLeod shows that this strategy forms an equilibrium of the repeated game, attaining profits in the interval between the Nash equilibrium level and the joint profit-maximising level. In what follows, we assume the joint profit-maximising level is reached.

If an explicit agreement to use an alignment rule had been discovered, the Commission could have distinguished the two equilibria. The problem is, of course, that no explicit agreement is needed for this type of collusion to work. MacLeod noted that an antitrust authority cannot find out whether an observed time path of prices is collusive or not, when this sort of game is being played, if it does not know the profit functions of the players, i.e., the demand and cost parameters. Indeed there are no systematic differences between the sizes of the price responses at the collusive and the static non-cooperative equilibria.

Suppose the inverse demand function for wood pulp in Europe is

$$p_m = a_m - bQ_m,$$

and that the Commission knows neither the intercept a_m nor the slope b. All the Commission knows about demand is that its seasonal character is a parallel shift reflected in changes of a_m, where the seasonal index m here represents quarters: $m = I, II, III, IV$. In this equation, p_m represents the price in US dollars/ton of wood pulp delivered in Europe in quarter m. Q_m represents total imports into the EC from North America and the Scandinavian countries in quarter m. Suppose also that the Commission knows the (constant) unit costs of producing and transporting wood pulp to Europe and that these costs turn out to be much lower for the American and Canadian producers than for the Scandinavian producers. (This was the case during the period of alleged collusion because of a favourable exchange rate of the dollar.)

If there is tacit collusion between all producers concerned, joint profit maximisation implies that the North American producers be allowed to produce at full capacity, with the Scandinavian producers satisfying the residual demand. Treating the North American producers as one single firm, an export cartel, with a production capacity of $\bar{q}_m$ in quarter m, and supposing that there are F Scandinavian firms involved, we have

$$Q_m = \bar{q}_m + \sum_{f=1}^{F} q_{fm}$$

where q_{fm} represents the sales quantity (to Europe) of individual Scandinavian firm f in quarter m. The capacity $\bar{q}_m$ is in fact the (aggregate) residual capacity of North American firms that remains after the North American market is served. The residual inverse demand curve for Scandinavian firms is

$$p_m = a_m - b \left(\bar{q}_m + \sum_{f=1}^{F} q_{fm} \right) = a_m - b(\bar{q}_m + Fq_m)$$

with the last equality invoking an assumption that all Scandinavian firms are of equal size: $q_{1m} = q_{2m} = \cdots = q_{Fm} = q_m$. Maximisation with respect to q_m of the joint profit gives

$$q_{fm} = \frac{(a_m - b\bar{q}_m) - c_h}{2bF}, \quad f = 1, \ldots, F \tag{8.8}$$

and

$$p_m = \frac{(a_m - b\bar{q}_m) + c_h}{2} \tag{8.9}$$

where c_h is the (higher) unit cost common to the Scandinavian firms.

If instead these firms are repeatedly playing a static Cournot equilibrium, then

$$q_{fm} = \frac{(\hat{a}_m - \hat{b}\bar{q}_m) - c_h}{\hat{b}(F+1)}, \quad f = 1, \ldots, F \tag{8.10}$$

and

$$p_m = \frac{(\hat{a}_m - \hat{b}\bar{q}_m) + Fc_h}{F+1} \tag{8.11}$$

on the assumption that the North American cartel exports its residual subsidy to Europe, no matter what the behaviour of the Scandinavian firms.

For the sake of argument, we shall suppose that the wood pulp producers were in fact adhering to the convention described above, so that the observed imports and prices were determined by equations (8.8) and (8.9) and the true values of the slope and intercepts of the seasonal demand functions are a_m and b. When interrogated by the Commission about the properties of the demand for wood pulp in Europe, what values of $\hat{a}_m$ and $\hat{b}$ should the economic experts testifying for the wood pulp industry have reported, to support the proposition that the market was in a static non-cooperative Cournot equilibrium in each quarter?

Of course, the values reported should have been obtained by equating (8.8) to (8.10) and (8.9) to (8.11), and solving the resulting system of eight equations (two equations per season). This solution is

$$\hat{a}_m = [a_m(F+1) - c_h(F-1) - b\bar{q}_m], \qquad \hat{b} = Fb. \tag{8.12}$$

Consider the years 1976 and 1977. For the four quarters of 1976, an identical price was announced: $p_m = 415$. The Scandinavian cost (of production and delivery) was (approximately) 300. Identical price announcements of eight Scandinavian firms are reported in the Commission's decision, so that we put $F = 8$. The North American sales in Europe totalled 2,078 thousand tons in 1976, so that $\bar{q}_m = 2,078/4 = 519.5$.[8]

What were the true values of the a_m (under the assumption of collusion)? Equation (8.9) gives

$$415 = \frac{a_m - 519.5b + 300}{2}$$

for $m = I, II, III, IV$. To compute the a_m, we need a value for b. Supposing $b = 0.1$ leads to $a_m = 581.95$. We can now use (8.12) to find

$$\hat{a}_m = 1,542.8, \qquad \hat{b} = 0.8.$$

Experts for the defence should have exaggerated the value of the intercept and the slope of the inverse demand function. In other words, they should have insisted that the price elasticity of the demand for wood pulp was low.

During the year 1977, the announced price was 415 for the first three quarters and dropped to 350 in the fourth quarter. With $\bar{q}_m = 2,092/4 = 523$, $b = 0.1$ and $c_h = 300$, the demand intercepts derived from assuming collusion are $a_I = a_{II} = a_{III} = 585.3$ and $a_{IV} = 473.8$. The values to report are

$$\hat{a}_I = \hat{a}_{II} = \hat{a}_{III} = 1,557.7, \, \hat{a}_{IV} = 1,055.9, \, \hat{b} = 0.8.$$

The true value of the downward shift of the inverse demand function is

$$a_I - a_{IV} = 585.3 - 473.8 = 111.5$$

[8] The Commission reported only the yearly imports of wood pulp into the Community. As it would be desirable to analyse quarterly data, we requested quarterly data on imports from EuroStat, which replied that quarterly data were never compiled. So this exercise illustrates under the presumption that imports from North America in each quarter were approximately one-fourth of the annual imports. While we have not explicitly included this sort of informational disadvantage in our analysis, it may often be the case that antitrust authorities are more limited than are the firms to data-gathering routines which were not selected for their relevance to antitrust analysis.

while the shift to report is

$$\hat{a}_I - \hat{a}_{IV} = 1{,}557.7 - 1{,}055.9 = 501.8.$$

In other words, experts for the defence should have exaggerated the seasonal character of the demand for wood pulp. (To our knowledge, at least one expert did exactly that on intuitive grounds.)

To the extent that the Commission had to rely on information which it did not know but the firms knew, it could not make a solid case. Recall that we have been assuming that the Commission knew costs exactly and presumed the demand curve to be linear and to shift in parallel, and we have been assuming that these presumptions were not only correct, but moreover were indisputable. Presumably smaller exaggerations, at least of intercepts, would be needed for the defence if they could argue that demand linearity was incorrect (arguing, for example, for a concave inverse demand curve).

To make our point, this example has supposed that there was collusion in order to find out what sort of information the industry should provide. Indeed, it would be hard to imagine a situation in which an industry would try to convince an antitrust authority that there is collusion when there is none. The difficulties illustrated here are fundamental.

8.4 The ICI–Solvay case[9]

Soda-ash, an alkaline chemical commodity, is mainly used as a raw material in the glass manufacturing industry. To a much lesser extent it serves for the production of detergents and in metallurgy. While natural soda-ash is extracted from mines in the US, Africa, Australia and Asia, Europe's entire output is produced by a synthetic chemical process invented by Solvay in 1865.

There are six suppliers of soda-ash in the EC among which Solvay is the largest single producer with 60 per cent market share in Western Europe. Solvay has plants in Austria, Belgium, France, Germany, Italy, Spain and Portugal. ICI is the second largest producer in the EC and serves the UK and Ireland (serving about 90 per cent of this market) from its two plants in the UK.[10] On the continent, Solvay faces competition from two German, one Dutch and one French producer, which mainly serve their domestic markets. Solvay is thus the only European producer that can be regarded as a multinational company. Despite this fact, the company never tried to gain access to the British market. Similarly, ICI does not sell soda-ash in

---

[9] This section is a shortened version of the paper by Barbara Böhnlein (1994a) on the soda-ash market in Europe.

[10] ICI closed one of its original three plants in 1984.

continental Europe. Other competitors from third countries (mainly from the US) play only a minor role in Europe's soda-ash market.

Transportation costs represent a considerable fraction of a firm's cost. Overseas shipping leads to additional costs, not only because of its expensive rates for freight and insurance, but also because the commodity has to be stored in the foreign harbour.

The ability of a firm to serve the commodity continuously on a daily or weekly basis is extremely important in the glass manufacturing industry. Most glass producers have established continuous process plants for which they hold stocks of soda-ash for a few days only.

The overall demand for soda-ash in Europe (and in the world market) went through a phase of stagnation in the early 1980s, but experienced a strong increase in sales towards the end of the decade. Since then production has been run at full capacity, due also to it being difficult, if not impossible, to get permission for the construction of a new plant in the EC.[11]

There have been long-standing commercial links between ICI and Solvay. After several cartel agreements dating back to the last century, the two firms settled a new agreement right after the Second World War. The essence of this so-called 'Page 1000' agreement consisted of a market sharing cartel for soda-ash. Continental Europe was assigned to Solvay while ICI agreed to restrict its activity to the British Commonwealth. After having obtained legal advice that the agreement was against Article 85 of the Treaty of Rome, ICI and Solvay formally terminated Page 1000 on 31 December 1972.

The Commission used the fact that neither ICI nor Solvay invaded each other's market, after the agreement was cancelled, as proof that market separation, and hence collusion, still continued.[12] The Commission argued that the absence of market penetration can only be explained by a tacit agreement to maintain the formerly explicit cartel agreement. Competition would have provoked mutual entry since prices were monopolistic in both markets thus providing positive profit opportunities for a foreign entrant.

To justify its reasoning, the Commission pointed to the price gap between the two markets which had existed over a long period of time. Before 1980, the price for soda-ash used to be lower in the UK than on the continent. During the last decade, however, UK prices rose by about 15–20 per cent above those of continental Europe. This price movement served as an indication that it would have been profitable for the firm in the lower price market to enter the higher price market. Furthermore, ICI purchased large

---

[11] As a result of increasingly restrictive EC environmental laws.
[12] *Official Journal*, No. L 152, 91/297/EEC, 19 December 1990.

tonnages of soda-ash from Solvay between 1985 and 1988 in order to meet its long-term contracts with its British customers. Hence, ICI's obvious difficulty in serving its home market should have given an additional incentive for Solvay to enter the UK market directly rather than selling soda-ash to a potential competitor. The Commission therefore accused Solvay of deliberately not having invaded the lucrative British market in the 1980s.

The theoretical framework: collusion detection and foreign entry

The question is whether the fact that neither firm entered the other's home market unambiguously reflects collusive behaviour or whether mutual staying out may also arise in a competitive equilibrium. The latter requires each incumbent to set the price such that the potential entrant cannot make profits by entering the foreign market.

Suppose inverse market demand is linear with intercept α_k in market k. For simplicity, let its slope be -1. Firms are supposed to play price strategies, an assumption based upon some characteristics of the soda-ash market. Usually, suppliers announce list prices and rebate schemes for one year in advance. Having long-term contracts with their customers, producers guarantee that prices remain fixed for the duration of these contracts. Consequently, producers adjust quantities according to demand throughout the year. Since the production process is rather simple (soda-ash is obtained through a fall-out process of some basic chemicals), it is fairly easy to increase or to decrease production in the short run.

There is one firm in each market k. Each firm is 'low cost' in its domestic market. All firms have the same low cost c_l for simplicity. Because of the cost of transportation, each firm is high cost (c_h) when it sells in a foreign market. Under these conditions the joint profit-maximising price per period is

$$p_k^M = \frac{\alpha_k + c_l}{2} \tag{8.13}$$

in home market k. In an infinitely repeated game, collusion protects firms from foreign entry whenever the discount factor δ is close enough to 1 and yields a market structure of k national monopolies.

In a competitive situation, the domestic firm, firm i, will set $p_{ik}^N \approx c_h$, where h indicates the foreign (high cost) firm. This involves slightly undercutting the foreign firm's marginal cost in order to prevent the rival from gaining any market share. Put differently, at a price of $p_{ik}^N \leq c_h$, there would be no profit opportunity and hence no incentive for the foreign firm to enter market k. Therefore, the competitive equilibrium requires incumbent i to set a price of

$$p_{ik}^N = c_h \tag{8.14}$$

in market k. Pricing at the rival's marginal cost level is a limit-pricing strategy to deter entry and a subgame perfect Nash equilibrium strategy.

Transferring this result to our indistinguishability problem, we can state the following. A monopoly price as in equation (8.13) indicates *unacceptable* behaviour from the point of view of the authorities. A Nash limit price as in equation (8.14) indicates *acceptable* behaviour.

These inferences can only be drawn if the authorities know the true values α_k, c_l and c_h.

Suppose the authorities know that price strategies are played and that price formation is as in (8.13) or (8.14). Let $\hat{\alpha}_k$, $\hat{c}_l$ and $\hat{c}_h$ denote estimates of the true values of the parameters and consider the following relationships. If

$$\hat{\alpha}_k = 2c_h - c_l \tag{8.15}$$

or

$$\hat{c}_l = 2c_h - \alpha_k \tag{8.16}$$

then acceptable behaviour is not distinguishable from unacceptable behaviour since $p_k^M = p_k^N$ when either (8.15) or (8.16) is substituted into (8.13).

Similarly, if

$$\hat{c}_h = \frac{\alpha_k + c_l}{2} \tag{8.17}$$

it is straightforward that acceptable behaviour cannot be distinguished from unacceptable behaviour.

A numerical example

Let firm 1 be ICI with home market a representing the UK and Ireland. Solvay is labelled firm 2, with home market b corresponding to continental Europe. ICI's home market is definitely smaller than Solvay's home market. This is due to the fact that the glass industry, which represents the prime demand for soda-ash, is an important industrial sector in all major EC member countries while Ireland has only a few glass manufacturers.

We have to be careful in defining the intercept, α_k, required to calculate monopoly prices in each market. For ICI's home market, we can take the intercept α_a to represent its entire home market: ICI is a monopolist in Ireland and in the UK, serving both countries from its two British plants. Matters are quite different for Solvay, which is confronted with several other EC competitors of respectable size. We know further that Solvay usually satisfies demand within national borders: French customers are supplied through French plants, German customers through German plants and so on. This provides important information about how to choose the intercept for the determination of the collusive outcome.

To illustrate, let us take a closer look at price formation in continental Europe. The product being homogeneous, firms have to agree to set a single price (including transportation cost) in each of the national (sub-)markets. In other words, p_b^M will differ in each national submarket according to the number of competitors in that market. Hence, the intercept α_b relevant to Solvay's entire home market will be defined as an average of the national intercepts.

Second, we have to split up the cost function. While production technology seems to be relatively mature and standardised, transportation costs differ. We specify total costs for firm i as follows

$$c_{ih} = c_{il} + t_{ik} \quad (k = a, b; i = 1,2) \tag{8.18}$$

where c_{il} includes the production as well as transportation costs of serving customers in the home market and t_{ik} is the cost of serving the overseas market. Although the cost of transportation clearly increases with distance to the customer, we approximate c_{il} by averaging continential transportation costs.

We first model prices consistent with the soda-ash market in the 1970s when prices in market a were lower than in market b. List prices in these markets differed from \$200 to \$240 per metric ton (MT). However, these list prices are not those effectively paid by the customers. First, a 5 per cent rebate on list prices seems to be common in the industry. Second, all suppliers try to bind customers through bulk discount schemes. If we take into account all rebates and discounts, we arrive at effective prices which lie around 10–15 per cent below list prices, that is, $p_a = 180$ and $p_b = 200$. Since both firms produce soda-ash with the same production technology, we suppose that the cost of production is the same for each firm, yielding a fob-mill price of \$95 per MT. Home market delivery costs, an important fraction of the firms' cost, account for some 25 per cent of production costs on average. We fix[13] these costs at \$25 per MT. Adding production and local transportation costs together, we get $c_{1l} = c_{2l} = c_l = 120$.

The cost supplement t_{ik}, incurred when serving the foreign market, can be split into overseas shipping and on-land delivering components. The cost

---

[13] ICI serves its home market (the UK and Ireland) from its two plants located in the UK. Although Solvay has a much larger home market in terms of geographical area, it also owns more plants than ICI. With six production facilities in six different EC countries, Solvay serves customers over distances similar to ICI's. We therefore assume that average transportation cost within the home market is the same for ICI and Solvay.

of shipping the product overseas is comprised of freight and insurance to the foreign harbour as well as warehouse and handling costs. Overseas shipping and warehouse costs are assumed to account for roughly $15 per MT. On-land delivery costs in the foreign market are the costs of transportation from the warehouse to the foreign market customer. Average transportation costs on the continent are relatively high for ICI because customers are widely spread throughout Europe. Hence, we add an average of $25 per MT to ICI's cost function when serving continental Europe. On the other hand, Solvay's delivery within the UK is less costly since most potential customers are located close to the southern shore. For the purpose of our example, we take these costs to be $15 per MT. From these figures we can compute total transportation costs for the foreign market. Serving continental Europe from its British plants would cost $t_{1a} = 40$ for ICI, whereas Solvay would have transportation costs of $t_{2b} = 30$ when delivering soda-ash to the UK.

Plugging our numerical values into (8.18) yields Nash prices of

$$p_a^N = c_{bh} = c_{2l} + t_{2b} = 120 + 30 = 150 \tag{8.19}$$

$$p_b^N = c_{ah} = c_{1l} + t_{1a} = 120 + 40 = 160. \tag{8.20}$$

If the overseas cost supplement, t_{ik}, were the same for ICI and Solvay, then differences in Nash prices would stem from differences in domestic transportation costs.

Equations (8.19) and (8.20) indicate that our effective prices of $180 and $200 respectively cannot be the result of the competitive game. Hence, these prices must be the result of collusive behaviour. This allows us to draw inferences about α_k from equation (8.13). We have

$$p_a^M = 180 = \frac{\alpha_a + c_{1l}}{2} = \frac{\alpha_a + 120}{2} \tag{8.21}$$

$$p_b^M = 200 = \frac{\alpha_b + c_{2l}}{2} = \frac{\alpha_b + 120}{2} \tag{8.22}$$

so that $\alpha_a = 240$ and $\alpha_b = 280$. In this example, differences in collusive prices across markets are due to differences in the intercepts. In general, we must have

$$\alpha_a + c_{1l} < \alpha_b + c_{2l} \tag{8.23}$$

for $p_a^M < p_b^M$ to hold. Price differences under collusive behaviour result from differences in intercepts, differences in home market costs or from a combination of both. Differences in foreign market transportation costs leave monopoly prices unaffected.

Equations (8.19) to (8.22) show that $p_a < p_b$ may hold with collusive as well as competitive strategies. In both cases, firms stay out of their rival's home market. Since the market reveals list prices only, the Commission would have to rely on the firms' data and on its own estimations to compute effective prices. Firms may manipulate the data to make collusion appear as acceptable behaviour in the following way. If

$$\hat{t}_{2b}=\frac{\alpha_a+c_{1l}}{2}-c_{2l} \quad \text{and} \quad \hat{t}_{1a}=\frac{\alpha_b+c_{2l}}{2}-c_{1l} \tag{8.24}$$

are reported as transportation costs to the foreign market, then collusive behaviour appears as competitive. Plugging in our true parameter values, we get $\hat{t}_{1a}=80$ and $\hat{t}_{2b}=60$. In other words, an overestimation of foreign market delivery costs by 100 per cent makes collusion look like competition.

While α_k influences only collusive prices and overseas shipping costs influence only competitive prices, costs of production and supply to the home market affect price formation for both strategies – compare equations (8.19) and (8.20) with (8.21) and (8.22). An overestimation of c_{il} such that

$$\hat{c}_{1l}=\frac{\alpha_b+c_{2l}}{2}-t_{1a} \quad \text{and} \quad \hat{c}_{2l}=\frac{\alpha_a+c_{1l}}{2}-t_{2b} \tag{8.25}$$

will lead to $\hat{c}_{1l}=160$ and $\hat{c}_{2l}=150$. Overestimating the true values of $\hat{c}_{il}$ by one fourth and one third causes collusion to be mistaken for competition when (8.25) is substituted into (8.18).

One might argue that the deviations from the true values in our example are so large that the Commission is not likely to accept these. However, the estimation of each parameter involves considerable uncertainty. Take t_{ik}, for example: Since transportation to the foreign market is subject to economies of scale, t_{ik} doubles or even triples when small quantities are shipped instead of large quantities. Accordingly, t_{ik} depends heavily on the market share the foreign firm could capture from the incumbent. Since both firms did not actually enter the foreign market, there are no available data on the entrant's (potential) market share. There is less uncertainty about α_k and c_{il}. Nevertheless, it is doubtful whether the Commission possesses reliable figures on any of these. The intercepts were inferred from effective prices in our example, while only list prices are publicly available. As for c_{il}, uncertainty arises from two sources. First, although production technology is the same for ICI and Solvay, the cost of production may vary because of differences in the cost of inputs (energy, labour, etc.). Second, average delivery costs in the home market may be different for each firm. Information on c_{il} is firm specific and hence cost reports by the defence have to be viewed with some caution.

Solving the indistinguishability problem under imperfect information

This is not to say that antitrust authorities face a totally hopeless task. Detection of collusion is possible in the following circumstances:

(a) When it is known that $c_{1l} = c_{2l}$ and that $\alpha_a = \alpha_b$, $p_a^M = p_b^M$ whatever the actual value of c_{il} and α_k. Then, any observed price differences between the two markets must be due to Nash pricing.

(b) When $c_{1l} = c_{2l}$ and $t_{1a} = t_{2b}$ and thus $p_a^N = p_b^N$, price differences between markets $k = a, b$ must be caused by $\alpha_a \neq \alpha_b$ and are hence due to collusion.

(c) When overseas transportation costs vary significantly between firms and markets. Nash prices then differ proportionally, as long as c_{il} is about the same for each firm i. Similarly, differences in α_k are reflected in monopoly prices in each market. Again, it is important to know whether the c_{il} differ. If so, cost differences may dampen the effect of the gap in intercepts. In other words, one can detect the nature of the game that is played from the differences in the values of a parameter. If the Commission knows that the c_{il} are almost equal, significant price differences between market a and b can only be caused by differences in α_k or in t_{ik}. If the Commission knows further that the differences in the values of one of these two parameters is small while the other is large, it can draw valid inferences.

Our numerical example in the previous section reflected conditions in the market for soda-ash in the 1970s when prices in market a were below prices in market b. According to the Commission, a crucial piece of evidence that a collusive price game is being played between ICI and Solvay is the reversal of this price gap in the 1980s. Given that prices in the UK were 15–20 per cent higher than on the continent during this decade, the Commission argues that Solvay should have had a strong incentive to enter the lucrative British market. The Commission claims that the only way to explain Solvay's absence in the British market is the existence of a tacit collusive agreement between the firms which allows ICI to raise its home market prices without provoking Solvay's entry. Our analysis provides several arguments to demonstrate the weakness of this reasoning. The basic point is that any reversal in the price gap must have been due to a change in one or more of the parameters that influence price formation – regardless of whether firms play the collusive or the competitive game. In addition, the fact that UK prices tended to be significantly higher than continental prices throughout the 1980s may have been the result of an increase in the price level in market a or of a decrease in the price level in market b or a combination of both.

The Commission's report gives no information on whether the reversal in the price gap comes from a rise in British prices or from a drop in continental prices. Since we already know that α_k and c_{il} determine the collusive price, any price change under collusive behaviour has to stem from a change in at least one of these two parameters. For p_a^M to have risen, α_a must have increased or c_{1l} must have increased (or a combination of the two) until the sign of (8.23) is reversed. Alternatively, a decrease in α_b, an increase in c_{2l} or a combination thereof would have had the same effect. Under limit pricing, on the other hand, an increase in c_{2l} and/or an increase in t_{2b} causes p_a^N to rise. Without knowing which of the above parameters actually changed and in which direction, no inference can be drawn about firm behaviour. The fact that prices in one or both markets changed, as such, is not of any further help in solving the indistinguishability problem.

Indistinguishability and price discrimination

Until now we assumed that firms set a common net mill price for each customer and that each buyer pays in addition 100 per cent of the transportation costs up to his location. Greenhut and Greenhut (1975) show that firms can increase profits by discriminating between customers when transportation costs play a significant role in the final delivery price. By definition, spatial price discrimination requires firms to set net mill prices that vary according to the customer's location. With considerable transportation costs, firms maximise profits by absorbing freight, that is, by charging the more distant customers less than the full cost of transportation. Compared with the previous strategy where each customer paid a uniform mill price and full delivery cost, this strategy enlarges the sales territory of a firm. The supplier charges the closer customers relatively more by shifting transportation costs from the distant customers to the closer customers. The counterpart of freight absorption is then a phantom freight by which closer customers subsidise delivery to the more distant customers.

In this section we postulate such a price discrimination strategy and examine whether the indistinguishability problem continues to exist. As Greenhut and Greenhut demonstrated, spatial price discrimination may well occur when two or more firms are located at two different production centres potentially serving the same geographical area.[14] Figure 8.1 illustrates this configuration, ICI being located at $x = 0$ in market a and Solvay being located at $x = 1$ in market b.

Customers are assumed to be distributed on a horizontal line of unit length. At each point in space, market demand is linear with slope $b = -1$

---

[14] Greenhut and Greenhut (1975) investigate price discrimination when firms are quantity setters. Further details can be found in Phlips (1983, chapter 3). For a spatial analysis with Bertrand strategies, see Thisse and Vives (1988).

and intercept α. Transportation costs increase proportionally with distance to the production centre. Thus, firm 1 faces transportation costs of tx and firm 2 faces transportation costs of $t(1 - x)$ as x ranges from 0 to 1. Point F indicates the frontier between the two markets. c_1 and c_2 represent marginal costs of production which are supposed to be constant and the same for each firm. For the purpose of this analysis, we assume $c_1 = c_2 = 0$. Transportation costs rise along the line $c_1 B_1$.[15] The straight line $p_1 B_1$ gives the prices at which firm 1 maximises its profits under monopoly by charging $p_1^M = (\alpha + tx)/2$. Note that there is a different price for each location but that prices increase by less than the increase in transportation costs. This is reflected in $c_1 B_1$ being steeper than $p_1 B_1$.

If firm 1 were the only supplier for markets a and b, it would deliver to customers located up to B_1. Thus, it would cover the entire market a and the part of market b that is closest to its production location. But the fact that a second firm located in market b sells the same products reduces the sales territory for firm 1 to point $1 - x^*$. Between x^* and $1 - x^*$ both producers offer the commodity. At x^*, $p_1^M = t(1 - x^*)$, i.e., firm 1's monopoly price is equal to the marginal cost of firm 2. At any location $x^* < x \leq 1$, $p_1^M > t(1 - x)$. In the absence of tacit collusion, p_1^M is not sustainable to the right of x^*, since firm 2 is able to undercut firm 1's monopoly price. The same argument is valid for p_2^M at locations to the left of $1 - x^*$. Equilibrium prices in the area from x^* to $1 - x^*$ follow Bertrand–Nash strategies. Prices are set equal to the marginal cost of the firm with the higher transportation cost at each point $x^* < x < 1 - x^*$. This corresponds to the V-shaped line dfe in figure 8.1.

Therefore, the competitive solution includes two areas of natural monopoly[16] close to the production centres as well as an area around F where prices are set at marginal cost by competing duopolists. Tacit collusion, on the other hand, allows each firm to set its monopoly price in its entire home market. Therefore, if we observe prices that increase continuously with distance from the production centre up to the frontier F, we know that firms are playing the collusive game. In this basic model our indistinguishability problem does not exist.

We must adjust the previous model to the specific cost situation in the soda-ash market, in which a firm that wants to enter the foreign market has to pay a transport cost supplement for overseas delivery. Figure 8.2 illustrates this. Line $c_1 B_1$ now has a break at point F.[17] The vertical

---

[15] Since the graph is symmetric for both firms, we discuss the situation from firm 1's viewpoint only.

[16] Natural in the sense that each rival would make a negative profit when serving the foreign market to the left of x^* and to the right of $1 - x^*$ respectively.

[17] This implies that the price line is also discontinuous.

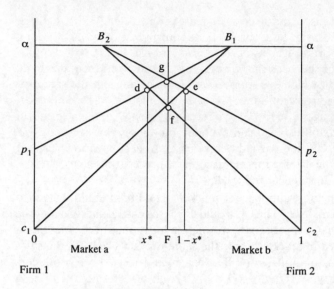

Figure 8.1 Duopoly with spatial price discrimination

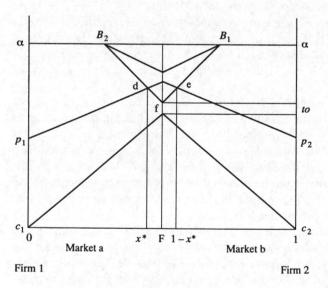

Figure 8.2 Price discrimination with a supplement for overseas delivery

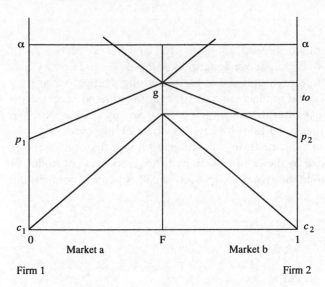

Figure 8.3 Indistinguishability with spatial price discrimination

difference, *to*, between these two segments measures the size of the supplement. While the collusive solution is not different from that of the previous figure, the competitive solution is characterised by an area of Bertrand–Nash prices that is smaller than before. That is, the area $x^* < x < 1 - x^*$ has shrunk. The overseas cost supplement allows firms to extend monopoly pricing to the more distant locations in their home markets, even though firms are playing the competitive game.

However, the price and marginal cost lines do not need to intersect at points d and e. Figure 8.3 illustrates a scenario in which we can no longer distinguish between collusion and competition.

Indistinguishability arises here because the transportation cost supplement, *to*, is higher than in figure 8.2 and such that the price and cost lines intersect exactly at F, the frontier between markets a and b. Staying-out can now be the outcome of a non-cooperative game because none of the firms can make a profit in its foreign market. In general, competitive behaviour will be compatible with staying-out whenever price and cost lines either cross at point F (or do not cross at all). This final result gives us a situation in which there is a separation of markets, with monopoly prices being charged in each of them, regardless of whether firms play the collusive or the competitive game.

Concluding remarks

Our investigation of the allegation against ICI and Solvay served as an empirical example to highlight our general hypothesis. We did not say that the Commission's interpretation of the facts is wrong. Rather, we argued that the Commission did not have all the information at hand necessary to exclude an alternative interpretation of ICI's and Solvay's behaviour. We examined under which conditions we can draw correct inferences on firms' behaviour when some information is lacking and found that the degree of information provided by the Commission in its final report is not sufficient to determine whether the two firms played a collusive or a competitive game. In dubio pro reo.

III

Semicollusion

9   Excess capacity and collusion

9.1 The concept of semicollusion

'Semicollusion' (or 'partial collusion' as it is sometimes called) arises when decisions have to be made in a competitive way but with the understanding that product market collusion will follow, or, alternatively, when collusive decisions are made with the understanding that they will be followed by competition on the product market. Typically, these decisions are about investments. Are the capacities chosen differently if the products resulting from the investment are going to be sold in a collusive way than if the product market is competitive? Conversely, do the independent choices of capacities by individual firms affect the type of collusive agreement these firms will make? Consider the choice of locations for these investments in the space domain or the choice of varieties of differentiated products (which is analytically the same problem: distance is interpreted as a measure of production differentiation). Will the choice of location depend on whether it is followed by collusive rather than competitive pricing? If so, will it in turn affect the collusive prices and profits that are to follow? Consider the choice of investments in R&D. Will these investments be affected by the knowledge that collusion in the product market is going to follow? Will they in turn affect the collusive outcome? What if, to the contrary, R&D is organised in a collusive way but followed by competition in the product market?

Clearly, these examples raise questions of considerable interest. In the literature on explicit or tacit collusion discussed in parts I and II, these questions are ignored: only 'full' collusion is considered. Recent research makes the distinction between full and partial collusion and asks the question how the latter affects the outcomes. Since there is a mixture of collusion and competition, intuition suggests that the outcomes are intermediate ones: production levels and prices somewhere between the collusive and the competitive levels, intermediate investment levels, locations that are not at a maximum distance, as in a competitive spatial model, but are more distant than in a collusive spatial model. This intuition is wrong. Friedman and Thisse (1993) were the first to emphasise this, to my knowledge. They draw a striking analogy between their own results (for a repeated game in which firms select their locations knowing that a particular trigger strategy equilibrium, arranged collusively, will ensue) and the results by Osborne and Pitchik (1987) for capacity choices followed by collusion and by Fershtman and Gandal (1994) for R&D investments followed by product market collusion. This chapter will show how the *non-cooperative* choice of *excess* production capacities can enforce collusion. The next chapter will demonstrate that *collusive* R&D efforts, followed by competition in the product market, are to be recommended. Location theory is outside the scope of this book.

9.2 Excess capacity and cartels in an historical perspective

Cartels break down under the pressure of excess capacity. Indeed, when there is excess capacity, individual cartel members have an incentive to undercut the collusive price because they can capture a large share of the market. This basic intuition is at the heart of the traditional view that there is a negative correlation between excess capacity and collusion. Recent game-theoretic contributions, however, stress that this correlation is positive rather than negative. Excess capacity gives colluders a stronger bargaining position in their negotiation about cartel quotas. In the case of tacit collusion, firms with excess capacity can punish deviators more harshly, so that deviations are less likely to occur. In the words of Davidson and Deneckere (1990, p. 525):

After all, when the level of excess capacity is substantial the threat of retaliation looms large in the eyes of a potential cheater since firms can (and will) easily dump a large amount of output on the market to punish any chiseller. Similarly, when the level of excess capacity is relatively small a cheater need not worry very much about retaliation since the industry cannot cheaply expand production by any significant amount.

There is an element of truth in both positions, which are not as conflicting as they may seem at first sight. The purpose of this chapter is to clarify this. Before going into theory, an examination of the historical evidence – however fragmentary – on the creation, strengthening and collapse of cartels should put the traditional as well as the game-theoretic view into the proper perspective.

Chapters 9 and 10 of my 1962 book on market integration are rather detailed historical studies of the cartelisation of the European market for cement and nitrogen fertilisers. In Germany, France, Italy and Belgium, the

1920s were characterised by what could be called a capacity race. Incumbent cement producers increased their capacities and many new firms came in, while national cartels were formed and market separation agreements (between national markets) were negotiated. This race led to huge excess capacity at the industry level and was followed, in the early 1930s, by a general price collapse. The cartels did not stop the race. Was the price collapse due to the excess capacity that had been built up? One could argue as well that the price war was the consequence of the extraordinary and world-wide drop in market demand, due to the big crisis, which forced the cement producers to struggle for survival.

As of 1920, the German nitrogen fertiliser industry produced much more sulphate of ammonia than the national consumption, while the neighbouring countries produced much less. As a result, Germany was the recognised price leader all through the 1920s. It set the price so high that an enormous amount of capital was attracted into the industry all over Europe. Between 1925 and 1930, national production capacities were increased in the following proportions: 500 per cent in Poland, 600 per cent in Italy, 900 per cent in France and 1,400 per cent in Belgium. Yet, prices remained under control. This tacit collusion with price leadership was transformed in August 1930 into an explicit agreement (the so-called *Convention Internationale de l'Azote*) signed by the German *Stickstoff Syndikat* (the German cartel), ICI, the French cartel and the dominant Belgian, Dutch, Italian, Polish and Czechoslovakian producers. Together, they controlled 98 per cent of the European production. Interestingly, while the agreement adapted the productions per country to the local consumption, capacity increases were *not* regulated. In the spring of 1931, prices collapsed and several firms (including a newly created Dutch firm) went bankrupt as a result of the crisis.

Citing Bloch (1932), Scherer (1980, p. 370) writes the following:

In Germany during the 1920s and 1930s, shares were allocated on the basis of production capacity. Cartel members therefore raced to increase their sales quotas by building more capacity. In the Rhineland–Westphalian coal cartel, for example, production capacity exceeded *peak* demand levels by 25% because of the competition in investment. Even when market shares are not linked formally to capacity, a cartel member's bargaining power depends upon its fighting reserves – the amount of output it can dump on the market, depressing the price, if others hold out for unacceptably high quotas. Recognising this, companies participating in market-sharing cartels will be tempted to invest in more capacity than they need to serve foreseeable demands at anticipated collusive price levels.

Summing up: in the 1930s, the excess capacity built up earlier during the collusive 1920s led to fiercer price wars, in the face of a sudden and important drop in market demand, than there would have been otherwise. In this sense, excess capacity and collusion were 'negatively correlated'.

Yet, they were also 'positively correlated' because the capacities were built during periods of high collusive prices. This sort of evidence clearly does not contradict a theory, such as the one developed in this chapter, which stresses the role of excess capacity in providing the means of enforcing collusion.

Osborne and Pitchik (1987) work out such a theory in a semicollusive framework. They set up a two-stage model. In the first stage, duopolists choose their production capacities in a non-cooperative way, knowing that they will collude explicitly (they are going to become members of a quota cartel) in the second stage. In this second stage, they negotiate about how to divide up the monopoly profit, with given capacities. To enforce the agreement, they issue the following threat: in the event of disagreement, they will fix the prices that are the Nash equilibrium strategies in a non-cooperative price-setting game with the same given capacities. This price-setting game is analysed in the next section. Section 9.4 is devoted to the second (collusive) stage, while section 9.5 explains how the individual capacities are chosen in the first stage. These capacities turn out to be such that their sum is larger than the sum of the quotas (outputs) in the cartel: there is excess capacity in the industry under collusion. Excess capacity is not the result of bad planning but is necessary for the cartel agreement to work! Section 9.6 then shows that the same is true (in a repeated game) with tacit collusion. The final section derives a few empirical tests that could facilitate the detection of collusion by antitrust authorities.

9.3 A non-cooperative price-setting game with given capacities

Osborne and Pitchik (1987) in fact take over the capacity-constrained duopoly model with price-setting strategies of Kreps and Scheinkman (1983). Using price strategies in the absence of capacity constraints leads to the Bertrand model, in which a firm that undercuts the price of its competitor serves the entire market when its product is a perfect substitute for that of its competitor. Each firm therefore undercuts the other so that both end up selling at a price equal to marginal cost in equilibrium. This is unrealistic: firms should realise what the outcome of the game is going to be and therefore refrain from competing in price. When their products are differentiated, price undercutting does not take the entire market away from one's competitor and price strategies make sense. They also make sense when the product is homogeneous but each firm has a limited capacity: then fixing a lower price allows one to produce up to capacity without serving the entire market.[1] Edgeworth (1897) introduced such a

---

[1] Such a situation was assumed in the discussion of threats of minimax punishments in section 6.2.

capacity-constrained Bertrand duopoly in the literature. Kreps and Scheinkman analyse its properties in detail.

They suppose that two firms produce the same commodity with given capacities K_1 and K_2. The sum of these capacities is $K = K_1 + K_2$. Without loss of generality, let $K_1 \geq K_2 > 0$. The unit cost of initially installing these capacities is the same for both firms and equal to u. Both firms also have the same constant unit production cost $c \geq 0$ up to capacity. p is the excess price over unit cost and $d(p)$ is industry demand. There exists a price p_0 above which $d(p) = 0$. If the smallest $K_i(i = 1,2)$ is larger than the intercept of aggregate demand $d(0)$, then each firm can serve the entire market, there are no capacity constraints and we are in the standard Bertrand model. There is no entry.

There is a large number of identical consumers. When one firm undercuts the other's price but is unable to serve all consumers, each customer is allowed to buy the same fraction of this firm's capacity.

The firms simultaneously and independently name prices p_i chosen from the interval $[0, p_0]$. If $p_1 < p_2$, then firm 1 sells up to its capacity or demand, that is

$$q_1 = \min(K_1, d(p_1)) \tag{9.1}$$

units of the good at price p_1, while firm 2 sells up to its capacity or the residual demand, that is

$$q_2 = \min(K_2, \max(0, d(p_2) - K_1)) \tag{9.2}$$

units at price p_2. When firm 2's residual demand $d(p_2) - K_1$ is negative, it sells nothing. If $p_2 < p_1$, symmetric equations apply. If $p_1 = p_2 = p$, Osborne and Pitchik suppose that demand is allocated in proportion to capacities when these are sufficient to serve that demand. Then

$$q_i = \min\left(K_i, \frac{K_i}{K} d(p)\right). \tag{9.3}$$

At any price pair (p_i, p_j) the profit of firm i is therefore

$$h_i(p_i, p_j) = \begin{cases} L_i(p_i) \equiv p_i \min(K_i, d(p_i)) & \text{if } p_i < p_j \\ M_i(p_i) \equiv p_i \min(K_i, \max(0, d(p_i) - K_j)) & \text{if } p_i > p_j \\ \phi_i(p_i) \equiv p_i \min\left(K_i, \frac{K_i}{K} d(p)\right) & \text{if } p_i = p_j = p. \end{cases} \tag{9.4}$$

L_i and M_i are difficult to interpret because they are simultaneously valid for any combination of p_i and p_j. Figures 9.1A and 9.1B should be of great help. If $p_1 < p_2$, then firm 1's profit function is represented by L_1 and firm 2's profit

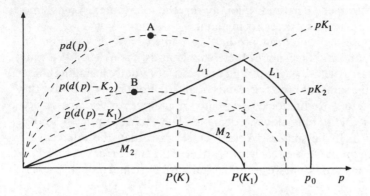

Figure 9.1A $p_1 < p_2$ and industry capacity is very small

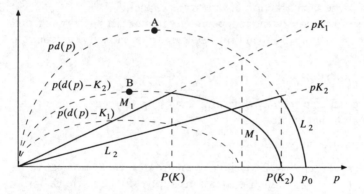

Figure 9.1B $p_1 > p_2$ and industry capacity is very small

function is represented by M_2 in figure 9.1A. If, to the contrary, $p_1 > p_2$, then firm 1's profit is M_1 and firm 2's profit is L_2 as depicted in figure 9.1B.

As prices increase along the horizontal axes, market demand $d(p)$ goes down. Let $P(q)$ be the inverse market demand function. All profit functions are straight lines through the origin with slope K_i at prices up to $P(K)$. (Remember that $K = K_1 + K_2$.) Indeed, at prices equal to or below $P(K)$, market demand is so high that both firms can sell their full capacity output. As long as $p_1 < p_2$, firm 1 can continue to sell at full capacity at higher prices until its price is equal to $P(K_1)$. At that price, firm 1 serves the entire market and M_2 is zero (see figure 9.1A). At even higher prices, firm 1's profit curve L_1 coincides with $pd(p)$. As long as $p_1 > p_2$, firm 2 can produce and sell at full capacity along L_2 at prices up to $P(K_2)$. At that price, M_1 is zero (see figure 9.1B). At higher prices, L_2 coincides with $pd(p)$.

Note that $P(K)$ is the price at which $pK_1 = p(d(p) - K_2)$ and pK_2

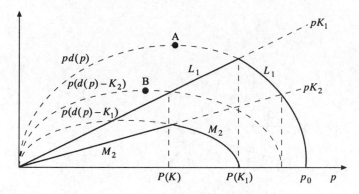

Figure 9.2A $p_1 < p_2$ and industry capacity is small

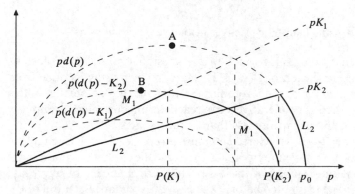

Figure 9.2B $p_1 > p_2$ and industry capacity is small

$= p(d(p) - K_1)$, the sum of the capacities being equal to market demand. $P(K)$ was put to the right of the price at which $pd(p)$ reaches its maximum (point A). This implies that, in figures 9.1A and 9.1B, *the sum of the capacities is very small*: industry capacity is *less* than the output that generates the unconstrained monopoly profit represented by point A (since $P(K)$ is higher than the price that would generate this unconstrained monopoly profit). In this situation, the best the duopolists can do is to name the same price $P(K)$, so that their equilibrium profits are $K_i P(K)$. Indeed, naming a price greater than $P(K)$ will not profit either firm (see figures 9.1A and 9.1B), and there is no incentive to name a lower price, since each firm is selling its full capacity output.

The price $P(K)$ is also a Nash equilibrium price in some cases when $P(K)$ lies to the *left* of the price that generates the unconstrained monopoly profit (point A). Figures 9.2A and 9.2B illustrate the case where *capacity is 'small'*

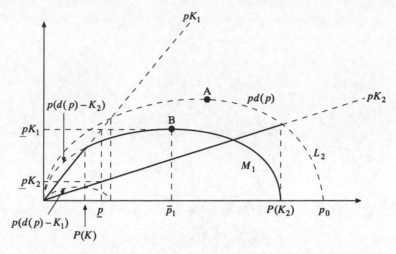

Figure 9.3 $p_1 > p_2$ and industry capacity is neither very large nor small

in the sense that point B (at which firm 1's residual profit M_1 reaches its maximum) lies to the left of $P(K)$. Therefore, by increasing its price from $P(K)$ firm 1 will *lower* its profits (compare with figure 9.3). Note that in this case both firms acting cooperatively can reach the unconstrained monopoly profit (point A) by producing less than at full capacity.

Next consider the case where *the industry capacity is very large* in the sense that each firm has enough capacity to serve the entire market or, more precisely, that the smallest K_i is larger than the intercept of aggregate demand $d(0)$. Then, as noted before, we are in the standard Bertrand price-setting game without capacity constraints. Price undercutting leads to an equilibrium price equal to zero.

For the intermediate case where *industry capacity is neither very large nor small*, an equilibrium in pure strategies does not exist. Figure 9.3 illustrates: the only candidate for equilibrium is $p_1 = p_2 = P(K)$, as was said before. However, there is now an incentive for firm 1 to increase its price p_1 up to $\bar{p}_1$ and make more profits. Kreps and Scheinkman (1983) show that in this case there is a mixed strategy equilibrium. There is a range of prices, between an upper limit $\bar{p}_1$ and a lower limit $p_1 = p_2 = \underline{p}$, inside which each firm names prices according to continuous and strictly increasing distribution functions, except that firm 1 names $\bar{p}_1$ with positive probability whenever $K_1 > K_2$. In addition, the firm with the larger capacity is more likely to name a higher price than the other firm and is thus 'less aggressive', loosely speaking.[2] Such a situation is depicted in figure 9.3, which is based on the

---

[2] More correctly, for a given price, the probability that firm 1 names a lower price is smaller than the probability that firm 2 names a lower price: firm 1's strategy 'stochastically dominates' the strategy of firm 2 in a strict sense.

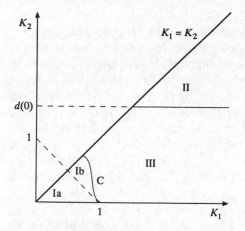

Figure 9.4 Three areas with different threats

assumption that $p_1 > p_2$ and industry capacity is neither very large nor small.

Note that (a) $\bar{p}_1$ is the price at which firm 1's residual profit M_1 reaches its maximum (point B), which is firm 1's minimax profit, (b) this minimax profit $M_1(\bar{p}_1)$ is firm 1's equilibrium revenue,[3] (c) firm 1 is selling less than its capacity output (if it were producing at full capacity it would have the same price $P(K)$ as firm 2), (d) firm 2 is selling its capacity output and (e) p is determined by the equilibrium level of M_1 and is above $P(K)$. As for (e), firm 1's equilibrium capacity is such that M_1 is maximised, given K_2. At this capacity $\underline{p}$ just yields that same profit (follow the horizontal dashed line from point B to pK_1) so that firm 1 would not want to price below $\underline{p}$, which is thus the equilibrium lower limit.

9.4 Cartel negotiation with given capacities

Suppose our duopolists negotiate a cartel agreement with given capacities K_1 and K_2 (and $K_1 \geq K_2$ as above). They use the following threats: if no agreement is reached, the non-cooperative price-setting game of section 9.3 will be played. That means that the prices will be the equilibrium prices defined in the previous section. Consequently the threats are credible. They correspond to the four cases in which industry capacity is defined as either 'very small', 'small', 'very large' or neither small nor very large. These cases are represented by areas Ia, Ib, II and III respectively in figure 9.4 (still on the assumption that $K_1 \geq K_2$).

Let us normalise the quantities such that $K = K_1 + K_2 = 1$ represents the total industry output that maximises $pd(p)$. Curve C separates area Ib from

---

[3] Used to compute the negotiated payoff in equation (9.7).

area III and represents[4] the values of K_1, corresponding to different values of K_2 (and therefore of $\bar{p}_1$) that maximise firm 1's residual profit M_1.

In area I the pair of threats is $(P(K), P(K))$. Indeed, 'since both firms are producing at capacity, neither can improve its bargaining position by threatening to cut prices (this only reduces its own payoff, and does not affect that of its opponent). That is, the "threat," of each firm is to set the price $P(K)$ ...' (Osborne and Pitchik 1987, p. 421). In area II, the equilibrium threat of each firm is to set the price equal to marginal cost, or $P(q) = 0$, which is the outcome of the standard Bertrand game. In the previous section, it was argued that it is unrealistic to suppose that duopolists would actually play the Bertrand game in the absence of capacity constraints. Here, however, a cartel agreement is at stake. In area II, both firms are capable of flooding the market and the threat of doing so in case no agreement is reached is *the* realistic alternative. The threat of reverting to $P(q) = 0$ is therefore credible. In area III, the threats involve randomisation and vary continuously between p and $\bar{p}_1$ (see figure 9.3). They can be interpreted as threats to hold 'sales' at reduced prices over a period of time.

What are the negotiated payoffs, given these threats? We know that, in area I, the non-cooperative profits are $v_i^* = K_i P(K)$. In the subarea Ia, $K \leq 1$ (see figures 9.1A and 9.1B) and the negotiated profits are equal to these non-cooperative profits. No firm can do better. In subarea Ib, however, industry capacity is high enough ($K > 1$) to reach the unconstrained monopoly profit (see figures 9.2A and 9.2B). Nash's (1950) bargaining solution is then to split equally the excess of the unconstrained monopoly profit over the payoffs obtained when the threats are carried out. In this solution, each firm thus gets

$$K_i P(K) + \frac{1}{2} [1 - K_1 P(K) - K_2 P(K)]$$

after normalising the unconstrained monopoly profit to 1. For firm 1, one obtains

$$v_1^* = K_1 P(K) + \frac{1}{2} [1 - K_1 P(K) - K_2 P(K)] = \frac{1}{2} [1 + (K_1 - K_2) P(K)],$$

$$(9.5)$$

which is larger than $1/2$, since $K_1 > K_2$. Firm 2's share of the unconstrained monopoly profit is

---

[4] Note that $K > 1$ in subarea Ib. In this subarea there is enough capacity in the industry to generate the unconstrained monopoly profit but firm 1 cannot reach point B in figures 9.2A and 9.2B.

$$v_2^* = 1 - \frac{1}{2}[1 + (K_1 - K_2)P(K)] = \frac{1}{2}[1 - (K_1 - K_2)] < \frac{1}{2}. \qquad (9.6)$$

In area II, the non-cooperative profits are zero. The Nash bargaining solution is then for each firm to get one half of the unconstrained monopoly profit, according to equation (9.5).

In area III, the firms play mixed strategies choosing prices between $\underline{p}$ and $\bar{p}_1$, with firm 1 being more likely to name a higher price than firm 2. At the upper limit[5] $\bar{p}_1$, firm 1 gets a cartel profit equal to

$$v_1^* = \underline{p}K_1 + \frac{1}{2}\left[1 - \underline{p}K_1 - \left(\frac{K_2}{K_1}\right)\underline{p}K_1\right] = \frac{1}{2}[1 + (K_1 - K_2)\underline{p}]. \qquad (9.7)$$

Remember, from figure 9.3, that $\underline{p}K_1$ is the profit that maximises M_1 and that firm 2 nets a proportion K_2/K_1 of it. Firm 1's share is larger than $1/2$ at $\bar{p}_1$. At that price, firm 2's cartel profit is

$$v_2^* = 1 - \frac{1}{2}\left[1 + \frac{K_1 - K_2}{K_1}\underline{p}K_1\right] = \frac{1}{2}\left[1 - \underline{p}K_1 + \frac{K_2}{K_1}\underline{p}K_1\right] < \frac{1}{2}. \qquad (9.8)$$

Note that the sum of v_1^* and v_2^* equals 1, as was the case in area Ib.

Summing up, we found that the profit shares of the firms depend on the nature of the available threats, so that the leverage of firms with different capacities at the bargaining table is not, in general, in proportion to these capacities. The smaller firm can obtain the same share as the larger firm, if it has built up a capacity that enables it to flood the market. Then the threats are the most damaging and the cartel negotiation is most likely to be successful. Needless to say, such a cartel solution would imply a huge waste of resources, both firms being able to serve aggregate demand at any price.

9.5 Non-cooperative capacity choices with explicit collusion

The preceding section solved the second stage of our semicollusive game (in which duopolists choose capacities non-cooperatively in the first stage knowing that they are going to negotiate a cartel agreement with the outcomes just described in the second stage). This solution supposed that the investment decisions had been made before: K_1 and K_2 were given and known. Will our duopolists actually go for overcapacity in the industry in the first stage? More precisely, will they put themselves in area II of figure 9.4? Or in area III? Or in subarea Ib?

The question whether one firm will build up a larger capacity than the others and which will turn out to be the bigger one is of no interest here.

---

[5] For further details, see Osborne and Pitchik (1987, appendix).

(Differences in size depend on differences in unit costs of capacity in this framework.) Osborne and Pitchik (1987) therefore make the simplifying assumption that the oligopolists have the same (constant) unit cost of capacity u although $K_1 > K_2$. They also suppose that the capacities are chosen independently (that is, non-cooperatively[6]) once-and-for-all by all firms before the cartel negotiation starts.

The capacities are thus neither objects of negotiation, nor strategic variables for the firm during negotiation. The idea is that, given some inflexibility of capacity, it is to the advantage of a firm to choose its capacity before entering negotiations. Of course, if the cartel lasts for a long time, there is scope for subsequent adjustments of capacity. Even so, in the absence of perfect enforcement, agreement on a capacity-reduction may be much less likely than agreement on a price-hike: if a firm cheats on the former, its opponent is in a weak position, while any change in price is easily reversible. (Osborne and Pitchik 1987, pp. 414–15)

They also add the following interesting remark:

Rather than assuming that the industry is starting from scratch, we could suppose that it is currently competitive, and that adjustments in capacity are being made, in anticipation of subsequent collusion. Or, the industry may currently be a monopoly, which is changing its capacity in response to an entrant with which it will collude. (Osborne and Pitchnik 1987, p. 414, footnote 3)

To characterise the equilibrium industry capacity K^*, use must be made of the negotiated profits (given in the preceding section) which are the outcomes of the second stage subgame. After deduction of the capacity costs uK_i, these are the payoffs of the capacity subgame in which the strategies are capacity choices.

Two results are rather straightforward. First, suppose each firm builds up a capacity such that each can serve the entire market, or $K_i \geq d(0)$ for $i = 1, 2$, so that $K \geq 2d(0)$. Both firms are then in area II. However, in this area an extra unit of capacity does not yield any marginal benefit: it only increases the cost of capacity. So no firm would want to build that much capacity. Second, the equilibrium level of industry capacity implies, for $K < d(0)$, that each firm has the same capacity $K^*/2$. To show this, differentiate the profits in each area: in an equilibrium, these derivatives must be zero. For example, looking at[7] area Ib and using equations (9.5)

---

[6] Fershtman and Muller (1986, p. 214) justify this assumption as follows: 'in many instances investment decisions must be made far in advance so that they are observed only with a time lag. As a result, a firm will be reluctant to enter an agreement on its capital stock, since a breakdown in the agreement may leave the firm either overcapitalised or, even worse, undercapitalised with a weak market position.'

[7] To do the same exercise for area III, one has to rewrite equations (9.7) and (9.8) as functions of the capacities.

and (9.6), the payoffs of the capacity subgame are

$$w_1^*(K_1, K_2) = \frac{1}{2}[1 + (K_1 - K_2)P(K)] - uK_1$$

and

$$w_2^*(K_1, K_2) = \frac{1}{2}[1 - (K_1 - K_2)P(K)] - uK_2.$$

Differentiating w_1^* with respect to K_1 and w_2^* with respect to K_2, and putting these derivatives equal to zero, one obtains

$$\frac{\partial w_1^*}{\partial K_1} = \frac{1}{2}[P(K) + (K_1 - K_2)P'(K)] - u = 0 \qquad (9.9)$$

$$\frac{\partial w_2^*}{\partial K_2} = \frac{1}{2}[P(K) + (K_1 - K_2)P'(K)] - u = 0. \qquad (9.10)$$

Therefore[8]

$$K_1 P'(K) - K_2 P'(K) = K_2 P'(K) - K_1 P'(K)$$

or

$$K_1^* = K_2^*.$$

The sum of equations (9.9) and (9.10) is

$$P(K) = 2u. \qquad (9.11)$$

The left-hand side is the joint marginal profit of an increase in the capacity of the industry. This must be equal to $2u$. If we now normalise the price, so that it is equal to 1 when the joint capacity output yields the unconstrained monopoly profit, that is, $K = 1$, then $P(1) = 2u$ implies $u = \frac{1}{2}$. When $K > 1$, the normalised $P(K)$ is smaller than 1, since $P(K)$ is decreasing in K, and u must be smaller than $\frac{1}{2}$. There is excess capacity in the industry ($K > 1$) if $u < \frac{1}{2}$. Going through areas Ia, Ib and III, it can be shown that the joint marginal profits are decreasing in K, so that there is a unique equilibrium $K^* < 2d(0)$, and $K^* > 1$, if and only if $u < \frac{1}{2}$. In words, the sum of the

---

[8] If the unit costs of capacity are different, say $u_1 < u_2$, then the same exercise leads to $(K_1 - K_2)P' = u_1 - u_2$. With a given slope of the demand curve, differences in capacity are proportional to differences in unit costs of capacity.

capacities chosen by the duopolists exceeds the total output that yields the unconstrained monopoly profit if the cost of capacity is less than half the monopoly profit margin (since prices are in excess of the cost of production). This implies that the duopolists locate themselves in area Ia when $u > \dfrac{1}{2}$. When $u < \dfrac{1}{2}$, they move into areas Ib or III depending on the level of u.

Whenever they located themselves outside area Ia, the sum of the capacities chosen exceeds the sum of the negotiated quotas (total sales). The firms know that part of their capacity is *not* going to be used for production. They build this capacity to make the punishments in case the cartel negotiation fails more severe: the larger is K, the lower are the threat prices. This is the consequence of their expectation that they will collude in the second stage of the game. Indeed, if they expected to compete in the second stage, they would be playing the Kreps–Scheinkman game in which there is no use for excess capacity.

When the Osborne–Pitchik game is played, the outcomes thus look like this. First, the duopolists choose simultaneously their capacities in such a way that their sum is $K \gtrless 1$ depending on $u \lessgtr \dfrac{1}{2}$, with $K < d(0)$. Then output quotas are negotiated. Indeed, the model can be interpreted as one of negotiation over output quotas, since the chosen capacities are always sufficient to allow a production that can be sold at the price $P(K)$ when $K \leq 1$ or at the monopoly price equal to 1 when $K > 1$. The demands for quotas are backed by threats to deviate from the monopoly price. Finally, the negotiated quotas are produced and sold at the monopoly price and the negotiated profits are realised by each firm without any side-payment.[9] Needless to say, this outcome is not efficient since excess capacity is costly.

9.6 Collusion detection

The Osborne–Pitchik model is most interesting, not only because it shows that it is rational for firms to build up capacities which they do not intend to use for production, but also because it provides a simple test that can be used by antitrust authorities to detect collusion, whether explicit or tacit. (Tacit collusion in capacity-constrained duopoly will be discussed in the next section.)

The idea is to examine the profit *per unit of capacity* and to compare it between competitive outcomes and collusive outcomes. Osborne and Pitchik (1987, p. 414) write:

---

[9] On efficient cartel agreements with side-payments, see section 4.2.

If we want to compare the outcome in our model with one which is 'competitive', there are two alternatives. In the standard 'perfectly competitive' outcome, both firms sell at the same price, so that their unit profits are the same. The outcome of price competition (between firms with limited capacities) predicted by the Bertrand–Edgeworth model involves the same unit profits for both firms for a wide range of capacity pairs (essentially, unless the large firm has more than enough capacity to serve demand at the break-even price; for the details, see Osborne and Pitchik (1986)). Thus whenever the industry capacity is neither very small nor very large relative to demand, the unit profit is the same for both firms in either of the 'competitive' outcomes, while the small firm fares better in the cartel. If the cartel outcome can be achieved by an implicit agreement, this provides a criterion to distinguish between competitive and collusive industries.

The small firm fares better in the cartel: it has the larger profit per unit of capacity!

To show this, consider first the case where $K < 1$. (We are in area Ia in figure 9.3.) The industry capacity is less than the unconstrained monopoly output, so that the duopolists are unable to obtain the monopoly profit. A cartel agreement would have no effect: the non-collusive profits $K_i P(K)$ are the highest that can be reached. So

$$\frac{v_1^*}{v_2^*} = \frac{K_1 P(K)}{K_2 P(K)} = \frac{K_1}{K_2}.$$

The profits are proportional to the capacities. In other words, the profits per unit of capacity (v_i^*/K_i) are equal.

When $K > 1$, this is no longer true. Now, with $K_1 > K_2$

$$\frac{v_1^*}{K_1} < \frac{v_2^*}{K_2}$$

or

$$\frac{v_1^*}{v_2^*} < \frac{K_1}{K_2}. \tag{9.12}$$

If the firms were in region II, this is obvious. Each firm would net $1/2$ of the excess over the competitive profits (which are zero). So each firm gets $1/2$ (given the normalisation which puts the unconstrained monopoly profit equal to 1). Therefore the firm with the smaller capacity has a higher profit per unit of capacity. When the firms are in region Ib, we have $v_1^* + v_2^* = 1$ from equations (9.5) and (9.6). To show that the smaller firm has a higher profit per unit of capacity, it suffices to show that $v_1^* < \dfrac{K_1}{K}$. Indeed, if this is the case, then

$$\frac{v_1^*}{K_1} < \frac{1}{K} = \frac{v_1^* + v_2^*}{K_1 + K_2}$$

or

$$v_1^* K_1 + v_1^* K_2 < v_1^* K_1 + v_2^* K_1$$

or

$$v_1^* K_2 < v_2^* K_1$$

or

$$\frac{v_1^*}{K_1} < \frac{v_2^*}{K_2}.$$

Now, according to (9.5), $v_1^* = \frac{1}{2}[1 + (K_1 - K_2)P(K)]$. On the other hand, when $K > 1$, the joint profit without collusion $(KP(K))$ is smaller than the unconstrained monopoly profit. So $(KP(K)) < 1$ or $P(K) < \frac{1}{K}$. Therefore,

$$v_1^* = \frac{1}{2}[1 + (K_1 - K_2)P(K)] < \frac{1}{2}[1 + (K_1 - K_2)/K] = \frac{K_1}{K}.$$

In area III, the proof is more complicated and can be found in Osborne and Pitchik (1987), who also note that the larger the joint capacity of the firms relative to market demand, the higher the profit per unit of capacity of the small firm relative to that of the large one.

I now wish to return to the great salt duopoly in the UK discussed in section 6.3 and see whether this collusion detector works and confirms Rees' (1991) conclusion that there was collusion during the period of observation (1980–4). Rees used a folk theorem based on mutual minimaxing. Here, the reasoning is based on a static model of capacity constrained duopolists.

We know that there are two producers of white salt in the UK: ICI Weston Point (WP) with a given capacity of 1,095 kilotonnes and British Salt (BS) with a given capacity of 824 kilotonnes. The smaller firm has a larger market share in the UK, but WP (only WP!) is exporting abroad. Both had considerable excess capacity during the period for which data are available, as can be seen from table 9.1. Both argued that this was caused by a decline in demand. However, over the period 1975–9, BS and WP still averaged 13 per cent and 17 per cent excess capacity respectively. Strengthening collusion is an alternative explanation of continuing excess capacity.

Table 9.1. *The great salt duopoly: excess capacities (in %)*

	1980	1981	1982	1983	1984
BS	15	29	21	31	33
WP	25	40	35	41	46

Table 9.2. *The great salt duopoly: shares in industry output*

	1980	1981	1982	1983	1984
BS output (KT)	702	587	649	570	553
WP output (KT)	824	670	722	636	707
Industry output (KT)	1,526	1,257	1,371	1,206	1,260
Total UK sales (KT)	1,294	1,099	1,125	1,007	1,003
BS output share (%)	46	47	47	47	44
WP output share (%)	54	53	53	53	56

I now compute the *total* output (exports included) of each duopolist and its share in total industry output. Table 9.2 shows that these shares were remarkably stable over time. If there was a quota agreement, these quotas corresponded to about 45 per cent of industry output for BS and 55 per cent for WP.

A tacit agreement may have reserved the foreign market for WP. As far as the UK market is concerned, a comparison of total sales in the UK with the firms' capacities shows that WP's capacity was larger than UK market demand in 1983 and 1984. But BS's capacity was always well below it. So the salt producers were not in area II. Total capacity was large enough to produce the monopoly output, so they were not in area Ia (see figure 9.4). Since there was price leadership, they did not randomise and were not in area III. Area Ib is the relevant one.

If they shared the excess monopoly profit, how was this profit split? Equations (9.5) and (9.6) suggest that the bigger firm (WP) should have had the larger share of the joint profit. Table 9.3 shows that this was not the case: in 1980 and 1981, the profit share was equal. In the following years, WP's share dropped sharply. This is not conflicting evidence, however, since the model supposed equal and constant average variable costs up to capacity. In fact, WP suffered, in 1982, 1983 and 1984, from higher and increasing average variable costs, relative to BS. The equality of the profit shares in 1980 and 1981, when BS's average variable cost was higher than WP's, is

Table 9.3. *The great salt duopoly: profits (£000) and profit shares*

	1980	1981	1982	1983	1984
BS profit	7,065	7,622	10,489	10,150	10,882
WP profit (incl. exports)	7,273	7,527	6,841	6,297	6,204
Joint profits	14,338	15,149	17,330	16,447	17,086
BS share (%)	49	50	61	62	64
WP share (%)	51	50	39	38	36

Table 9.4. *The great salt duopoly: profits per unit of capacity*

	1980	1981	1982	1983	1984
BS profits per unit of capacity (£)	8.57	9.25	12.73	12.32	13.21
WP profit per unit of capacity (£)	6.64	6.87	6.25	5.75	5.67
Industry capacity/total UK sales	1.483	1.746	1.706	1.905	1.913

more difficult to reconcile with equations (9.5) and (9.6), however. Perhaps WP's exports were smaller than planned?

The ultimate test of the presence of collusion is to look at the profits per unit of capacity, to check whether these are larger for the smaller firm (BS). From table 9.3, it is clear that they are. Table 9.4 shows in addition that they increase as the joint capacity of the two firms increases relative to market demand. There is strong indication that BS and WP were indeed colluding during the period 1980–4.

9.7 Non-cooperative capacity choices with tacit collusion

The preceding section suggests that excess capacity also occurs when collusive outcomes are sustained in a repeated game that is played non-cooperatively. This is precisely the outcome of Davidson and Deneckere's (1990) two-stage duopoly game. In the first stage, capacities are determined with the expectation that tacit collusion will arrive in the second stage. Firms are not allowed to collude in capacity. In the second stage, they play an infinitely repeated non-cooperative price-setting game in which they charge the highest sustainable price in any collusive agreement, that is, at or below the monopoly price. If at any time anyone is detected cheating, the duopolists revert to the static Nash equilibria of the Kreps–Scheinkman game described in section 9.3.

Cheating will not occur if the immediate gain from cheating is smaller than the capitalised value from losses due to retaliation. This argument was developed in section 6.1. The rate of interest r therefore plays a crucial role together with the cost of building capacity. If the rate of interest is above some critical value (so that the discount factor is below a corresponding critical value and firms discount the future heavily) no sustainable price exists that yields profits above what would be earned in the static non-collusive equilibrium. We saw that there also exists a critical value of the cost of capacity u above which there will be no excess capacity in the Osborne–Pitchik Game.[10] In this repeated game the critical value of u depends on the value of r.

Davidson and Deneckere (1990) work out an example, using a linear market demand $d(p) = 1 - p$, to show the following. When u and r are sufficiently low, there is at most one 'unconstrained' semicollusive equilibrium, characterised by high levels of capacity and considerable excess capacity. The equilibrium price is the price a monopolist with zero costs of capacity would choose. Increases in u and/or r give rise to a continuum of 'constrained' semicollusive equilibria with some excess capacity and prices above the static Bertrand–Nash level but below the monopoly level, as long as u and r remain below a critical level. Equilibrium profits are lower than their fully cooperative equivalents for two reasons. First, the extra cost of sustaining a given profit stream with excess capacity would not have to be incurred by a monopolist.[11] Second, the firms make no efforts to reduce excess capacities: to the contrary, a capacity 'race' develops, each firm trying to strengthen its ability to retaliate when cheating occurs. Note that the level of collusion that can be sustained is a decreasing function of the difference between the capacities. As the bigger firm becomes relatively bigger, the equilibrium price must go down: the profit share of the smaller firm decreases and collusion becomes less attractive (and cheating more attractive) to this firm. The collusive price must fall in order to keep the small firm from cheating. Finally, if u and r get above their critical levels, there is at most one non-collusive equilibrium in which the price is down to its static Bertrand–Nash level and each firm sells at capacity.

Davidson and Deneckere (1990, pp. 525–6) note that the empirical evidence on the correlation between excess capacity and tacit collusion is weak: see Esposito and Esposito (1974) and Mann, Meehan and Ramsey

---

[10] See equations (9.9), (9.10) and (9.11)
[11] Benoit and Krishna (1987) already showed this for a semicollusive repeated game in which firms are allowed to collude in capacity.

(1979). The most convincing evidence, perhaps, is to be found in Rosenbaum's (1989) econometric analysis of the United States' primary aluminium ingot market in the mid 1950s and 1960s. Rosenbaum uses *industry* excess capacity as a proxy for the expected extent of deterrence oligopoly members may impose on a price defector. He notes:

An appropriate measure of the extent of retaliation the industry can impose against a firm i might be $\sum_{j \neq i} EX_{jt}/\sum_{j=1}^{N} PROD_{jt}$ where EX_{jt} and $PROD_{jt}$ measure firm j's absolute levels of excess capacity and production respectively. The worst retaliation the industry could impose on firm i depends on the relative extent of excess capacity available to all but firm i. Individual firm levels of excess capacity, however, are unavailable for the aluminium industry. Hence the use of an industry-wide proxy in the empirical work. If, however, levels of excess capacity, firm sizes, and retaliations are sufficiently symmetric, the use of this proxy should not matter greatly. (Rosenbaum 1989, p. 233, footnote 3)

This note introduces an interesting distinction between individual (or firm) excess capacity and rivals' (industry) capacity. It is further argued that firm excess capacity provides an incentive to cheat (an idea that was not emphasised in the preceding discussion), so that high levels of firm excess capacity should reduce price–cost margins while industry excess capacity should enforce collusion and thus increase price–cost margins. Hence the regression equation

$$PCM_{it} = \beta_0 + \beta_1 FXC_{it} + \beta_2 IXC_t \tag{9.13}$$

where PCM_{it} is firm i's price–cost margin in period t, FXC_{it} is firm i's excess capacity as a percentage of its own production in period t, and IXC_t is industry capacity divided by industry production in period t. β_1 should be negative and β_2 should be positive. In the absence of data on individual levels of excess capacity, this equation has to be transformed so as to apply to industry data. Multiplying both sides of equation (9.13) by firm i's share of industry production and summing across all firms gives (assuming the β's are identical for all firms)

$$PCM_t = \beta_0 + (\beta_1 + \beta_2)IXC_t = \alpha_0 + \alpha_1 IXC_t \tag{9.14}$$

where PCM_t is the industry price–cost margin in period t and $\alpha_1 = \beta_1 + \beta_2$. If the estimated value $\hat{\alpha}_1$ turns out to be negative, this could imply $\beta_1 < 0$. If $\hat{\alpha}_1$ is positive, this is compatible with $\beta_2 > 0$ and larger in absolute value than β_1. If $\hat{\alpha}_1 = 0$, either β_1 and β_2 are both zero or opposite in sign but equal in magnitude. Since the purpose of the econometric exercise is not to accept or reject the theory (how could a data set, which is by definition particular and most of the time inadequate to some extent, ever reject a carefully worked out theory?), and since the theory is convincing, I am most willing to interpret the computed values of α_1 in the sense just given.

Table 9.5. *Effect of excess capacity, number of firms and inventories on aluminium ingot price–cost margins*

	1955–75	1967–81
Constant	0.4632	0.7301
	(12.692)	(7.746)
Excess capacity (%)	0.0349	0.2989
	(0.3450)	(1.527)
Number of firms	−0.0101	−0.0336
	(−2.479)	(−3.664)
Inventories (%)	−0.5523	−0.1182
	(−2.717)	(−1.103)
N	21	15
$\bar{R}^2$	—	0.55
R-squared between observed and predicted	0.60	—

Equation (9.14) is to be expanded in various ways. First, since fixed costs are significant and closing down and restarting production facilities is very costly, there is inventory accumulation among the producers of primary aluminium ingots. Large inventories may act like excess capacity by reinforcing the threats of retaliation. But they may also provide incentives to cut prices. Rosenbaum expects their net impact on price–cost margins to be negative. Second, the number of producers increased, from 1955 to 1981, from three to twelve. This number should have a negative impact on industry price–cost margins (since four are few and six are many). Third, there is a simultaneity problem: greater margins may generate greater excess capacity. Rosenbaum therefore adds an equation explaining IXC_t in terms of capacity changes, GNP divided by capacity and changes in unit material costs and wage costs. The true basic equation to be estimated becomes

$$PCM_t = \alpha_0 + \alpha_1 IXC_t + \alpha_2 INV_t + \alpha_3 N_t + \mu_t \qquad (9.15)$$

where INV_t is the level of inventories held relative to production for primary producers and N_t is the number of producers in period t, with $\alpha_2 < 0$ and $\alpha_3 < 0$.

The regression results are given in table 9.5 (t-statistics in parentheses).

During 1955–75, $\hat{\alpha}_1$ is small and statistically insignificant. One interpretation is that neither firm nor industry excess capacity influenced pricing. Another more plausible interpretation is that β_1 and β_2 were similar in magnitude and opposite in sign. Fortunately, excess capacity had a clear positive impact on price–cost margins during the 1967–81 period. While β_1 may be negative, β_2 is positive. In this period at least, industry excess capacity helped maintain price–cost margins.

10   Collusion in R&D

The policy question raised in this chapter is the following: should antitrust authorities authorise collusion, in particular joint ventures, in R&D? Competitors who are not allowed to collaborate in R&D might not invest enough, because innovations cannot be appropriated by the inventor: his competitors will copy the invention and thus 'free ride', that is, benefit from it without paying for it. However, competitors who are allowed to collude in R&D will have an incentive to also collude on the product market, restrict output and increase prices. In March 1985, the Commission gave a thirteen year block exemption under Article 85(3) of the Treaty of Rome, so that joint R&D ventures do not have to be notified to the Commission and exemptions do not have to be requested. Collusion on the product markets is not allowed, however. Was this a good decision? Intuition suggests that it was. Game theory confirms this intuition.

Joint R&D ventures have a number of organisational advantages and disadvantages (Jacquemin 1988). They are a flexible form of cooperation, compared to a merger, which would create rigid research structures. They allow firms to avoid the principal–agent problem which would arise if they had to work with external research contracts: with such contracts, it is difficult to monitor the agent's research efforts and to appropriate his findings. Joint ventures allow to spread risks and sunk costs among the participants, especially when there are indivisibilities. Above all, duplication of efforts can be avoided and complementary expertise can be combined. Yet, joint ventures are often short-lived, because cooperation is difficult as such, the more so since a partner remains a potential competitor once the new product is put on the market. Success may depend on the possibility of collusion on the product market.

To the extent that joint R&D ventures succeed, their main feature is that externalities or 'spillovers' are internalised: all partners collectively benefit from cost reductions that result from an investment made by any one of them. Free-riding is thus eliminated. This internalisation is at the heart of the basic game-theoretic model used to answer the question which solution is the best: cooperative R&D followed by competition on the product market, rather than collusive R&D followed by collusive selling, or competitive R&D followed by collusion, or competitive R&D followed by competitive selling.

10.1 The basic model

In their seminal 1988 paper, d'Aspremont and Jacquemin[1] set up the following model to analyse some of these solutions. Consider a duopoly selling a homogeneous product. Let the inverse market demand function be $p = \alpha - \beta Q$, where $Q = q_1 + q_2$ is total production and $\alpha, \beta > 0$.

Each firm i ($i = 1, 2$) individually benefits from a spillover that results from the R&D investment made by the other firm. Indeed, each firm has the cost function

$$C_i(q_i, r_i, r_j) = [A - r_i - \gamma r_j] q_i \quad (i \neq j)$$

where

q_i: own production rate of duopolist i

r_i: own research effort (investment)

r_j: rival's research effort (investment)

$$p > A > 0$$
$$0 < \gamma < 1$$
$$A \geq r_i + \gamma r_j$$
$$Q \leq \frac{\alpha}{\beta}.$$

When the rival invests r_j, it is as if firm i had done that investment itself and reduced its cost by γr_j.

Each firm also has a quadratic cost of R&D function $\frac{1}{2} \delta r_i^2$, which reflects diminishing returns to R&D expenditures.

The coefficient γ measures the spillover effect, that is, the reduction in i's unit production cost due to j's investment in R&D. The larger is γ, the more difficult it is for an investor to appropriate the benefits resulting from his innovation. Intuition suggests that the value of γ is higher in basic research than in applied development activities where the results are more easily appropriable.

---

[1] See also Henriques (1990) and d'Aspremont and Jacquemin (1990) for comments and corrections.

D'Aspremont and Jacquemin consider four two-stage games, in which the investments r_i are the strategies of the first stage, followed by the quantities q_i in the second stage. The four games are the following:

(1) a non-cooperative game in both R&D (first stage) and output (second stage);
(2) a game with explicit collusion (joint profit maximisation) in the first stage but non-cooperative Cournot strategies in the second stage;
(3) a game with explicit collusion in both stages;
(4) a game where social welfare is maximised in both stages. The solutions of the fourth game, namely socially optimal R&D and socially optimal output, are used as benchmarks.

The solution concept is subgame perfect equilibrium. Therefore each game is solved backwards: first the second stage, for given R&D expenditures, then the first stage, incorporating the solution (production) of the second stage. This analytical procedure is detailed in table 10.1, which is self-explanatory.

10.2 The results

The computations required to solve these games are cumbersome and will not be detailed here. The solutions are given in table 10.2 and will be discussed in the order they are obtained, that is, first for stage 2, then for stage 1 and finally for total output in subgame perfect equilibrium.

Consider the *second stage* and compare total outputs obtained in the four games with given research efforts (to be determined). Needless to say, social welfare maximisation leads to the highest total production, Q^{**}, which turns out to be exactly twice the total output $\tilde{Q}$ obtained with collusion in both stages. The latter is in turn smaller than $Q^* = \hat{Q}$, that is, total output in a non-cooperative Cournot equilibrium, when research efforts are equal. No surprises here. (Of course, a larger output implies a lower price.)

Next consider the *first stage* and the R&D investments corresponding to the subgame equilibrium outputs of stage 2. First compare cooperation limited to R&D, $\hat{r}_i$, with non-cooperative R&D, r_i^*. The expressions in table 10.2 imply

$$\hat{r}_i r_i^* \quad \text{iff} \quad 1 + \gamma > 2 - \gamma \qquad (10.1)$$

$$\text{or} \quad 2\gamma > 1$$

$$\text{or} \quad \gamma > 0.5.$$

For large enough spillovers ($\gamma > 0.5$), the research effort is larger when firms are allowed to cooperate. This makes sense, since large spillovers imply that it is difficult for an individual firm to appropriate the benefits of its research efforts. Cooperation solves the free-riding problem.

Table 10.1. *Analytical procedure to find subgame perfect R&D effort and output*

	Non-cooperative in both R&D and output *Game 1*	Cooperative in R&D Non-cooperative in output *Game 2*	Cooperative in both stages *Game 3*	Social welfare *Game 4*
Second stage *Output* Conditional on r_1 and r_2	$Max_{q_i} \Pi_i$ $= [\alpha - \beta Q]q_i$ $- [A - r_i - \gamma r_j]q_i - \delta \dfrac{r_i^2}{2}$ for given r_1 and r_2. Find $Q^* = q_1^* + q_2^*$ conditional on r_1 and r_2	idem Find $\hat{Q}(=Q^*)$ conditional on r_1 and r_2	$Max_{q_1,q_2} \Pi = \Pi_1 + \Pi_2$ $= [\alpha - \beta Q]Q - AQ +$ $(r_1 + \gamma r_2)q_1 + (r_2 + \gamma r_1)q_2$ $- \delta \sum_{i=1}^{2} \dfrac{r_i^2}{2}$ Find $\tilde{Q}$ conditional on r_1 and r_2	$Max_{Q} W(Q) =$ $\dfrac{1}{2}(\alpha - p)Q$ $+ [\alpha - \beta Q]Q - AQ$ $+ (1+\gamma)rQ - \delta r^2$ where $r_1 = r_2 = r$ Find Q^{**} conditional on r
First stage *R&D effort*	Insert q_i^* in $\Pi_i \to \Pi_i^*$ $Max_{r_i} \Pi_i^*$ to find r_1^* and r_2^*	$Max_{r} \hat{\Pi} = \Pi_1^* + \Pi_2^*$ where $r_1 = r_2 = r$ (symmetric) to find $\hat{r}$	Insert $\tilde{q}_1$ and $\tilde{q}_2$ in $\Pi \to \tilde{\Pi}$ $Max_{r} \tilde{\Pi}$ where $r_1 = r_2 = r$ to find $\tilde{r}$	Insert Q^{**} in $W(Q) \to W^{**}$ $Max_{r} W^{**}$ to find r^{**}, the socially efficient level of R&D
Subgame perfect equilibrium Output	Insert r_1^* and r_2^* in Q^*	Insert $\hat{r}$ in $\hat{Q}$	Insert $\tilde{r}$ in $\tilde{Q}$	Insert r^{**} in W^{**} to find the socially efficient output incorporating the efficient level of R&D

Table 10.2. *Results: equilibrium R&D effort and output*

	Second stage: Output conditional on r_1 and r_2	*First stage:* R&D effort	*Subgame perfect equilibrium output*
Non-cooperative in both R&D and output *Game 1*	$Q^* = q_1^* + q_2^*$ $Q^* = \dfrac{2(\alpha - A)}{3\beta} + \dfrac{2(1+\gamma)}{3\beta} \cdot r_i^*$	$r_i^* = \dfrac{(\alpha - A)(2-\gamma)}{4.5\beta\delta - (2-\gamma)(1+\gamma)}$ $i = 1,2$	$Q^* = \dfrac{2(\alpha - A)}{3\beta}\left[\dfrac{4.5\beta\delta}{4.5\beta\delta - (2-\gamma)(1+\gamma)}\right]$
Cooperative in R&D Non-cooperative in output *Game 2*	$\hat{Q} = \hat{q}_1 + \hat{q}_2$ $\hat{Q} = \dfrac{2(\alpha - A)}{3\beta} + \dfrac{2(1+\gamma)}{3\beta} \cdot \hat{r}_i$	$\hat{r} = \dfrac{(\alpha - A)(1+\gamma)}{4.5\beta\delta - (1+\gamma)^2}$ where $\hat{r} = \hat{r}_1 = \hat{r}_2$	$\hat{Q} = \dfrac{2(\alpha - A)}{3\beta}\left[\dfrac{4.5\beta\delta}{4.5\beta\delta - (1+\gamma)^2}\right]$
Cooperative in both stages *Game 3*	$\tilde{Q} = \tilde{q}_1 + \tilde{q}_2$ $\tilde{Q} = \dfrac{\alpha - A}{2\beta} + \dfrac{(1+\gamma)}{2\beta} \cdot \tilde{r}$	$\tilde{r} = \dfrac{(\alpha - A)(1+\gamma)}{4\beta\delta - (1+\gamma)^2}$ where $\tilde{r} = \tilde{r}_1 = \tilde{r}_2$	$\tilde{Q} = \dfrac{\alpha - A}{2\beta}\left[\dfrac{4\beta\delta}{4\beta\delta - (1+\gamma)^2}\right]$
Social welfare *Game 4*	$Q^{**} = q_1^{**} + q_2^{**}$ $Q^{**} = \dfrac{\alpha - A}{\beta} + \dfrac{(1+\gamma)}{\beta} \cdot r^{**}$	$r^{**} = \dfrac{(\alpha - A)(1+\gamma)}{2\beta\delta - (1+\gamma)^2}$ where $r^{**} = r_1^{**} = r_2^{**}$	$Q^{**} = \dfrac{\alpha - A}{\beta}\left[\dfrac{2\beta\delta}{2\beta\delta - (1+\gamma)^2}\right]$

When cooperation is possible in both stages, research efforts are even greater

$$\tilde{r}_i > \hat{r}_i. \tag{10.2}$$

Collusion in the product market allows firms to capture more of the surplus created by R&D and induces more R&D investments. However, a comparison of $\tilde{r}_i$ with the non-cooperative r_i^* shows that

$$\tilde{r}_i > r_i^* \tag{10.3}$$

iff $\quad \dfrac{(1+\gamma)}{4\beta\delta - (1+\gamma)^2} > \dfrac{2-\gamma}{4.5\beta\delta - (2-\gamma)(1+\gamma)} \quad$ or $\quad \gamma > 0.41$.

Again, the spillover effect should be large enough.

Putting the stage 1 results together gives

$$r_i^{**} > \tilde{r}_i > \hat{r} > r^* \tag{10.4}$$

for large enough spillovers: collusion in both stages leads to the research effort closest to the social optimum.

Since total output determines the market price in these games, it is of considerable interest to take a closer look at the *subgame perfect equilibrium outputs* reported in table 10.2. The block exemption given under Article 85(3) implies $\hat{Q}$. We have

$$\hat{Q} > Q^* \tag{10.5}$$

iff $\quad 1 + \gamma > 2 - \gamma \quad$ or $\quad \gamma > 0.5$.

For large spillovers, the non-collusive output is higher and the price is lower with cooperative R&D than in the fully non-cooperative solution. This is a surprising result! Furthermore, the fully collusive output $\tilde{Q}$ may be larger than Q^*: it is smaller if and only if $5\gamma^2 + 4\gamma - 1 > 3\beta\delta$. Notice, however, that $\hat{Q}$ is larger than the fully collusive output $\tilde{Q}$, although the reverse is true for the corresponding research efforts (see equation (10.2)). The final result is that, for $\gamma > 0.5$

$$Q^{**} > \hat{Q} > Q^* > \tilde{Q}. \tag{10.6}$$

Cooperation limited to R&D leads to the second-best output. Intuitively, one would have expected an intermediate result, such that $Q^* > \hat{Q} > \tilde{Q}$.

To summarise the policy implications: while an exemption under Article 85(3) for both R&D and output would have led to the second-best level of research (see equation (10.4)), the exemption limited to collusive R&D actually given leads to the second-best output and therefore to the lowest prices in the absence of social planning.

Time has come to emphasise that these conclusions are valid for games as defined by d'Aspremont and Jacquemin (1985), and to wonder to what extent these[2] capture the essence of R&D joint ventures. The reader will have noticed that the words 'cooperation' and 'collusion' were used indistinctly: they both simply meant joint profit maximisation. Yet, 'cooperation' inside a joint venture should imply that the results of R&D efforts are fully shared among the partners and that duplication of efforts is avoided. But then the individual spillover effects should reach their maximum value, that is, γ should be made equal to 1. However, in d'Aspremont and Jacquemin's model the value of γ remains the same whether there is cooperation (collusion) in R&D or not. This is the point made by Kamien, Muller and Zang (1992), who therefore distinguish between an R&D 'joint venture' *stricto sensu* (defined by the fact that $\gamma = 1$) and an R&D 'cartel', which corresponds to what d'Aspremont and Jacquemin called cooperation (with a given $\gamma < 1$).

Kamien, Muller and Zang also generalise the approach by considering differentiated commodities, more than two firms and Bertrand competition. This leads to a large number of games which cannot be described here. Only the general conclusions, which are of considerable interest, are reported here. First of all, the results discussed above remain valid. Second, when joint profit maximisation is combined with full cooperation, so that $\gamma = 1$, R&D investments are even higher than $\hat{r}_i$ and total production is even higher than $\hat{Q}$, implying even lower prices. Third, the worst case of all is that where there is a 'joint venture' *stricto sensu* ($\gamma = 1$) but no joint profit maximisation in R&D.

The policy implications are important. Antitrust authorities should encourage the creation of joint ventures in R&D (which, by definition, share all information to make γ equal to 1) but on two conditions: (a) the partners should maximise joint profits in R&D, and (b) they should not collude in the product markets. One implication is that information sharing alone is to be avoided: the worst situation is one where a joint venture is created just to share information.

A further result, obtained by Kamien and Zang (1993), is worth mentioning. Consider an industry which is partitioned into a number, λ, of competing R&D 'joint venture (JV) cartels', that is, joint ventures ($\gamma = 1$) whose members maximise joint profits. Is it better to have one grand JV

---

[2] There have been a number of extensions to the d'Aspremont and Jacquemin model. See Choi (1989), De Bondt and Veugelers (1991), De Bondt *et al.* (1992), Simpson and Vonortas (1994), Suzumura (1989) and Ziss (1994). De Bondt and Henriques (1994) consider asymmetric spillovers leading to price leadership situations. Hinloopen (1994) argues, taking the d'Aspremont and Jacquemin model as a starting point, that subsidising R&D optimally raises social welfare and is more effective in promoting R&D investments than permitting R&D cartels.

cartel including all n firms in the industry ($\lambda = 1$) or several? Which solution gives the lowest price?

Suppose each JV cartel has the same number of members n/λ. As the number of JV cartels (λ) declines, three effects occur simultaneously: (1) there is less competition among the cartels, so that the overall competitive stimulus to R&D investment declines; (2) membership inside each cartel increases (for given n) so that the scope over which an innovation applies increases and R&D investment is stimulated; (3) each cartel becomes a more formidable rival (for the other cartels) because its membership has increased. This stimulates R&D investment. It is possible, therefore, that on balance R&D investment is greater with several JV cartels than with just one grand cartel. This happens when (a) membership is big enough and (b) the spillover effect *between* JV cartels, γ_c, is *small* enough (so that it is not profitable to combine them). The precise condition is

$$\frac{n - \lambda}{\lambda} > \frac{\gamma_c}{1 - \gamma_c}$$

(when the commodity is homogeneous). When this condition is satisfied, the greatest research effort *and* the lowest price are obtained when $\lambda = 2$, that is, when the industry is partitioned into exactly *two* competing JV cartels.

10.3 Overinvestment in R&D and collusion

A last case of semicollusion in R&D has to be considered: what if there is collusion in the product market while investments in R&D are made non-cooperatively? Our discussion, in chapter 9, of overcapacity and collusion suggests that collusion in the second stage would lead to overinvestment in the first stage. Fershtman and Gandal (1994) show that this intuition is correct. This overinvestment may be large enough so that the overall semicollusion equilibrium profits are smaller[3] than when the firms compete in both stages.

Fershtman and Gandal (1994, p. 142) note that

for a given choice of variables in the first stage, the firms always are better off colluding in the second stage. Thus, when collusion in the output market yields lower overall profits than competition, the decision not to collude in the second stage must be accompanied by some type of commitment mechanism. Otherwise the

---

[3] Sevy (1992) shows that semicollusion in which collusion occurs only in the second stage may increase consumer surplus when the firm with the lower production cost is granted a monopoly in the second stage. See also Matsui (1989) who considers capacity choices in the first period and collusive quantity choices in the second period.

firms will wish to renegotiate and the decision not to collude in the second stage will not be credible.

The basic model is very close to the d'Aspremont and Jacquemin model, in that market (inverse) demand is linear and the cost of R&D is quadratic $\left(\dfrac{1}{2}\delta r_i^2\right)$. The firms' cost of production function, however, is simplified to

$$c_i(q_i, r_i) = (A - r_i)q_i,$$

where $A \geq r_i$. Computations analogous to those explained in the previous section lead to the following propositions:

1 The equilibrium level of investment in R&D is higher when firms cooperate in the second stage.
2 When investment costs are relatively small ($\delta < 1.4$), semicollusion results in *lower* equilibrium profits than the non-cooperative interaction.
3 However, semicollusion results in *higher* equilibrium prices than the non-cooperative interaction. Thus prices are still lower in the non-cooperative interaction despite the higher-level investment in the semicollusive setting.

So, even when semicollusion lowers profits and stimulates R&D efforts, this should not be used as an argument to weaken the enforcement of competition policy.

IV

Predatory pricing

11   Predation in theory

The theory of economic predation has a special and rather uncommon feature. Great sophistication is needed to show that predation can occur at all, and perhaps even greater sophistication is needed to show what distinguishes predatory prices from other types of prices. One reason is that predation appears, on simple intuitive grounds, as irrational or at least as impossible to reconcile with profit maximisation. Another reason is that one well-known line of reasoning in game theory leads to the conclusion that predation cannot be an equilibrium strategy.

To show that predation can be a profit-maximising equilibrium strategy, a number of particular circumstances have to be modelled. To begin with, for predation to make sense it has to be defined as an attack (in the form of a low price) by a monopolist against an entrant, after the latter has actually entered one of the monopolist's markets. Otherwise predation would be synonymous with entry-preventing limit pricing.

Second, this aggressor is typically a multimarket monopolist. If the aggressor operates in one market only, it can always protect it profitably by absorbing the entrant. Predatory pricing without merger has a chance to be the best strategy only if a low profit (or a loss) in one market can be compensated by larger profits in other markets. Predation thus appears in one market in order to protect the aggressor's other markets.

A further feature is that entrants must have incomplete information. If they know that predation is profitable, they will not enter and predatory prices will never be observed. If they know that predation is not profitable, they will enter without hesitation and, again, predation will not be observed. It is essential, therefore, that entrants have some doubts about the monopolist's response and are not sure that predation will occur. The standard way to model this is to assume that the monopolist they are facing may belong to different more or less aggressive 'types' and that they cannot distinguish these types. A probability is therefore attached to each type. At most, the entrants know the probability distribution of these types. An additional sophistication is to model the fact that the entrant may find it difficult to identify low prices set by the monopolist as being predatory rather than the result of normal competition, that is, prices corresponding to a non-cooperative Nash equilibrium in their local market.

Entry implies not only a fixed cost but also an adjustment cost: it is not instantaneous – hence the assumption that a particular entrant can enter at most one market in any period. (The question then arises whether each entrant should be allowed to enter several markets or just one market.)

What about the predator? Should one try to allow for (and to rationalise) the possibility that, after one or several attacks, the predator stops preying? This seems more realistic than a solution in which the predator continues to prey once preying has begun. Similarly, it seems more realistic to look for a model in which the predator's aim is to slow down entry (in other markets) rather than to stop entry entirely.

Finally, the predator's markets can be supposed to be identical, in order to emphasise the purely intertemporal aspect of the problem, according to which a low profit today (in any market) is more than compensated by a flow of higher profits later (in the other markets). However, part of this compensation may not be due to predation as such but to (non-predatory) geographical price discrimination based on differences in demand elasticities. The question then arises how predatory and non-predatory price discrimination can be distinguished.

11.1 Why predatory pricing is rare and unimportant

The Standard Oil case[1] of 1911 is probably the best known and most widely discussed case of predatory pricing. Allegedly, Standard established a monopoly in oil mining and maintained it mainly through the systematic use of a particular type of geographical price discrimination, namely local price cutting. It thus eliminated its competitors in one local market at a time and preserved its monopoly by selective price cuts wherever entry occurred.

McGee (1958) made himself a reputation by challenging this commonly held view. He not only showed that the available evidence brought before the court was not convincing, but also accumulated sound economic reasons why predatory pricing is, in general, rare and not an important problem for competition.

Evidently, he says, because the predator is supposed to have important monopoly power (the 'war chest' for supporting the unprofitable raids and forays), local price cutting cannot explain the monopolisation of a market. But suppose sufficient monopoly power is achieved through some other

---

[1] Standard Oil Co. of New Jersey v. United States, 221 US 1 (1911).

means. How would this monopolist go about using predatory techniques?
McGee (1958, pp. 139–40) writes

Assume that Standard has an absolute monopoly in some important markets, and
was earning substantial profits there. Assume that in another market there are
several competitors, all of whom Standard wants to get out of the way. Standard
cuts the price below cost. Everyone suffers losses. Standard would, of course, suffer
losses even though it has other profitable markets: it could have been earning at least
competitive returns and is not. The war could go on until average variable costs are
not covered and are not expected to be covered; and the competitors drop out. In the
meanwhile, the predator would have been pouring money in to crush them. If,
instead of fighting, the would-be monopolist bought out his competitors directly, he
could afford to pay them up to the discounted value of the expected monopoly
profits to be gotten as a result of their extinction. Anything above the competitive
value of their firms should be enough to buy them. In the purchase case, monopoly
profits could begin at once; in the predatory case, large losses would first have to be
incurred. Losses would have to be set off against the prospective monopoly profits,
discounted appropriately. Even supposing that the competitors would not sell for
competitive value, it is difficult to see why the predator would be unwilling to take
the amount that he would otherwise spend in price wars and pay it as a bonus.

Acquisition or merger is thus a feasible alternative to local price cutting.
It always gives a higher present value, because revenues during the price war
are always less than revenues gotten immediately through purchase and are
not higher after the war is concluded. Predation can therefore make sense
only if the direct costs of a price war were small compared to the difference
between the takeover price to be paid to a competing firm and its
competitive value. However, this can never happen, because the costs of the
price war must be higher for the predator than for the individual competitors. As McGee (1958, p. 140) puts it:

To lure customers away from somebody, he must be prepared to serve them himself.
The monopolist thus finds himself in the position of selling more – and therefore
losing more – than his competitors. Standard's market share was often 75 per cent or
more. In the 75 per cent case the monopolizer would sell three times as much as all
competitors taken together, and, on the assumption of equal unit costs, would lose
roughly three times as much as all of them taken together.

Purchase must be cheaper than price cutting. Since competitors know
this, they will simply stick it out. Or they will shut down operations
temporarily, letting the predator take all the business and all the losses, and
resume operations when he raises prices again. Indeed, plants do not
necessarily wear down and may be reopened at low cost, by the same owner
or by some opportunist who knows that the predator will have, sooner or
later, to buy these up. And it is not likely that a price war would sufficiently

depress the purchase price of these properties, because everybody knows that the artificially low price cannot be permanent.

It remains true that Standard did, in fact, discriminate geographically by local price cutting, as is the case in some form or another in most historical examples of alleged predatory pricing. To rationalise this discriminatory behaviour, McGee (1958) notices that these discriminatory prices simply reflect changes in local demand elasticities, but do not imply or establish that anybody is preying on anybody else. In today's terminology, the argument would be reformulated by saying that geographical price discrimination is a property of a non-cooperative Nash equilibrium when oligopolists are serving submarkets in which demand elasticities differ.[2]

Twenty years after his initial article, McGee (1980) still maintains his position against an impressive flood of articles in which predation is taken seriously and numerous (competing) rules for establishing whether predation has occurred are proposed. He also offers a string of arguments, some old and some new, among which I pinpoint the following.

The predator may, because of its size and activities in other markets, have larger financial reserves – a 'longer purse' – and thus be able to sustain larger losses and sustain them longer. McGee (1980, p. 297) answers:

Military analogies are not apt. Among other differences, business lacks pipes, drums, and flags, and it does not have conscription. A firm plotting a predatory campaign would require disproportionately greater liquid reserves, and, in one way or another, it will have to pay for them. Liquid reserves are costly, and disproportionately large reserves are disproportionately costly. Reserves are a cost, not an inherent advantage. No one has yet demonstrated why predators could acquire the reserves they will need, while victims cannot. In any case, if this is predation, the present value of assets in this trade is positive. Why not stick it out, since the long-run returns are there?

McGee (1980, p. 300) also notes that the very presence of an antitrust rule against predation creates an incentive for a small firm to make a complaint to the antitrust authority in order to prevent a big competitor from undercutting it:

so long as people in authority can be made to listen and perhaps persuaded to do something, it may pay competitors to complain that someone is preying on them. They have a natural interest in tying the hands of those who compete for consumers' favors. If law permits, they also have an interest in collecting damages from those who compete with them. These are good reasons for doubting that predation claimed is predation proved. These are also good reasons to be cautious in developing rules against 'predatory' conduct.

---

[2] Neven and Phlips (1985) have worked out an example.

Finally, let me quote a passage (McGee 1980, p. 296) in which McGee hints at the role of incomplete information and suggests that if the game is played under complete and perfect information, then predation is impossible for the simple reason that the victim will not give up, so there is no point in even trying to kill it:

[The predator] will be disappointed, if for no other reason than that it will pay the victim to stick it out. If things go back to where they were before the predatory price cut, it would pay both the predator and victim to replace their plants. And, of course, if prices were somehow raised even more. It only seems paradoxical, therefore, that if a victim were sure this is a predatory campaign, rather than normal competition or a response to a collapsing market, he would surely want to stick it out.

If, under complete information, predation is impossible – an intuition that will be shown to be correct for game-theoretic reasons in what follows – then predation can occur only to the extent that the potential victim has doubts about the predatory nature of a price cut and that the predator manages to manipulate these doubts to its own advantage – another intuition that is at the core of the discussion that follows.

11.2 The chain store paradox or the impossibility of predation

To show that predation is logically impossible from a game-theoretic point of view, Selten (1978) imagines the following game, in which a firm operates in a number of identical markets. For concreteness, he supposes it is a chain store, also called player A, which has branches in twenty towns, numbered from 1 to 20. The game is played over a sequence of twenty consecutive periods $1, \ldots, 20$. In each of the towns there is a small businessman, called player k, who might raise money to establish a shop of the same kind.

As time goes on, each of these businessmen will, in turn, have accumulated enough capital to start a new business so that they must in turn – first player 1, in town 1, then player 2, in town 2, and so on – decide whether they want to enter the local market or use their capital in some other business. In other words, at the beginning of period k, player k must decide between IN or OUT. Player k's decision is immediately known to all players. Incumbent A enjoys its monopoly position without further threat if player k, at time k, decides not to enter.

Incumbent A can react in two ways in each market. It either decides to 'cooperate', that is, to share the market, or to be 'aggressive', that is, to prey on the entrant. Again, this decision is immediately common knowledge so that information is perfect. The incumbent gets the highest immediate profit, in period k, if player k stays out. If he enters, and if A's reaction is

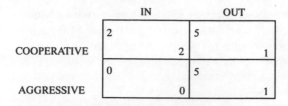

Figure 11.1 Player A's immediate payoffs and player k's payoffs

cooperative, then A's immediate profit is lower. But it is even lower if A's reaction is aggressive, because predation is costly (McGee's argument!). As for player k, his profit is the highest if his entry is met by a cooperative response. When it is met by predation, his interest is to stay out and invest his capital elsewhere.

The problem for the incumbent is to maximise the sum of the immediate payoffs over the periods 1 to 20. It would be the highest if all twenty potential entrants decided to stay out. If all decided to enter, then this sum is the highest if player A cooperates with all of them. If some decided to enter, it might be worthwhile to prey on them, although that gives A the lowest immediate profit, if that could convince the others to stay out. The trouble is that each one-period game has to be played after the other in a sequence, and that in each of these the then potential entrant has an interest to come in if the incumbent cooperates.

Notice that the game is to be played in a non-cooperative way, that the players cannot commit themselves to threats and promises, and, in particular, that the chain store cannot purchase the shops possibly opened by the entrants (to ignore the McGee argument that acquisition is cheaper than predation and thus to be able to analyse the profitability of predation as such in the long run). More generally, binding contracts and side-payments are not permitted. Selten also emphasises that the players are not allowed to talk during the game.

The numbers in the payoff matrix in figure 11.1 represent the potential predator's immediate payoffs (in the upper left corner) and the payoffs of player k (in the lower-right corner). These numbers are known to all players, so that information is complete. In this example, the prey loses as much (-2) as the predator.

If all potential entrants decide to stay out, player A's intertemporal profit is $20 \times 5 = 100$. If all decide to enter and A shares a local market with each of them, then A gets $20 \times 2 = 40$. If all enter and A preys on each of them, A's total profit is $20 \times 0 = 0$. (There is no discounting to simplify the argument.)

What is A's best policy? Notice that A cannot hope to make a total profit of 20×5, because to keep potential entrants out, at least one aggression is necessary. And this implies that at least one entry has occurred, leaving a profit of at most $0 + (19 \times 5) = 95$. At best, this one predation in period 1 might create such a reputation of aggressiveness that players 2 to 20 prefer to stay out. Perhaps a sequence of two or more predatory acts (each giving zero profit) might be necessary to build up such a reputation. But even then, why should the remaining players be afraid? They know the rules of the game as well as player A. In particular, they know the numbers in figure 11.1 as well as the incumbent. They therefore realise that the best policy for A is never to prey at all and to share all markets with the local entrant, because it is profit maximising for each potential entrant to actually enter. To see this, consider what must happen in market 20 in the last period. Selten (1978, p. 131) writes the following:

If in period 20 player 20 selects IN, then the best choice for player A is the COOPERATIVE response. The COOPERATIVE response yields a higher payoff. Long run considerations do not come in, since after period 20 the game is over. This shows that it is best for player 20 to choose IN. Obviously the strategic situation of period 20 does not depend on the players' decisions in periods $1, \ldots, 19$.

Now consider period 19. The decisions in period 19 have no influence on the strategic situation in period 20. If player 19 selects IN, then the COOPERATIVE response is best for player A. The AGGRESSIVE response would not deter player 20.

It is clear that in this way we can go on to conclude by induction that each player k should choose IN and each time player A should use the COOPERATIVE response. The strategic situation in the remainder of the game does not depend on the decisions up to period k. If it is already known that in periods $k+1, \ldots, 20$ players $k+1, \ldots, 20$ will choose IN and player A will always select the COOPERATIVE choice, then it follows that also in period k a choice of IN should lead to a COOPERATIVE response.

The induction theory comes to the conclusion that each of the players $1, \ldots, 20$ should choose IN and player A should always react with his COOPERATIVE response to the choice of IN. If the game is played in this way, then each of the players $1, \ldots, 20$ receives a payoff of 2 and player A receives a total payoff of 40.

The logic of this reasoning is implacable: In equilibrium, predation cannot occur, because the equilibrium strategies of the game (over twenty periods) must also be equilibrium strategies for every subgame (a game starting at any period k and ending at period 20). This is the 'perfect equilibrium' concept for non-cooperative games introduced by Selten (1965). Even if the players were to observe A to behave differently, for example, to prey systematically during the initial periods, they would not be impressed and the next potential entrant would expect its entry not to meet an aggressive response.

The entire reasoning clearly hinges on the assumption that all players know everything: They know all possible strategies and all possible outcomes (such as in figure 11.1), so that their information is 'complete'; they also are immediately informed about all decisions, so the history of the game as it is being played is perfectly known and information is 'perfect'. When this assumption is relaxed, the logic of backwards induction (starting with period 20 and then going backwards to period 19, 18, etc.) breaks down, because actions taken in the past may become a useful guide to future behaviour. If one wants past predation to impress potential entrants, it is necessary therefore to admit some incompleteness or imperfectness of the available information. Only then could something like a reputation of aggressiveness effectively deter entry.

11.3 The lack of common knowledge can generate predation

It is easy to imagine a game in which a slight imperfection of the information can lead to predation in equilibrium. Consider the following example, based on Milgrom and Roberts (1982a, appendix B). For simplicity, the chain store (player A) faces only two possible entrants, player 1 and player 2, in that order. However, the situation is complicated by the fact that there are three possible states of the world, a, b and c, all equally likely, and by the fact that the three players differ in their information. Although firm 1 has perfect information and is thus able to distinguish a, b and c, firm 2 cannot distinguish between states a and b. The chain store, on the contrary, cannot distinguish between b and c. The information structure is thus

player A: $[\{a\}, \{b, c\}]$,
player 1: $[\{a\}, \{b\}, \{c\}]$,
player 2: $[\{a, b\}, \{c\}]$.

The three states could be three events leading to price cutting. State b could be a cost decrease and state c could be a demand decrease, but any other interpretation could do. At any rate, state a is such that entry results automatically in predation. The chain store is a fanatic predator. In the other states, predation (AGGRESSIVE) is one of two possible strategies (COOPERATIVE is the other one) according to the payoff matrix in figure 11.2, which applies to players 1 and 2.

The only difference with figure 11.1 is that the market-sharing payoffs are slightly reduced, for a reason that will become clear in the discussion.

What is the chain store's best long-run policy? It is to prey if firm 1 enters,[3] whatever the state! And since firm 1 knows this, it is deterred from entering! As for firm 2, it will enter only in state c.

[3] If firm 2 enters, A preys automatically in state a. If the state is b or c, it should not prey, because this is the last period of the game.

	IN	OUT
COOPERATIVE	1.5 1.5	5 1
AGGRESSIVE	0 0	5 1

Figure 11.2 Player A's immediate payoffs and the payoffs for players 1 and 2

To see this, note first that A cannot distinguish states b and c and must therefore take the same act in both states. It can prey against firm 1 in both states or in neither. If it does not prey against firm 1, its expected return is 3. Indeed, if c is the actual state, firm 2 recognises it and also enters so that A's return is $1.5 + 1.5 = 3$. If the state is b, failure to prey against 1 allows 2 to infer that the state is b, that it will therefore not meet predation and that it should enter. Again, A's return is $1.5 + 1.5 = 3$.

However, if A does prey against firm 1, then A's expected return is 3.25. Indeed, if the state is b, firm 2 cannot distinguish a and b and must allow for the possibility that it might meet predation (case a), in which case its return is zero. If A is not a fanatic predator (state b), then entry would give firm 2 a return of 1.5. Its expected return is thus, because a and b are equally likely $1/2 (0 + 1.5) = 0.75$. This is less than the return (1) if it stays out. So firm 2 prefers to stay out. On the contrary, if the state is c, which firm 2 recognises, it enters without fear. So, from A's point of view, predation yields equal chances of firm 2 staying out or not, so that A's expected return is $1/2(0 + 5) + 1/2(0 + 1.5) = 3.25$. Because this exceeds the return of 3 resulting from failure to prey, A preys no matter what the state. Therefore firm 1 does not enter.[4]

Note that firm 1 is deterred from entering although there still is a lot of common knowledge in this game. It is common knowledge between firm 1, firm 2, and the chain store that the latter is not a fanatic predator, when state c occurs. In period 1, both firm 1 and the chain store know that to share the market is directly more profitable for the latter. Yet, the confusion of the chain store about b and c and the confusion of entrant 2 about a and b, which require both to reason in terms of expected returns, suffices to turn predation into an equilibrium strategy.

---

[4] If I were to keep the market sharing payoffs at 2, failure to prey would give A the largest return. A would not prey, firm 2 would be indifferent between IN and OUT, and firm 1 would enter in equilibrium. So the equilibrium is sensitive to the numbers chosen.

11.4 Reputation and predation

In a sense, the example just given worked too well. Predation had a deterrent effect without even having to actually occur! It was the common understanding that predation is A's equilibrium policy that prevented entry. One might wish to construct a game whose equilibrium implies that predation has to occur at least once in order to have a deterrent effect. Intuition suggests that the real-life solution to the chain store's problem is to be aggressive in the early stages of the game and to share the market (be 'cooperative') when the game comes close to its end. And intuition is, for once, more convincing than correct game-theoretic reasoning. This is, by the way, the opinion of Selten himself and the reason why he called his game the chain store 'paradox'.

It thus remains to show how the lack of complete information can imply an equilibrium in which entry is not only deterred by predation but predation has to actually be practised. Kreps and Wilson (1982a) and Milgrom and Roberts (1982a) construct models that have these properties. What drives them is the idea that to establish a reputation (that will make further punishments unnecessary) it is necessary to first carry out a few punishments,[5] because any other attitude would be misinterpreted as weakness and encourage further disobedience (entry). This in turn implies that some potential entrants did prefer to enter in the early stages of the game although they could expect to be attacked. Such entry seems to make sense only in a very lucrative market.

One possible approach, followed by Kreps and Wilson, is to allow for some positive probability that predation is immediately more profitable, in any given period, than peaceful market sharing. This assumption looks rather unrealistic and, furthermore, leads to complicated arguments. I shall therefore follow the Milgrom–Roberts approach, which sticks to the idea that predation is always costly in the short run but allows that the entrants entertain some possibility that the chain store may follow some simple behavioural rule, such as being a fanatic predator or a fanatic pacifist.

Take Selten's chain store model but modify it in the following two ways. First, introduce the possibility that past behaviour is relevant in forecasting future behaviour, to destroy the induction argument. For this purpose, allow the entrants to think that a predatory response, if they meet one, might be part of a general aggressive pattern (the chain store is a fanatic predator) and a cooperative response might be part of a general cooperative pattern (the chain store is a fanatic pacifist). This amounts to admitting that

---

[5] See also Scharfstein (1984), Roberts (1986), Fudenberg and Tirole (1986b) and Milgrom and Roberts (1987).

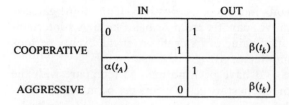

	IN	OUT
COOPERATIVE	0 1	1 $\beta(t_k)$
AGGRESSIVE	$\alpha(t_A)$ 1 0	1 $\beta(t_k)$

Figure 11.3 Player A's immediate payoffs and player k's payoffs

one of three possible games (with twenty periods each) are played and that only the chain store knows which of the three actually obtains. The first game has a one-period payoff matrix structured as in figure 11.1 or 11.2; the second game only admits the aggressive response (and the corresponding payoffs); the third game only admits the cooperative response (and the corresponding payoffs). The entrants attach a probability to each of these three possibilities, say of

$1/(1 + \varepsilon + \delta)$ to the first game
$\varepsilon/(1 + \varepsilon + \delta)$ to the second game (automatic predation)
$\delta/(1 + \varepsilon + \delta)$ to the third game (automatic sharing)

so that the three values add up to 1. Think of ε and δ as being small. In Selten's model $\varepsilon = \delta = 0$, so there is no reason for an entrant to suspect that any observed behavioural pattern might continue.

To this uncertainty on the entrant side, a second modification of the chain store model adds a lack of information that affects all players and relates to the other players. Suppose the entrants are not sure about the costs of predation for the chain store, and the chain store is not sure about the payoffs of the potential entrants if they stay out. To model this, suppose that to each player is associated a random variable τ_i which is uniformly distributed on [0,1] and independent of the τ_j associated with the other players. Refer to a realisation t_i of τ_i as the 'type' of player i ($i = $ A, 1, ..., 20). The cost of predation $\alpha(t_A)$ is then a function of the type of chain store, increasing with t_A between $- \infty$ and 0 (0 not included, i.e., always negative; see McGee!). The payoff of staying out is then $\beta(t_k)$, where $k = 1, ..., 20$, and is normalised between $- \infty$ and 1 (not included). This payoff also increases with the type of entrant. The entrant of type $t_k = 1$ has the highest opportunity cost of entry. The assumption that β may be negative allows for the possibility that a particular entrant might prefer to enter even if preyed upon, so predation may fail against a particular entrant.

If the first game is played, player A's immediate payoffs and player k's payoffs are given in figure 11.3, in period k. If the second game is played, only the 'aggressive' payoffs indicated are possible. If the third game is played, only the 'cooperative' payoffs are possible. Player A's intertemporal profit is the discounted value of its profits over the twenty periods calculated with the discount factor ρ.

The numbers in figure 11.3 have been normalised (compare with the previous figures) so that the chain store gets 1 in any period in which it does not experience entry and 0 in case of peaceful market sharing. Similarly, player k gets 0 if it meets predation and 1 if its entry elicits a non-aggressive response. These numbers are chosen solely to ease computations. I could have retained the corresponding numbers of the previous payoff matrices.

It is worth emphasising that all players know the values of δ and ε, the α and β functions, the distributions of the τ_i and figure 11.3. The rules of the game are thus known by all players, so a situation with incomplete information is modelled as a game with complete information as far as these rules are concerned. However, the model is simultaneously a game with imperfect information, because the historical realisations are not known to all players. Only the chain store knows which of the three games is being played (was selected by Nature, which could be treated as an additional player). Only player k knows his type (realisation t_k, drawn by Nature from the distribution of τ_k) and the corresponding payoff $\beta(t_k)$. Only player A knows his type and the corresponding payoff $\alpha(t_A)$. Although each player is immediately informed about the moves of all other players, and thus knows the history of the moves taken to each point in the game by it and the other players, the history of player A's payoffs is not known to the others.

In this game, predation *must* occur! The basic intuition is that if, during the game, the chain store ever failed to prey all other players immediately know with certainty that it is not a fanatic predator. And then the chain store paradox is valid again!

Let us therefore begin by examining the equilibrium of the game if A ever fails to prey. Knowing that it is not a fanatic predator, player 20 enters because everybody knows that A will not prey in period 20 (Selten's argument applies). But then, A cannot gain by preying in period 19, nor in period 18, nor in any other period. Thus if A ever fails to prey, it will never prey again in equilibrium. And entry will occur in every period, because $\beta(t_k)$ is always less than 1 (the payoff for unopposed entry). Then the present value of A's intertemporal profit is zero (a sum of 0's).

On the contrary, if entry just occurred in period k *and firm A has never failed to prey*, then one or more successive predatory aggressions gives an intertemporal profit to firm A of $P\alpha(t_A) + M$, where P is the number of future predatory acts and M is the number of future periods with unshared markets (in which A's payoff is 1 each time).

Since P is a number equal or larger than 1, and $\alpha(t_A)$ is increasing in t_A, the whole payoff is increasing in t_A. If this payoff is positive for a value $\tau_A = t$ at period k, it is therefore also positive (it pays to prey) if $\tau_A = t' > t$. On the other hand, if future payoffs increase with t_A, their maximised value also increases with t_A. The strategy to follow (to prey or not) can thus be determined without ambiguity for each type of chain store: it is a 'pure' strategy (as opposed to a 'mixed' strategy which would involve choosing different strategies with a probability attached to each).

If we then consider the history of play up to period k and the collection of critical values that triggered off predation, it makes sense to call the highest of these values firm A's current 'reputation', x.

Call the maximised value of the expected future payoffs $V(t,x)$, noting that it depends only on the value (t) taken by τ_A and firm A's current reputation x [because entrants only look at the chain store's reputation, whereas the revision of the latter's reputation depends only on its current actions (prey or share)]. Firm A will prey at period k if and only if its current return plus the maximum present value of future payoffs, that is $\alpha(t) + \rho V_{k+1}(t, x_{k+1})$, is larger than the value of the payoffs resulting from failure to prey (which is zero), or

$$\alpha(t) + \rho V_{k+1}(t, x_{k+1}) > 0. \tag{11.1}$$

What is firm A's reputation when period $k+1$ starts, x_{k+1}? If no entry occurred in period k, its reputation is still x (we assume throughout that it has never failed to prey in the past). If entry did occur in period k and firm A did not fight, everybody knows it will never fight in the future and it has lost its reputation. If entry occurred and firm A did fight, then x_{k+1} is at least as high as a value of t just large enough to make predation worthwhile, that is, to satisfy the profitability condition given earlier. If its reputation x was in fact larger than this minimum, it remains intact at the beginning of period $k+1$.

Therefore, predation necessarily occurs in period k if firm A is at least of type $t = x_{k+1}$. A fortiori, there is predation if its current reputation x is larger, because $V_{k+1}(t, x_{k+1})$ is increasing in t. And this aggressive strategy in period k implies that firm A at least keeps its reputation of aggressiveness during the next period, so its reputation is either constant or growing over time by repeated predation. Whenever future entrants observe a predator, they can correctly forecast that he will continue to prey. Whether they enter or not depends on whether their expected payoff in case of entry exceeds their $\beta(t_k)$.

The entire reasoning was based on a given discount factor ρ. When this factor increases, because the interest rate decreases, then the future reward to preying increases in present value terms and the chain store is willing to incur larger immediate losses. A reduction in interest rates thus allows the predator to use the reputation effect with less delay between uses, because an increase in p in period k makes predation more attractive in period $k + 1$. The incentive for building and maintaining a reputation increases.

We thus get an effect that goes in the opposite direction of the effect established by Friedman (1972) with relation to the incentive for colluders to deviate from a collusive price. A reduction of the interest rate increases the present value of a deviator's future losses due to retaliation by loyal colluders (who push the price down to its Nash equilibrium level). Low interest rates thus make immediate gains due to cheating less worthwhile, so cartels are more stable and price wars (leading to Nash equilibria) less likely. We just saw that low interest rates simultaneously make predatory price cutting more likely, because future gains get a higher weight compared to immediate losses for the predator. The argument is entirely symmetric.

11.5 Nash equilibria and predation

The Milgrom–Roberts model has the merit of showing that predation in one market to protect another market is theoretically possible. However, it does this at the cost of a number of restrictive assumptions, which it shares in part with the Selten model. First, there is the assumption that entry occurs sequentially, in one market at a time by a different entrant. (In each period a new entrant appears.) Consequently, if predation occurs today, its aim is to prevent entry in a later period, not to prevent simultaneous entry in other markets. In addition, if predation has begun in any market there is no reason why it should stop. Finally, though it seems inevitable to assume that there are different types of monopolists between which entrants cannot distinguish before they have revealed themselves, it is unfortunate and unsatisfactory that these types correspond to pathological cases (a fanatic predator or a fanatic pacifist).

Easley, Masson and Reynolds (1985) have managed to relax these assumptions. They allow for the possibility that entry may occur simultaneously[6] in several of the monopolist's markets, possibly to stop or prevent predation. They allow for a monopolist to prey only to gain extra time, that is, to slow down entry in other markets, with full knowledge that eventually entry will occur. They also are able to explain why a monopolist may decide to stop preying after preying once or twice, and so on. Above all, Easley *et al.* define different types of monopolists (which the entrant cannot distinguish) according to the nature of the post-entry non-predatory Nash equilibrium that would occur in the entrant's local market if a

---

[6] Each entrant can enter at most one market in any period, though, to take adjustment costs into account.

particular type of monopolist were active in it. This definition of types has the advantage of incorporating (admittedly in a complicated way) the often observed simple fact that, in practice, predatory prices are difficult to distinguish from prices corresponding to a local non-cooperative Nash equilibrium (or 'normal' competition).

Indeed, suppose the monopolist is drawn from a sample composed of 'type 1' and 'type 2' monopolists. If he is a type 1, then the local market considered in isolation has a post-entry Nash equilibrium that yields a negative entry value to any of the potential entrants. Entry is non-remunerative in the present value sense. Profits are competitive, and the present value of their future flow is smaller than the fixed sunk entry costs of any potential entrant. If he is a type 2, then the local Nash equilibrium considered in isolation yields a positive entry value (defined in the same present value sense).

Predation occurs when the monopolist is a type 2, which means that entry is remunerative in the local market considered in isolation, but acts as a type 1 in that market to make entry non-remunerative. (For that purpose, the monopolist must sacrifice immediate local profits.) When the entrant observes a positive entry value, it can conclude without error that the monopolist is not a predator (that he is a type 2 monopolist and acts as such). But when the entrant observes a negative entry value, it has no way of figuring out whether this is the result of predation (a type 2 monopolist feigning the reaction of a type 1) or whether the market it entered into is inherently competitive (the monopolist is a type 1).

At this point, the reader will have realised that the reasoning in terms of different types of monopolists is a technical necessity, in order to be able to model the incompleteness of the entrants' information in terms of a known probability distribution over types (from which probabilities can be taken to compute expected values and so on). In simple words, the preceding paragraph says that entry into a local market would be profitable in the long run without predation (and without collusion), but predation makes it unprofitable in a way that cannot be distinguished from normal competition by the entrant, because the latter does not know whether the monopolist acts to prevent (or slow down) entry in its other markets or not.

Can such predatory pricing be an equilibrium of a game? Yes.[7] Given a particular distribution of types and a behaviour rule for each monopolist type, Easley *et al.* (1985, p. 451) are able to show,[8] in a first step of the proof, that the best replies for the entrants can lead to the following entry sequence, on the assumption that the monopolist has three markets:

---

[7] It can be a 'sequential equilibrium' in the sense of Kreps and Wilson (1982b).

[8] By computing entrants' expected entry values.

Time

Market	1	2	3
1	Π2	Π2	Π2
2	ΠM	Π2	Π2
3	ΠM	Π2	Π2

Figure 11.4 No predation in period 1

Time 1: entrant 1 enters market 1.
Time 2: entrant 1 enters market 2.
Time 3: if the entry value is positive in markets 1 and 2, then entrant 2 enters market 3. If the entry value is negative in markets 1 and 2, there is no further entry.
Time 4 (anon): no entry. The profit steady state is that of time 3.

Given this entry sequence, the best reply for a type 2 monopolist could be to prey in response to a period 1 entry and to not prey in response to the second entry.

To prey in period 1 is profitable if the period 1 profits foregone are smaller than the gains made by retarding entry into market 3 by one period. These gains and foregone profits can be computed by comparing the flow of profits in the three markets with and without period 1 predation.

If this type 2 monopolist *does not* prey in period 1, entry has a positive present value, and this fact reveals that the monopolist is not of type 1. As a result, all other markets will be entered in period 2, and the situation is represented by the matrix in figure 11.4. $\Pi 2$ is the monopolist's post-entry profit (when he does not prey), and ΠM is his profit in the absence of entry. If this monopolist does prey in period 1, however, his profits in his different markets evolve over time as depicted in figure 11.5. Predation in period 1 is profitable if

$$\Pi 2 - \Pi P < \frac{\Pi M - \Pi 2}{1 + r}, \tag{11.2}$$

where ΠP designates the profits made in market 1 with predation (possibly their absolute value if they are negative), ΠM is the additional period 2 monopoly profit made in market 3 because entry into that market is retarded by one period, and r is the real rate of interest.

Not to prey in period 2 is certainly profitable if preying also in the second

Time

Market	1	2	3
1	ΠP	Π2	Π2
2	ΠM	Π2	Π2
3	ΠM	ΠM	Π2

Figure 11.5 Predation in period 1

Time

Market	1	2	3
1	ΠP	ΠP	ΠP
2	ΠM	ΠP	ΠP
3	ΠM	ΠM	ΠM

Figure 11.6 Preying twice to stop all entry

market leads to foregone profits that are higher than the gains made if this were to stop all future entry in market 3. Figure 11.6 represents the flow of profits resulting from two successive predations, continued over time to make sure that no entry occurs in market 3. (The additional infinite sequence of columns which replicate the time 3 profits is not represented, because the profit steady state is reached after time 3.)

The foregone profits by preying twice are found by comparing figures 11.5 and 11.6. They are equal to the difference between $\Pi2$ and ΠP in markets 1 and 2 in perpetuity as of time 2 and thus have a present value of $2(\Pi2 - \Pi P)/r$. The gains are equal to $\Pi M - \Pi2$ in the third market in perpetuity (starting at time 3) and have a present value of $(\Pi M - \Pi2)/r(1+r)$. Not to prey twice is therefore profitable if

$$\frac{2(\Pi2 - \Pi P)}{r} > \frac{\Pi M - \Pi2}{r(1+r)}.$$

(11.3)

Putting conditions (11.2) and (11.3) together and multiplying by r, we see that a type 2 monopolist preys once in a way that mimics a type 1 Nash equilibrium (negative entry value) and then stops preying if

$$2(\Pi2 - \Pi P) > \frac{\Pi M - \Pi2}{1+r} > \Pi2 - \Pi P, \tag{11.4}$$

because conditions (11.2) and (11.3) are thus seen to be consistent. The foregone profits by preying twice must be larger than the gains from retarding entry, which must be larger than profit foregone by preying only once.

Of course, this is not the only possible predatory strategy. Easley *et al.* also show that an equilibrium strategy may be to prey in some markets (two in the example given) in perpetuity to protect others (the third market in the example) in perpetuity. To that effect, they introduce a 'type 3' in the sample from which the monopolist is supposed to be drawn.

11.6 Geographical price discrimination and predation

The reader who takes McGee's arguments against the possibility of collusion seriously, as we do, may wonder how, at the end of this lengthy discussion, we can nevertheless conclude that both transitory and permanent predation is a real possibility. There is no contradiction, because McGee reasons under two restrictive assumptions which were relaxed during the discussion.

The first assumption is that of complete information on the entrant side. McGee himself made the qualification that his impossibility arguments are based on the condition that his businessman (the entrant) is 'sure this is a predatory campaign, rather than normal competition'. He thus pointed the way to the discovery of the chain store paradox and to the subsequent game-theoretic treatment under incomplete information.

The second assumption has become clear in the presentation of the model by Easley *et al.* Although McGee talks about a multimarket monopolist, especially when he mentions the possibility of geographical price discrimination, he ignores the fact that the control of several markets provides the possibility of compensating immediate foregone profits (or losses) in one market by future gains in other markets. This possibility is at the core of the model by Easley *et al.*

Notice that it is different from the 'long purse' argument, which says that the predator must have larger financial reserves because of its activities in other markets. McGee correctly rejects this argument, and so do Easley *et al.* (1985, p. 453):

In 'deep-pockets' predation firms are alleged to use earnings from profitable markets to finance predation in others. That is certainly not the causality underlying this example. In fact the predatory markets may yield non-negative cash flows ($\Pi P \geq 0$). Thus, a 'long purse' (see Telser 1966) is not required for predation to have anticompetitive effects in some markets in perpetuity.

However, to demonstrate this feature of multimarket control, Easley *et al.* make another simplification, which should be emphasised now. They suppose that all the markets controlled by the monopolist are identical. This makes it possible to consider the entrant's market in isolation and to define a Nash equilibrium for it as if the monopolist was active in this market only. (Each monopolist type is defined that way.) Indeed, when all markets are identical, then the Nash equilibrium in one market is not affected by the fact that the monopolist also operates in other markets.

This amounts to excluding the possibility that the local Nash equilibrium may imply a price that is discriminatory when compared with the equilibrium prices in the other markets. Indeed, when markets are different (display different demand elasticities) for the same commodity and the marginal cost of production is not constant, then the monopolist will find it profitable to price discriminate by equating marginal revenues across markets.[9] Then the price in one market is linked to the prices in the other markets, the maximisation of profits over all markets is not synonymous with profit maximisation in each market separately, and its implications are to be added to those, emphasised by Easley *et al.*, of intertemporal profit maximisation over all periods in a number of identical markets.

As a consequence, part (or all) of what may appear as foregone immediate profits, as a result of a low price in the entrant's market, may in fact reflect the low *ex post* profit made in that market that is necessary (to maximise profits over all geographical markets) because demand is more elastic in that local market. Indeed, entry in a market should make the demand for the monopolist's product more elastic in that market, so price discrimination is to be expected.

When the Nash equilibrium implies discriminatory prices, predation must be redefined as implying a price cut below the (already low local) discriminatory price to make the entry value negative in present value terms. In the terminology of Easley *et al.*, a discriminatory type 2 monopolist (positive entry value at the local discriminatory Nash equilibrium) behaves like a discriminatory type 1 monopolist. To distinguish this behaviour from normal discriminatory competition must be difficult for the entrant; hence, incomplete information is likely and the possibility of

[9] See Neven and Phlips (1985).

predation is greater than in a world of identical markets. The actual occurrence of predation presupposes that the discriminatory Nash equilibrium in the entrant's market implies a positive entry value. Predation then appears as a particular case of geographical price discrimination, made possible by the possibility to compensate immediate foregone profits by later gains in other markets.

Along the same lines, one might consider a monopolist that sells different commodities in different markets. Such a multimarket monopolist is also a multiproduct monopolist. All that has been said about a price discriminating monopolist carries over to this case, because the prices of a multimarket monopolist deviate from marginal cost in the same way as discriminatory prices – they have the common property that their percentage deviation from marginal cost is inversely proportional to the absolute value of the price elasticity.[10]

11.7 Necessary conditions for predatory pricing

To sum up, economic theory suggests that predatory pricing is a real possibility only when the following five conditions are simultaneously met:

1 The aggressor is a multimarket firm (possibly a multiproduct firm).
2 The predator attacks after entry has occurred in one of its markets.
3 The attack takes the form of a price cut in one of the predator's markets, which brings this price below a current non-cooperative Nash equilibrium price at which the entry value is positive for the entrant (possibly below a discriminatory current Nash equilibrium price with the same property).
4 The price cut makes the entry value negative (in present value terms) in the market in which predation occurs.
5 Yet the victim is not sure that the price cut is predatory. The price cut could be interpreted by the entrant as implying that its entry value is negative under normal competition. In other words, the victim entertains the possibility that there is no room for it in the market under competitive conditions.

Notice that immediate exit of the entrant from the market it entered into, as a result of predation, is not essential because predation, as defined, does not necessarily make the post-entry cash flow negative for the entrant. Similarly, the price cut does not have to take the price below the predator's marginal cost. Notice also that the market in which the attack takes place is not necessarily the one in which entry occurred. It may be another market in which the entrant was already established (for example, entry in market 2

---

[10] See Phlips (1988a, section 3.3).

leads to predation in market 1 in which the entrant entered earlier). On the other hand, although the theory is cast in terms of an incumbent who has the monopoly of the submarket in which entry occurs, this does not exclude the possibility that 'the monopolist' (or 'the chain store') is in fact an oligopolist. The presumption is then that it has a dominant position. Finally, predation is more likely in periods when the real rate of interest is low.

12 Evidence on predation

In the previous chapter, I asked whether predation is a theoretical possibility. In this chapter, I search for empirical evidence on predatory pricing, using the conclusion of the theory (in particular the five necessary conditions for predatory pricing) as a guideline. Four sources of evidence will be discussed. The potentially most interesting source is of an experimental nature. It asks whether predatory pricing is an observable phenomenon that can be induced in a laboratory environment. Its interest stems from the fact that a direct link with economic theory can be established by imposing a set of structural features that are favourable to the emergence of predatory pricing on theoretical grounds. I then move to an overview of American antitrust litigation, to get an idea of the relative importance of the number of cases of alleged predation brought before court, knowing that predation claimed is not predation proved. In section 12.3, direct evidence is gathered by analysing a few historical cases that are referred to in the literature. In section 12.4, a modelling approach, based on the theory developed in chapter 11, shows how the presence or absence of predation can be inferred for a particular market, namely the market for bus services in a particular town.

12.1 Experimental evidence

Experimental games[1] have provided new insights in the working of industrial markets. Instead of collecting statistical industry data and computing econometric estimates or running numerical simulations, the idea is to let people play games under conditions which the experimenter has under control. The experimenter can thus reproduce the assumptions made by the theory that is to be verified and come close to the laboratory environment set up by experimenters in the so-called exact sciences.

---

[1] An overview and general discussion of experiments in the field of industrial organisation can be found in Plott (1982, 1989).

206

The results of a well-known experiment on the possibility of predatory pricing, conducted by Isaac and Smith (1985), are discussed first. Isaac and Smith organise a series of market games lasting at most twenty-five periods each. The sellers are two graduate students. They receive information about their own costs of production (and possibly about the costs of production of their competitor), are given initial endowments (and possibly cash bonuses), and are required in some games to pay entry permits. In each period, they must post a price, which constitutes an irrevocable offer, after a computer has given them the corresponding quantity sold and the corresponding immediate profit.

Since they are in search of predatory pricing, as the title of the paper indicates, Isaac and Smith introduce a number of features that they think are favourable to predation. In all games played, there is one large firm (firm A) and one small firm (firm B). The larger firm is given a cost advantage, in the sense that its marginal cost and its average cost of production are always below those of the smaller firm. (At a competitive equilibrium there is room for a profitable firm B.) If predation occurs, A is the predator. In addition, A is given a 'deep pocket', that is, the initial endowment to A is double the endowment to firm B.

In some games, additional features are added to make predation more likely to occur. One feature is the introduction of sunk entry costs. It is achieved by requiring the two firms to buy an 'entry permit' before they are allowed to participate in the market. Each permit is good for only five consecutive periods. The incumbency advantage is created by requiring A to purchase two permits (good for periods 1 to 10) and not allowing B the option of entering until period 6.

In the games just described, the firms did not know one another's cost structure and neither knew demand. Three further games were played with complete cost information, the assumption being that predation is more likely if the potential aggressor (firm A) knows that the prey (firm B) has a cost disadvantage. (In all games, the demand curve remains unknown. All a firm knows is what quantity will be sold at a particular posted price.)

In further games, a motivation other than profit maximisation is introduced, to allow for the possibility that fanaticism or any abnormal intent may cause predation. For this purpose, player A is told privately that he or she will receive a cash bonus for each period in which B chooses not to enter the market.

To make sure that nothing artifactual about the experimental design inhibits B's being driven out of the market, secret instructions were given to A, in further games, to post predatory prices (and quantities sold) in periods 1 to 11. (As a result, B refused to renew his entry permit in period 11, which shows that the experimental design did not prevent B from exiting.)

Finally, an antitrust programme was incorporated in the game with sunk entry costs and uncertainty about the cost structure, to see how the firms would spontaneously react to antitrust rules. According to the rules imposed, A faces (a) an output expansion limitation for two periods whenever B enters, and (b) a price reduction regulation. If A reduces its price during periods in which B could be in the market, A is required by this regulation to maintain the low price for at least five consecutive periods. The authors' conjecture (p. 333) is that tacit collusion would be more likely under these rules:

At a collusive high price this constraint makes it more costly for A to punish B for defection. Firm B, knowing that any cut in price by A cannot be reversed for 5 periods, may be hesitant to defect and risk being locked into a lower price pattern. Similarly, at low prices if A signals with a price increase, this action may have greater credibility under the PPAP (Predatory pricing antitrust program) for firm B and may increase the probability that B will follow.

Unfortunately, after creating these conditions favourable to predatory pricing, Isaac and Smith define it in a very restrictive way. For them there is predation if two conditions are satisfied. First, the predator's price p_A must be below the predator's marginal cost of production (measured at the announced quantity sold q_A). The assumption is one of short-run (myopic) profit maximising by a firm that cannot produce for inventory (the quantity sold is equal to the quantity produced). The authors therefore ignore the possibility of intertemporal profit maximisation, which was found to be essential in the theoretical analysis above, and the resulting possibility of foregone immediate profits being compensated by later gains. The second condition for a price to be predatory is that it should be lower than B's average cost (AC_B), so that either B's entry is prevented, or B is driven out or its re-entry is prevented. Again, this condition ignores the possibility that (a) B may also maximise intertemporal profits and may rather be concerned about the sign of its entry value (in present value terms), (b) predation may be compatible with a positive cash flow $(p_A > AC_B)$, and (c) predation may aim at delaying rather than preventing entry.

Isaac and Smith acknowledge the fact that they ignore reputation effects. What they do not seem to realise, however, is that the multimarket aspect of the problem is essential. Each of their firms has only one market! It is not too surprising, then, that predatory behaviour did not show up in any of their experimental games. (In fact, the predominant outcome is that of a dominant firm equilibrium, in which the leader A moves first and B moves last, responding with the quantity that maximises instantaneous profit given the price quoted by A). This result does not imply that predatory pricing is impossible, but rather suggests that a narrow concept of predation based on a single-market monopolist that maximises instantaneous profits is not likely to have descriptive value.

Since the antitrust rules introduced *in fine* are valid for several periods, so that players may be supposed to consider long-run effects, as hinted at in the given quotation, the outcome of the games played under these rules may be of greater practical relevance. Figure 12.1 reproduces the evolution of a typical game played under cost uncertainty with sunk entry costs, and figure 12.2 displays the evolution of the same game under the two antitrust rules described. The upper horizontal line represents the monopoly price p_M that firm A would charge if all production were allocated to it given the supposed cost and demand parameters. The dominant firm equilibrium price is then p_{df}. The competitive equilibrium price must lie in the interval 2.66 to 2.76, and the potential predatory price range is 2.60–2.66. (Prices in that range are below marginal cost if the quantity sold is at least equal to eight units.) The prices posted by A and B are indicated by the solid and open circles. The circle is open when the quantity sold is zero. (Remember that B enters in period 6 in these games). The letters A and B are followed by a number that indicates the number of units sold by each firm.[2] Isaac and Smith's conjecture that tacit collusion is facilitated by the antitrust programme is confirmed. In figure 12.1, the prices fluctuate mostly around p_{df}; in figure 12.2 they cluster around the monopoly price!

The results of the Isaac–Smith experiment were reported at almost the same time as incomplete information models designed to resolve the chainstore paradox were providing a rationale for predatory pricing (see section 11.4). As a result, the Kreps–Wilson model was not taken into account. It was therefore of great interest to set up an experiment that would allow for incomplete information about the incumbent's type and correct the errors made in the design of the Isaac–Smith experiment. This was done by Jung, Kagel and Levin (1994). Not surprisingly, they found high levels of predatory pricing (to be defined in a moment).

First, instead of having one incumbent facing one entrant in one market, Jung *et al.* have one incumbent facing a known, finite number of different potential entrants, as in Selten's chain store game. Second, in the Isaac–Smith experiment, the incumbents were not given (and thus had to discover) the demand curve. This turned out to be a difficult task and prevented them from finding the monopoly price, which in turn led to 'a profit level so low that it did *not* pay to prey in any given period, even if they were certain of forestalling entry in the next period. In our game, optimal monopoly pricing was automatic' (Jung *et al.* 1994, p. 91).

---

[2] The heavy black arrows near the bottom of figure 12.2 denote periods in which A has triggered a price ceiling on himself (of 3.15 and 3.17, respectively).

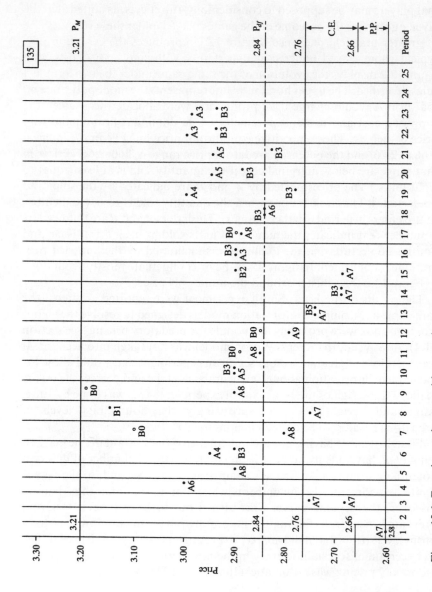

Figure 12.1 Experimental game without antitrust programme

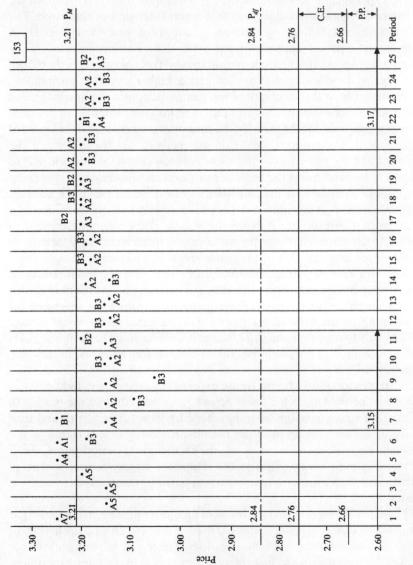

Figure 12.2 Experimental game with antitrust programme

To operationalise the Kreps–Wilson (1982) model, two types of monopolists are introduced: a 'weak' monopolist who prefers not to fight entry and a 'strong' monopolist who always fights (fighting is his dominant strategy). In the experimental sessions, the monopolists were told their type, but *the entrants did not know a monopolist's type* until the end of the game. The prior probability of facing a strong monopolist was fixed at 0.33. A monopolist's payoff depends on his type: if an entrant enters, a weak monopolist gets a higher (single-period) payoff from playing soft than from fighting, while a strong monopolist gets a higher payoff from fighting. Everything about this structure of the game was common knowledge, but the instructions were couched in neutral terms (for example, an artificial currency was used for the payoffs, the monopolists were called B players of type X or Y, the entrants were called A players and the actions of the entrants and the responses of the monopolists were coded numerically) to minimise responding on the basis of prior expectations regarding 'correct' responses. To make sure that the identity of the player making a decision was not known, the entrants and the monopolists sat on opposite sides of a room with a curtain drawn down the middle. They were not allowed to speak. In a given play, one of the monopolists faced eight entry threats. In other words, a single play of the game involved a sequence of eight stage games with a single subject as monopolist. This gave the monopolists an incentive to build reputation. However, the subjects playing the monopolist were changed between plays of the game to minimise the incentive for developing reputations across games. On the other hand, each entrant played only two periods and in a random order unknown to the monopolist they were facing, to minimise the incentive for entrants to develop reputations.

Weak monopolists who maximise expected income *always* fight entry in the initial periods of such a finite-period game according to the model. In mimicking strong monopolists, they hope to deter further entry and thus make up for their losses in future periods. Knowing this, entrants do *not* enter in early periods, in equilibrium. In this eight-period game, weak monopolists will always fight in the first three stages, assuming that all subsequent stages are on the equilibrium path. Entrants begin to enter in period 4.

The experiment revealed high levels of predatory pricing, in the sense that *weak monopolists did fight all entrants in early periods*. During the first three periods, inexperienced weak monopolists started out playing soft 46 per cent of the time during the first thirty games played in the same experimental session. In the following plays this percentage dropped to 15 per cent. However, experienced monopolists (who had played in one prior experimental session) virtually never played soft in the initial three periods. In

Table 12.1. *Frequencies of soft play by experienced weak monopolists*

Stage	Predicted	Games 1–30	Games 31–end
(1 to 3)	0.000	0.068	0.000
1	0.000	0.150	0.000
2	0.000	0.000	0.000
3	0.000	0.000	0.000
4	0.188	0.000	0.000
5	0.346	0.111	0.000
6	0.416	0.083	0.182
7	0.560	0.269	0.425
8	1.000	1.000	0.926

Source: Jung *et al.* (1994, table 4).

later periods, the frequency of soft play increased, even for inexperienced monopolists, as predicted by the Kreps–Wilson model. This can be seen in table 12.1 which reports the results for experienced players. The table gives predicted and observed frequencies of soft play. The predicted frequencies are based on the assumption that entry occurs as of period 4.

Note that soft play started one period later than predicted, because there was essentially no entry until stage 6. Note also that the observed frequencies of soft play are lower than those predicted by Kreps and Wilson.

What about entry? During periods 1 to 4, given the aggressive policy of the monopolists, there should be no entry. In fact, entry rates were quite high for inexperienced entrants and represent out-of-equilibrium play and learning. Indeed, with experienced entrants, there was essentially no entry during these periods. The threat of predation was sufficient to forestall virtually all entry (see table 12.2).

Remember that all entrants knew that there was a positive probability (0.33) of facing a strong monopolist. This created the uncertainty about the monopolist's type that is directly responsible for weak monopolists fighting. The chain store paradox indeed shows that without this uncertainty there will be entry and *no* aggressive play in each stage of the game. It was therefore of interest to repeat the experiment with no experimenter-induced strong types among the monopolists. In such games, the subjects turned out to be much less aggressive during the initial periods. This was true especially for the inexperienced players. However, only 10–15 per cent of the experienced players were playing soft in the early periods!

Table 12.2. *Frequencies of entry with experienced subjects, games 31–end*

Stage	Total entry		Entry in previous period		No entry in previous period	
	Actual	Predicted	Actual	Predicted	Actual	Predicted
(1–4)	0.015	0.000	0.000	0.000	0.012	0.000
(5–8)	0.402	—	0.727	0.357	0.346	1.000
1	0.024	0.000	—	—	—	—
2	0.000	0.000	0.000	0.000	0.000	0.000
3	0.012	0.000	0.000	0.000	0.012	0.000
4	0.024	0.000	0.000	0.000	0.024	0.000
5	0.048	—	0.000	0.357	0.049	1.000
6	0.169	—	0.333	0.357	0.163	1.000
7	0.679	—	0.750	0.357	0.667	1.000
8	0.906	—	0.815	0.357	1.000	1.000

Source: Jung *et al.* (1994, table 5).

Turning to periods 5 to 8, the Kreps–Wilson model predicts that entry will occur with probability 1 if there was no entry in the previous period. This was not the case with experienced entrants (table 12.2). In addition, contrary to the prediction, entry rates increased (instead of being stationary) and were not greater after periods with no entry than after periods with entry. The entrants largely ignored whether or not there was entry and fighting in the previous period. This result suggests a lack of Bayesian updating: human beings do not seem to use Bayes' rule.

To conclude, predatory pricing appears as a real possibility in the Jung–Kagel–Levin experiment, because the economic structure of the game is quite different from the one Isaac and Smith employed. Jung *et al.* (1994, p. 91) conclude:

Clearly, no one structure is the 'right' one, or the more 'natural' one, to test for the possibility of predatory pricing. What the data are telling us, and theory suggests, is that some structures give rise to predatory pricing more easily than others. It is important to experimentally explore, and to understand, the economic forces at work in a variety of structures, to have some reference point against which to evaluate claims of predatory pricing outside the laboratory. Our results demonstrate that one can find predatory pricing and that it pays under some economic structures, so that allegations of such activity outside the laboratory cannot be simply dismissed as sour grapes on the part of the prey, or economically 'irrational' actions on the part of the predators.

Table 12.3. *Illegal practices alleged in complaints*

	Primary allegations	Combined primary and secondary allegations
Horizontal price fixing	15.7%	21.3%
Vertical price fixing	3.5	10.3
Dealer termination	4.4	8.9
Refusal to deal	12.0	25.4
Predatory pricing	3.1	10.4
Asset or patent accumulation	2.5	5.6
Price discrimination	5.0	16.4
Vertical price discrimination	1.7	5.8
Tying or exclusive dealing	9.6	21.1
Merger or joint venture	2.6	5.8
Inducing government action	0.5	0.8
'Conspiracy'	3.0	5.9
'Restraint of trade'	4.3	10.0
'Monopoly' or 'monopolisation'	3.7	8.8
Other	8.6	8.9
No information	25.2	13.4

Note: Percentages sum to more than 100 per cent because a complaint may have more than one allegation.
Source: Salop and White (1988).

12.2 Antitrust litigation

Turning to allegations appearing in courtrooms, a number of questions arise. Are complaints based on predatory pricing relatively important? Are there more and more complaints of that nature? Are judgements generally favourable to plaintiffs? No systematic evidence on these questions seems to be available for Europe.[3] For the United States, the answers are: no.

The Georgetown Project on Private Antitrust Litigation collected suitable data on all private antitrust cases filed in the years 1973–83 in five district courts chosen to provide breadth and depth to the sample. The following tables are taken from an introductory presentation of this material by Salop and White (1988).

Table 12.3 shows that horizontal price fixing was the most frequent

---

[3] An extensive survey of cases of predatory pricing handled by antitrust authorities and courts in all OECD member countries can be found in the 1989 OECD report.

primary allegation (16 per cent), with predatory pricing representing only 3 per cent, and table 12.4 confirms the intuition that competitors are the main parties who allege predatory pricing.

Table 12.5 shows that the share of (primary and secondary) allegations of predatory pricing has fallen sharply in the 1980s. Salop and White suggest that this may be due to the spread of the Areeda–Turner predatory pricing rule (according to which there is a presumption of predation when a large firm prices below its marginal cost, as in the Isaac–Smith definition). To the extent that this rule was accepted by an increasing number of courts, the burden of proof on plaintiffs was increased.

Finally, table 12.6 indicates that settlement rates in cases of predatory pricing were above average, with plaintiff win rates deviating in the opposite direction. We know, from theory that such pricing can arise only in situations where the victim is not sure about its predatory nature. One may suspect, therefore, that some litigations are initiated with the sole purpose of obtaining a settlement favourable to the plaintiff.

On the other hand, when there is a conviction, this is not proof that the plaintiff was aggressed in a predatory way. Koller (1971) studied twenty-three cases of convictions in detail and found that, indeed, only dubious cases come before the courts. According to Bork (1978, p. 155), Koller concluded that 'predatory price cutting was attempted in only seven cases, succeeded to some extent in four, and had harmful effects upon resource allocation in only three (and these three involved predation not to eliminate a rival but to precipitate merger or collusion)'. However, it should also be said that Koller's criteria were too severe, because he recognised predation only when a competitor was eliminated or merged or when 'improved market discipline' resulted.

12.3 The historical record

After all these negative considerations, one wonders whether the historical record does not contain well-documented cases in which all the ingredients of predatory pricing are clearly present. One thus looks for cases where a multimarket firm attacks an entrant by cutting the price in the latter's local market (possibly for a particular product or brand) to make his entry value negative in a way that could be interpreted as normal competition, without necessarily forcing the entrant to exit. A few such cases were put forward by Yamey (1972).

One convincing example is provided by the use of 'fighting brands' by a monopolist to meet the competition of an entrant in those parts of the market where it is trying to become established or to extend its operations. In Yamey's words (1972, p. 136),

Table 12.4. *Cross-tabulation of business relationships and alleged illegal practices*

	Horiz. price fix	Vert. price fix	Dealer term.	Refusal to deal	Pred. price	Asset accum.	Price discrim.	Vert. price discrim.	Tie; excl. dealing	Merger; joint vent.	Induce govt. action	Consp., restr., monop.	Other	No info.	Total
Competitor	141	68	36	214	138	77	141	53	161	82	10	240	83	18	1,462
Dealer	105	112	159	211	56	19	138	68	165	19	2	125	30	5	1,214
Customer comp.	85	39	8	102	23	13	63	17	55	11	0	44	10	3	473
Franchisee	3	3	6	9	6	1	12	3	23	1	0	5	3	0	75
Licensee	2	1	1	3	1	2	0	0	12	0	0	25	2	0	49
Final cust.	97	4	0	25	7	6	29	4	35	6	0	39	13	3	268
Supplier	23	8	3	35	10	3	23	4	0	4	1	25	15	2	176
Employee	10	3	4	18	8	8	6	3	11	6	1	15	15	1	109
State/local govt.	13	0	0	1	0	3	0	0	0	2	2	9	1	1	34
Other	48	14	6	59	4	11	15	14	39	10	3	86	55	7	371
No information	13	2	2	2	4	3	6	2	10	1	0	20	3	228	296
Total	540	254	225	679	257	146	433	168	531	142	19	633	232	268	4,527

Note: The totals of the cross-tabulations sum to more than 1959 because individual cases can have more than one type of business relationship and/or more than one alleged business practice.
Source: Salop and White (1988).

Table 12.5. *Frequency of alleged illegal practices,^{a} by year of filing*

	Horizontal price fixing (%)	Vertical price fixing (%)	Dealer termination (%)	Refusal to deal (%)	Predatory pricing (%)	Price discrimination (%)	Tying or exclusive dealing (%)
1973 and before	24.4	16.3	9.1	26.3	12.4	23.4	29.2
1974	25.7	13.6	12.1	28.0	9.8	18.7	26.6
1975	20.5	7.3	11.7	25.4	10.2	20.0	29.8
1976	28.6	8.5	7.7	21.4	10.7	14.1	19.2
1977	17.3	7.3	6.4	21.8	11.4	17.7	18.2
1978	18.9	15.8	10.0	34.7	11.6	14.7	18.9
1979	18.2	13.3	11.5	33.9	13.3	21.8	19.4
1980	17.2	4.5	8.2	26.1	9.7	13.4	15.7
1981	19.6	7.1	10.1	24.4	8.3	10.1	16.7
1982	23.1	8.3	4.6	15.7	7.4	9.2	12.0
1983	32.1	8.0	2.7	15.2	5.4	9.8	17.9
All cases	21.3	10.3	8.9	25.4	10.4	16.4	21.1

Note:
^{a} Combined primary and secondary allegations.
Source: Salop and White (1988).

Table 12.6. *Settlements and judgements, by alleged statute violation,*
alleged illegal practice and business relationships

	Broad definition of settlement*		Narrow definition of settlement**	
	Settlement as a % of terminated cases	% of judgements favourable to plaintiffs	Settlement as a % of terminated cases	% of judgements favourable to plaintiffs
Alleged statute violation				
Sherman, Sec. 1	87.7	27.9	70.7	11.8
Sherman, Sec. 2	88.6	27.4	71.7	11.0
Clayton, Sec. 2	91.0	34.5	73.4	11.4
Clayton, Sec. 3	84.9	26.7	71.4	14.0
Clayton, Sec. 7	92.5	37.5	74.8	11.2
*Alleged illegal practice****				
Horizontal price fixing	84.2	24.6	68.3	12.3
Vertical price fixing	88.5	19.0	72.5	8.0
Dealer termination	86.2	43.5	74.5	23.8
Refusal to deal	85.6	25.4	68.6	11.6
Predatory pricing	92.9	23.1	77.6	7.3
Price discrimination	88.9	34.4	73.0	14.1
Tying or exclusive dealing	87.7	28.9	72.2	12.7
All horizontal	88.5	23.8	72.2	9.8
All vertical	86.9	27.9	72.3	12.7
Plaintiff's business relationship to defendant				
Competitor	91.1	20.8	73.4	7.4
Dealer	86.2	23.9	69.8	11.1
Customer company	92.0	5.9	77.9	2.1
Final customer	86.6	26.3	74.9	10.9
Supplier	96.9	25.0	74.4	4.5
All cases	88.2	28.1	70.8	11.3

Notes:
  * Includes dismissals in settlements.
  ** Includes dismissals in judgements for defendants.
  *** Combined primary and secondary allegations.
Source: Salop and White (1988).

A special brand is introduced for the purpose. Its sale is confined to the affected areas; the quantities offered are controlled so as not to make unnecessary sacrifices of profit; and it is withdrawn as soon as the objective has been attained, namely the acquisition of the independent by the monopolist, or the withdrawal of the independent, or its abandonment of plans of enlarging its share of the market. Good examples of the use of fighting brands are provided by the activities of the match monopoly in Canada from its creation, by merger, in 1927 to the outbreak of the Second World War. The dominant firm used the device at various times, and this suggests that the firm was convinced of its efficacy.

Another well-documented example is the use of 'fighting ships' by shipping cartels (conferences) as in the Mogul case, which Yamey (1972, pp. 138–42) describes as follows.

In December 1891 the law lords in the House of Lords pronounced upon the activities of a conference of ship owners in the China-England trade designed to exclude competitors so as to maintain a monopoly. This important decision, Mogul Steamship Co. v. McGregore, Gow and Co. *et al.*, terminated litigation which had been started in 1885 and concerned events of that year.

Ship owners regularly engaged in the China trade had formed a conference in 1879 to regulate freight rate and the sailings of the ships of each member. The object was to improve the profitability of the trade by removing competition among members, especially at the height of the tea harvest (May and June) when large quantities of tea were shipped from Hankow and elsewhere down the Yang-tse-Kiang river to Shanghai, and thence to London. At some time before 1884 the conference introduced a 5 per cent rebate payable to such shippers as gave all their business to conference companies during the particular year. This was designed to discourage shippers from giving business to interlopers who might be attracted into the trade, particularly at the height of the tea season when demand for shipping space was high and, presumably, also relatively inelastic.

The plaintiff company, Mogul, was formed in 1883, with ships engaged primarily in the Australia trade. It had an interest in picking up freights in China at the time of the year when homeward freight was plentiful in China but hard to come by in Australia. In the 1884 season the conference allowed two sailings to Mogul ships, although the company was not admitted as a full member. In the next year Mogul asked to be admitted as a full member of the conference, and threatened to cut rates if its request was not granted. The conference refused the request, and decided to treat Mogul as an outsider which had to be excluded from the trade....

In 1885 the conference decided 'that if any non-Conference steamer should proceed to Hankow to load independently the necessary number of Conference steamers should be sent at the same time to Hankow, in order to underbid the freight which the independent ship owners might offer, without any regard to whether the freight they should bid would be remunerative or not'. Three independent ships were sent to Hankow, two of them being Mogul ships; and the agents for the conference lines responded by sending such ships as they thought necessary. Freight rates fell dramatically.... Apparently in the event the losses of the conference were larger than those of the outsiders, since some conference ships sailed empty from Hankow, while all the outsiders' vessels were able to load up with some cargo and did not have to sail in ballast. . . . The fact that shipping companies continued to use fighting ships after the Mogul affair suggests that predatory pricing and the standing threat of such action were considered efficacious. . . .

The point is frequently made in the literature on predatory pricing that the practice makes little sense where entry into the industry or trade in question is easy. However, the Mogul story serves to illustrate a general point, namely, that predatory pricing, or the threat of its use, may itself operate as an effective hindrance to new entry even in situations where the conventional barriers to entry are weak or absent. In this request predatory pricing, like certain other pricing practices, should be given a place in the analysis of barriers to entry.

This lively story was worth telling, because it brings together all basic ingredients. The aggressor is a multimarket cartel. The victim is also a multimarket firm. The direct aim of the price cut is to slow down entry by the latter into a submarket and to deter further entry into that submarket. The fight could be interpreted as normal competition. Only the shipping conference knew whether the immediate foregone profits are compensated by later gains in the China trade. That it did consider such intertemporal compensation to be possible is indicated (though not proved, of course) by the fact that it continued to send fighting ships.

McGee might object that this alleged predation was a failure, because the losses for the shipping conference were eventually larger, while the outsiders might have made some small immediate profit. That is, at any rate, one of the conclusions of his 1960 study of the ocean freight rate conferences and of his 1964 study of the history of the Spanish sugar industry. My answer is that it is immaterial whether the immediate cash flow is negative for the victim or the predator. The key features are the possibility, for the predator, to compensate immediate losses or foregone profits by other gains in the long run, and the deterrence of further entry.

12.4 The bus war: a modelling approach

Dodgson, Katsoulacos and Newton (1992, 1993) provide a modelling framework which is explicitly designed for the identification of predation and closely follows the conclusions drawn in the last section of chapter 11. The basic message of that chapter was that predation turns a profitable entry opportunity for an entrant into an unprofitable one. To discover whether such an opportunity exists, that is, whether there is room for an additional firm in a market, it is necessary to find out whether the entrant would make a positive profit in a non-cooperative post-entry Nash equilibrium. This in turn requires the construction of a model for the product market involved, so that the equilibrium values of the prices and quantities can be computed.

Typically for my approach to the identification of predatory pricing is that the investigator or the antitrust authority shifts the focus of attention to the *entrant's* profits, to check whether they could be positive in the circumstances under investigation. This seems to be a new idea, to the extent that in antitrust proceedings the conventional approach concentrates attention on whether the incumbent is pricing below cost. Antitrust authorities generally take a close look at the incumbent's costs, not at the entrant's! (This will become clear in the discussion of the rules followed by US courts in the next chapter and is exemplified in my analysis of the Commission's AKZO decision in section 13.3. As we shall see in this section, the UK authorities also tend to investigate only the alleged predator's cost situation.)

In their 1992 paper, Dodgson *et al.* carefully construct a model that takes the peculiarities of bus competition in a medium-sized British town into account. In 1986, local bus services were deregulated in Great Britain, so that bus operators were free to operate commercial services on any route in town. Until that year, the town under investigation had been served by a municipally owned public bus company which operated traditional British double-deck vehicles. In 1987, a new, privately-owned firm operating small minibuses entered, matching the incumbent's fare and providing high frequency minibus services on all the town's main corridors. The incumbent soon reacted by introducing minibus services of its own to reduce its costs and by increasing service frequency. The end result was that both firms made losses. The entrant went bankrupt. Was this a case of predatory behaviour by the incumbent?

The model considers two bus operators competing on a single route of a given length. (Each route is a different market.) These duopolists compete on both price (fare) and service level (total bus-miles[4] operated by each firm on the route as a proxy for frequency). Bus operating costs are a linear function of fixed costs, bus-miles and patronage (passenger journeys). The demand function of a firm is a constant-elasticity function of the fares and the bus-miles of the two competitors. This function could not be estimated econometrically for lack of suitable data on patronage and also because the two firms charge the same fares in each period.

To obtain own- and cross-fare elasticities and own- and cross-service elasticities, simulation exercises were undertaken, altering observed fares and bus-miles. The corresponding demands are numbers of passenger trips

---

[4] Total bus-miles is the total number of buses times the number of trips per bus times the length of the route.

calculated from the available timetables for each competitor. The assumption is that potential passengers are evenly distributed over a straight line representing the part of the day over which passengers' preferences for travel are defined.[5] Along any small section of this line, the proportion of potential passengers depends on the travel cost for a passenger (the fare paid, walking time, in-bus travel time and the 'schedule delay' cost of not finding a bus at the preferred departure time). The actual patronage (passenger trips) for a particular bus departing at a particular time can be found by (a) locating the 'marginal' passengers who are indifferent between travelling on that bus and taking the earlier bus or the next bus and (b) integrating potential demand over the time the inframarginal passengers are willing to lose to take that bus at the particular departing time under investigation. In the specialised literature on transportation economics, estimates of travel costs for individual passengers are available. Yet, the computation of the patronage levels for each bus at each departure time for each competitor is a considerable task, which Dodgson *et al.* had the courage to carry out with great care. (This example shows how demand functions can be calibrated when econometric methods break down.)

Once the demand elasticities are available, the remaining parameters of the constant elasticity demand functions can be computed. Together with the cost functions, they give the profits of the two competitors. First-order conditions derived from these give a pair of reaction functions, which can be solved in the usual way to obtain the Nash equilibrium. It was found that there was a profitable entry opportunity, since at the non-cooperative Nash equilibrium the entrant would have made a positive profit. In fact, both competitors made losses. This is compatible with predation.

Dodgson *et al.* do not conclude that there was predation, however. A situation where the entrant has a positive entry value but in fact makes losses is a necessary but not a sufficient condition for predation to have happened. The entrant may have made mistakes, initially at least, so that it is necessary to check how the situation evolved in the post-entry period. The incumbent, in turn, may not be responsible for the entrant's losses, if it is the entrant who acts aggressively and imposes losses on himself and on the incumbent. Such aggressive behaviour make sense: it may be a fight to establish leadership in the market. Such a strategy is called Stackelberg warfare in the literature.[6] Dodgson *et al.* (1992, pp. 66–7) suggest that this is precisely what happened, namely, the entrant came in with too many buses

---

[5] This is a model of the Hotelling type. The Hotelling model was originally defined for preferences for product varieties. See Phlips (1983, pp. 210–12 and 1988b, pp. 42–5) and Dodgson *et al.* (1992, pp. 62–3) for details.

[6] More on this in sections 13.2 and 13.3.

per period and the incumbent overreacted by putting in too many buses in turn:

Both firms were operating higher levels of bus-miles than the Nash equilibrium. The bus-miles reaction curves (which show each firm's profit-maximising bus-miles, given the bus-miles and associated maximum profit fare of its rival) are downward-sloping. This means that the incumbent could have unilaterally increased its actual profits by reducing its own bus-miles, while the entrant could have unilaterally reduced its losses by reducing its own bus-miles. Moreover, the incumbent's bus-miles were not at a level so high that the entrant could not convert its losses into profits by such an action. Thus, although the entrant made losses, it could have been profitable (given the service level of the incumbent) if it had chosen to operate fewer bus-miles on the route. The incumbent was not therefore by its actions denying the entrant a profitable entry opportunity, though both firms were (in choosing service levels higher than the Nash equilibrium) reducing the maximum profits that could be earned by their rival. In this sense, the situation is akin to Stackelberg warfare, where each firm seeks to establish market leadership but *not* to eliminate its rival.

In their 1993 paper, Dodgson, Katsoulacos and Newton discuss the investigations held by the British Office of Fair Trading (1989a, 1989b, 1989c, 1990 and 1992) and the Monopolies and Mergers Commission (1990) on the bus industry and apply their modelling approach to the bus war that broke out in Inverness, the major town in the Scottish Highlands.

The Office of Fair Trading is concerned only with the issue of whether an observed behaviour is anticompetitive. If it is judged to be anticompetitive, the Director-General of Competition (the head of the Office) can refer the case to the Monopolies and Mergers Commission, which also judges whether action is anticompetitive and, in addition, whether it operates against the public interest. There were five formal bus industry investigations. Three were judged to involve predatory/anticompetitive action, and two were referred to the Monopolies and Mergers Commission.

In the Inverness case, the public company Highland Scottish Omnibuses (HSO) had been operating a network of local bus routes. In May 1988, an entrant, Inverness Traction Ltd. (ITL), started eight minibus routes. In August it expanded its operations with a further seven minibus routes. In March 1989, it went bankrupt and was taken over by Alexanders (North East) Ltd., which was not profitable either and was taken over by Magicbus (Scotland) Ltd., a subsidiary of the largest British bus operator. On 13 September 1991, HSO withdrew from the town.

Using the conventional approach, the Office of Fair Trading noted that HSO had reduced its fares on the day that ITL entered the market, considered HSO costs and revenue (not ITL's!) and judged that it had significantly restricted ITL's ability to compete, since HSO had not earned enough revenue to cover total costs (including overheads) on their Inver-

Table 12.7. *Competition in the Inverness bus markets: key data for competitors*

	One month after entry[*]		One year after entry[**]	
	Incumbent	Entrant	Incumbent	Entrant
Fare per passenger journey (pence)[***]	25.5	25.5	27.7	27.7
Bus miles operated	71,700	48,400	102,300	71,900
Patronage (number of journeys)	198,700	82,300	227,300	113,000
Cost per bus mile (pence)[***]	90.0	77.5	72.9	72.0
Profit/loss (£)[***]	− 29,700	− 20,400	− 26,200	− 24,400

Notes:
[*] The period one month after entry is the four weeks 20 June–17 July 1988.
[**] The period one year after entry is the four weeks 24 April–21 May 1989.
[***] All financial figures have been converted to constant (May 1988) prices.
Source: Dodgson *et al.* (1993, table 1).

ness town services. HSO's costs had increased by one third despite a fall in unit costs, due to a 60 per cent increase in its bus miles in a year. The Monopolies and Mergers Commission (1990, p. 1) concluded that HSO 'went too far: its provision of new services and of duplicates[7] was grossly excessive, incurring losses that were unjustified ...'.

Dodgson *et al.* modelled the Inverness market for bus services for each of the twelve four-week periods starting on 20 June 1988, three weeks after entry, and finishing on 21 May 1989. Table 12.7 summarises key data for both HSO and ITL in the first full period after entry and in the last period modelled, a full year after entry.

The computed demand elasticities (averaged across competitors and across the sample period) are:
Own-fare   − 1.02
Cross-fare   + 0.13
Own-service   + 0.43
Cross-service   − 0.21.
They were used to solve for the constants in the demand equations. These indicate that with equal fares and bus miles HSO would capture 62.5 per

---

[7] HSO continued operation of duplicate services on one route.

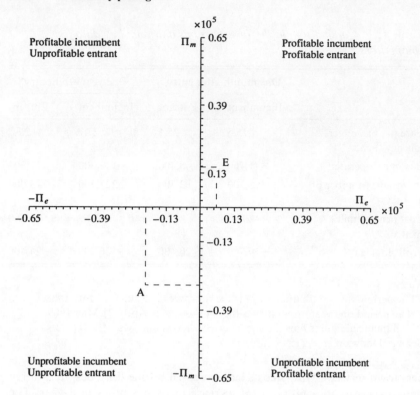

Figure 12.3 Actual and Nash equilibrium profits in Inverness one month after entry
Source: Dodgson *et al.* (1993, figure 2).

cent of the market and ITL 37.5 per cent, so that HSO had a considerable competitive advantage, possibly because of the loyalty of its old customers.

Figure 12.3 relates to the first period modelled (20 June–17 July 1988). Point A represents the losses made by both firms. Point E represents the positive Nash equilibrium profits, indicating that there was room in the market for two firms. Figure 12.4 shows that the same was true a year later but that the Nash equilibrium had become more asymmetric, in the sense that HSO could have made larger profits because of cost-cutting measures. In fact, HSO only slightly reduced its losses while those of the entrant were slightly increased. This is consistent with there being predation.

However, these losses were avoidable, as can be seen by examining the reaction functions for the corresponding periods depicted in figures 12.5 and 12.6. In the first period, the reaction curves intersect at the point where the incumbent operates 25,000 bus miles and the entrant 7,000 miles. In

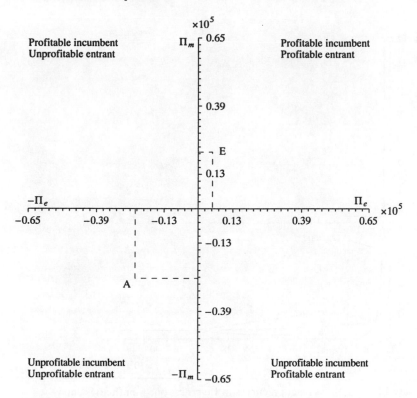

Figure 12.4 Actual and Nash equilibrium profits in Inverness one year after entry
Source: Dodgson *et al.* (1993, figure 3).

fact, they operated 72,000 and 48,000 bus miles respectively (point A). The entrant could have earned profits by (considerably) reducing its bus miles unilaterally.[8] A year later, after HSO had reduced its costs,[9] it could also have avoided losses by reducing its bus miles unilaterally (see figure 12.6). Instead it operated 102,000 bus miles (30,000 more) while the entrant added 44,000 (up to 72,000). While the incumbent produced more output than in a

[8] The vertical line CC′ touches the entrant's zero isoprofit curve ($\Pi_e = 0$). The horizontal line BB′ touches the incumbent's zero isoprofit curve ($\Pi_m = 0$). To turn the profitable entry opportunity into a negative one, the incumbent would have had to operate bus miles to the right of CC′, that is, more than 320,000! To make it impossible for the incumbent to make profits, the entrant had to operate bus miles above BB′, that is, more than 45,000. Since the entrant actually did just that, in the first period, the incumbent could not eliminate his losses.

[9] As a consequence, the incumbent's zero isoprofit curve moved upwards, pushing BB′ upwards.

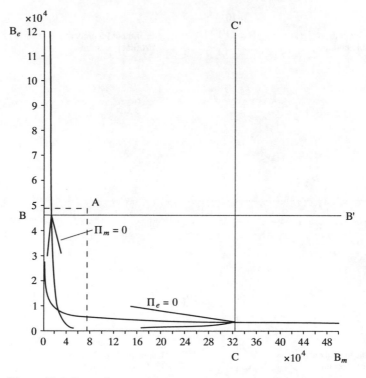

Figure 12.5 Bus miles reaction curves in Inverness one month after entry
Source: Dodgson *et al.* (1993, figure 4).

competitive equilibrium in the first period after entry, the entrant entered
with a level of output which was not only excessive but even so high as to
deny the incumbent the possibility of a profitable response. During
subsequent periods, they both engaged in Stackelberg warfare in order to
secure a more favourable market position in the future.

Dodgson *et al.* (1993, pp. 166–7) conclude:

It seems unreasonable to penalise only one of the combatants in this competitive
battle, that is, to expect an incumbent to acquiesce when faced by very aggressive
entry and not to fight back with a similarly aggressive response. This conclusion is
strengthened by the fact that . . . the entrant could have *avoided* losses by a different
response to the incumbent's post-entry bus-mile choice.

In the event, the incumbent did have an advantage in the form of a larger purse.
The entrant did not respond by retreating to the much lower, but profitable, output
level which our model has identified, but instead continued its Stackelberg-type
warfare until it went bankrupt. . . .

Further, account must be taken of the fact that, throughout this period of

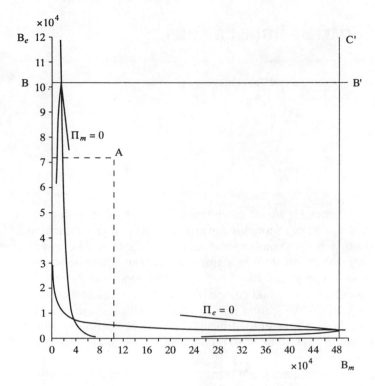

Figure 12.6 Bus miles reaction curves in Inverness one year after entry
Source: Dodgson *et al.* (1993, figure 5).

warfare, consumers have benefited from better services than would otherwise have been provided.

Let me add that entry did continue, with ITL replaced first by Alexanders and then by Magicbus, a nation-wide operator capable of assessing profitability prospects. Their managers must have been convinced that there was room for two operators on the Inverness market.

This fascinating episode has shown that a competitive battle can be (and is easily) misinterpreted as predation. A similar misinterpretation did show up in the Commission's AKZO decision. The informational requirements that make it difficult for an antitrust authority to distinguish between Stackelberg warfare and predation will be emphasised in the next chapter, after a critical discussion of the conventional rules followed in antitrust proceedings.

13   Antitrust implications

As shown in chapter 11, recent game theory is able to demonstrate that predatory pricing can be rationalised in an intertemporal profit maximisation approach, when a number of conditions are met. The essential conditions are that the predator be a multimarket firm, otherwise McGee's (1980) objections apply, and that his pricing behaviour can be misinterpreted by an entrant as normal competition. Although the first is easy to recognise in practice, the second implies that identification of predatory behaviour is a fortiori inherently difficult for both the economist and the antitrust authority. Yet, difficult to identify or not, predatory pricing is a real possibility.

Chapter 12 suggests that clearly identified cases of predatory pricing are hard to find. In the vast majority of cases, alleged predation is doubtful predation, which should not come as a surprise given that true predation requires the presence of such doubts. For the very same reason, predatory pricing may be more frequent, in the real world, than is generally thought.

Even if it were in fact rare, antitrust authorities could not simply disregard it. Indeed, to preserve free entry is one of the main objectives of any antitrust policy. When there is room in a market for new entrants (their entry value is positive under normal competition), predation should not be allowed to make this entry value negative and thus to discourage or delay further entry (or, in the limit, force exit). The issue is an essential one. One should at least try to see what policy implications can be derived from the recent theoretical advances. Hopefully, they should indicate what can be done in an operational way, which policy actions could deter predation, and what side effects these actions could have. At any rate, they should indicate what antitrust authorities should not do.

13.1 Rules

At least three policy attitudes are possible. The simplest is to do nothing and hope that 'market forces' will do the job in the long run. A second attitude is to devise a per se rule, according to which a dividing line between legitimately competitive prices and prices that are properly regarded as predatory is drawn and/or well-defined obligations are imposed on potential predators. The third attitude is to use a rule of reason, implying that each case is judged on its own merits, using all the available evidence.

No standard

According to McGee (1980, p. 317), the best thing to do is to do nothing – the best standard against predation is no standard at all. The argument is that predatory pricing is rare, while the danger of condemning what is in fact active competition by the more efficient firm is great, so more harm than good is likely to be done. I cannot follow this argument in view of the unduly restrictive assumptions of McGee's analysis and in view of the fact we do not and cannot know how rare predation actually is. Not detecting the guilty is as probable as punishing the innocent.

Another argument also leads to the conclusion that no standard should be used. It says that a prohibition, even if it is effective, does not necessarily lead to more entry, because predatory pricing is but one of a series of means to deter entry. A prohibition of predatory pricing may increase the incentive for a dominant firm to make investments prior to entry (e.g., investments in productive capacity, in advertising, in retail capacity, in R&D) to reduce the need for predatory pricing after entry has occurred. And it may be impossible to provide policy rules about such pre-entry investments. As argued by Spence (1981) an attack on predation may therefore not be the most important weapon in dealing with abuses of market dominance. Again, this argument is not convincing. It is of the same nature as the one that says that price agreements should not be made illegal because such a prohibition will promote mergers. With this type of argument, the whole of antitrust policy is under attack.

Price below marginal cost

It would be nice if a neat dividing line could be drawn between a price resulting from normal competition and a predatory price. Areeda and Turner (1975) have proposed what they call a meaningful and workable test[1] for making such a distinction, to replace such empty formulae as 'below cost' pricing, ruinous competition or predatory intent. The simplicity of their test may explain why it was adopted with remarkable speed by American judicial circles. (It has become the standard in a number of cases.) The test provides a floor below which a price is presumed predatory:

[1] Alterations and refinements by Posner (1976) and Greer (1979) will not be discussed here.

'Unless at or above average cost, a price below reasonably anticipated (1) short-run marginal costs or (2) average variable costs should be deemed predatory, and the monopolist may not defend on the grounds that his price was "promotional" or merely met an equally low price of a competitor' (Areeda and Turner 1975, p. 733). To establish predation, the antitrust authority 'simply' has to show that a price is below (reasonably anticipated) average variable cost, treated as a proxy for marginal cost. To escape indictment, the alleged predator 'simply' has to show that his price is not below (reasonably anticipated) average variable cost. Consideration of threats is disallowed.

After recalling the standard textbook definitions of fixed and variable costs, Areeda and Turner first discuss a general price reduction by a single-product single-market monopolist. (We know that predatory pricing cannot be rationalised under these circumstances.) Predatory pricing is defined (p. 698) as

a temporary sacrifice of net revenues in the expectation of greater future gains. Indeed, the classically-feared case of predation has been the deliberate sacrifice of present revenues for the purpose of driving rivals out of the market and then recouping the losses through higher profits earned in the absence of competition.

Although the elimination of the victim is an unduly severe criterion, this definition has at least the merit of being cast in terms of intertemporal profit maximisation (future profits compensate immediate losses). Quite surprisingly, however, Areeda and Turner then proceed to analyse predation in terms of myopic instantaneous profit maximisation and concentrate entirely on the sacrifice of short-run profits (p. 703):

We would normally expect a profit-maximising firm, within the limits of data and convenience, to attempt to maximise profits or minimise losses in the short run – the competitive firm by producing where marginal cost equals price, and the monopolist by producing where marginal cost equals marginal revenue.

Two exceptions to short-run profit maximisation are deemed non-predatory. One is 'limit pricing', that is, a price permanently set above average cost but below the profit-maximising price to prevent entry (that has not yet occurred) by newcomers with a higher average cost. The other one is a temporary price reduction to average cost when entry is relatively costly. These two pricing policies are deemed analytically indistinguishable and are not presumed illegal because they exclude only less efficient rivals and would require continuous supervision by the antitrust authority. (One might as well argue that they are also indistinguishable from predatory pricing.)

What is presumed illegal is pricing below marginal cost, when marginal cost is below average cost – pricing at marginal cost being tolerated (p. 712):

We have concluded above that marginal-cost pricing by a monopolist should be tolerated even though losses could be minimised or profits increased at a lower output and higher price, for the reasons, among others, that marginal cost pricing leads to a proper resource allocation and is consistent with competition on the merits. Neither reason obtains when the monopolist prices below marginal cost. The monopolist is not only incurring private losses but wasting social resources when marginal cost exceeds the value of what is produced. And pricing below marginal cost greatly increases the possibility that rivalry will be extinguished or prevented for reasons unrelated to the efficiency of the monopolist. Accordingly, a monopolist pricing below marginal cost should be presumed to have engaged in a predatory or exclusionary practice.

Subsequently, Areeda and Turner consider devices other than a 'general' price cut, namely, selective price cuts on particular products or particular geographical markets. In both cases, it is claimed that the same conclusions apply (except that a monopolist should have the benefit of any defences, such as 'promotional' pricing or 'meeting competition', available to other sellers in any market in which he lacks monopoly power).

In view of our theoretical analysis, the Areeda–Turner approach obviously lacks serious analytical underpinning, even if a 'general' price cut by a single-product single-market monopolist is left out of the analysis. To begin with, I can hardly think of an economist who would be willing, today, to interpret the marginal-revenue-equal-marginal cost rule as more than a mathematical tautology without descriptive value.[2] But above all, Areeda and Turner totally ignore the behaviour of firms as sophisticated players in an intertemporal game and the requirements of a non-cooperative Nash equilibrium between such players. From a game-theoretic point of view, the distinction made between the elimination of newcomers with higher average costs than the incumbents (called 'competition on the merits', apparently) and the elimination of at least equally efficient newcomers seems pointless. What matters is whether there is room for the newcomer in a competitive Nash equilibrium, that is, whether its entry value is positive, and whether the incumbent's pricing policy makes this entry value negative, that is, whether the entrant's fixed sunk entry costs are no longer compensated by the present value of future profits. The precise relationship between price and marginal cost plays no essential role at such a competitive equilibrium as far as predatory pricing is concerned.

From a policy point of view, the line drawn by Areeda and Turner is underinclusive. As noted by Easley et al. (1985, p. 457), none of the predators described in their model could be held in violation of the Areeda–Turner standard or similar standards defined in terms of price–cost relationships. Prices are not below average variable cost or marginal cost in

---

[2] On this, see chapter 6 of my 1983 book on price discrimination.

their model, and exit is not induced. Ironically, standards such as Areeda and Turner's 'may constitute the instruction manual on how to prey with impunity'.

On a pragmatic 'administrative' level (Areeda and Turner put heavy weight on the costs of administrative supervision and litigation), it may be added that average variable costs are not as easily defined in practice as they are in elementary textbooks. In addition, no judge, or academic or antitrust authority has adequate means of checking the correctness of a defendant's evaluation of average variable costs (whether 'reasonably anticipated' or not). For all practical purposes, the Areeda–Turner price–cost relationship is impossible to measure and makes the proof of predation too difficult.

Limit pricing

Instead of a dividing line between a price that is predatory and a price that is not, as in the Areeda–Turner rule, Williamson (1977) proposes an 'output restriction rule' which stipulates that a dominant firm cannot, in the period after entry occurs, increase output above the pre-entry level even if the resulting market price exceeds the dominant firm's average variable cost. This rule results from a reasoning in terms of limit pricing, which is apparently considered by Williamson as the type of pricing that correctly describes the behaviour of dominant firms (or collusive oligopolists). It is necessary, therefore, to briefly discuss limit pricing.

Limit pricing has been a major topic in industrial economics. It goes back at least to Modigliani's classic 1958 paper 'New developments on the oligopoly front'. The basic idea is that 'potential entrants behave as though they expected existing firms to adopt the policy most unfavourable to them, namely, the policy of maintaining output while reducing the price (or accepting reductions) to the extent required to enforce such an output policy' (Modigliani 1958, p. 217, note 26).

Figure 13.1 makes this statement more precise. The incumbent is supposed to maintain output (sales) at the level Q_L to which corresponds the limit price p_L. This price is below the monopoly price p_M, which the incumbent would fix if there is no prospective entry and no fear of it. The limit price (and the corresponding output Q_L) is found by drawing a line that is parallel to the industry demand curve AB and simultaneously tangent to the given long-run average cost curve (LRAC). The parallelism results from the assumption that the incumbent maintains sales at Q_L, so that DB is the residual demand curve on which the entrant can operate. This segment DB is shifted to the left. The tangency with the LRAC curve (which is the same for the potential entrant and for the existing firm) represents the policy most unfavourable to the potential entrant. Indeed, any quantity of

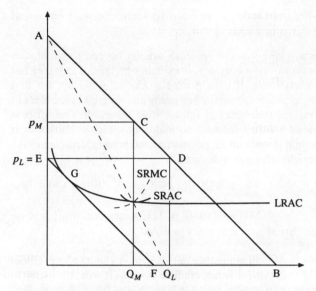

Figure 13.1 Limit pricing

the (homogeneous) commodity put on the market by an entrant leads to losses or at most to the break-even point G. Entry is thus deterred. The incumbent prefers the immediate reduction in profit (due to the fact that $p_L < p_M$) to the larger reduction in profit that would result if entry occurred.

Suppose entry somehow occurs. Then the dominant firm will allegedly flood the market to reduce the price below the entrant's LRAC curve and force it to exit. An output expansion is necessary, because lowering the price without increasing sales would create excess demand and make it easier for the entrant to establish itself. Hence the rule that a post-entry output expansion above the pre-entry level Q_L should be presumed predatory, even if the resulting price were still above the dominant firm's average variable cost.

Needless to say, this is an oversimplified presentation of limit pricing[3] and of the output restriction rule.[4] It will do for my present purpose, because I do not believe an output restriction rule to be a valid standard against predatory pricing.

---

[3] For important refinements see Gaskins (1971), Kamien and Schwartz (1971), Pyatt (1971) and Salop (1979).

[4] Williamson (1977) also discusses rules which allow post-entry output expansion on the condition that price does not fall below short-run marginal cost or below short-run average cost.

First of all, limit-pricing theories are hard to reconcile with empirical evidence. In McGee's strong words (1980, pp. 312–13)

if – as the theory asserts – long-run average costs are flat beyond the minimum efficient size, taken as it stands the theory cannot explain why there is anything but single-firm monopoly everywhere. If limit pricing works, why did not the first member of each industry practice it from the beginning and keep everyone else out forever? This is a serious question because, among other things, the limit price is determined by the slope of industry demand, no matter how big the market is. It would be difficult to explain the evolution, prosperity, and present structure of the U.S. economy if limit-pricing theories were right.

In particular, one wonders how entry and hence predation could ever occur.

On a more analytical level, McGee (1980, p. 311) notes that limit pricing rests upon an implicit threat which is not credible:

The monopoly threatens that it will not reduce output if entry should occur. Under the circumstances posited, the threat is not credible because it would not pay to carry it out. Suppose an entrant decides that it will come in at the smallest scale at which it can achieve minimum average cost. As Figure III [see my figure 13.1] shows, it is true that if the monopolist holds output constant in the face of entry, the entrant would lose money. But so would the monopoly. Indeed, the monopoly would lose much more than the entrant. Holding its output constant at that scale would hurt the monopoly more than it hurts the entrant, and the ex-monopoly has more attractive alternatives if entry actually does occur. As a result, the entrant should assume that the monopoly will not act like that. More attractive alternatives may include so-called dominant-firm pricing, Cournot-style duopoly pricing, a cartel, or other attempts to divide the market peacefully, and so on.

At this point, it should be clear that a game-theoretic treatment of limit pricing is the only way to disentangle the rights and the wrongs. Both the existing firm and the potential entrant should be treated as rational players in a well-defined game, and one should study the properties of the resulting equilibrium, to clarify the 'strategic' possibilities alluded to by both McGee and Williamson.

This is exactly what Friedman (1979) has done. His conclusion is that *if the incumbent and the entrant are completely informed* about demand and about each other's costs, as is implicitly assumed in the foregoing discussion and in the construction of figure 13.1, *no limit pricing can emerge in equilibrium.*

The argument is essentially the same as the argument leading to the chain store paradox. Post-entry profits are completely independent of the pre-entry price, under the usual assumption that pre-entry price does not affect post-entry demand. Under complete information, the post-entry profits are also fully known when the entry decision is made. Hence the entry decision is independent of the pre-entry price. Reducing this price to the limit price p_L amounts to throwing pre-entry profits away. As long as pre-entry actions do not influence post-entry costs and demand, this argument is valid and the traditional theory of limit pricing has no game-theoretic foundation.

The implication is that limit pricing can be rationalised only if information is incomplete, exactly as is the case with predatory pricing. It then remains to see how limit pricing could arise in equilibrium under incomplete information and especially whether such deviation from myopic profit maximisation would effectively deter entry in equilibrium. Milgrom and Roberts (1982b) have tackled these questions and shown that, while traditional limit pricing can arise under incomplete information, it does not bias the entrant's expectations of the profitability of entry. The only consequence of limit pricing, when it occurs, is therefore to reduce the price without limiting entry. Antitrust authorities should thus not worry about it. A reduction in price with no effects on entry cannot be objectionable from their point of view.

In the games analysed by Milgrom and Roberts (1982b), neither the incumbent nor the potential entrant is perfectly informed about the other firm's unit costs. Therefore, no player is able to compute the post-entry profits with certainty. However, the pre-entry price becomes a *signal* concerning the incumbent's costs and thus concerning the price and market share to be expected after entry. By signalling lower costs, a lower pre-entry price is an attempt to influence the entry decision.

The modelling is done, as in the analysis of predatory pricing, with the help of a probability distribution, which is here defined over the possible values of the unit costs of the players. A third player, 'Nature', moves first and draws a particular value of the unit costs out of the given probability distribution. The incumbent is informed about its own unit cost, but not about the unit cost of the potential entrant, and vice versa. In addition to its own unit cost, the potential entrant can observe the pre-entry output chosen by the incumbent. The game is thus transformed into a game with 'complete' information (the probability distribution is known to all, so all possible outcomes are known). But the information is 'imperfect' in the sense that the players must make a move at some point without having been fully informed about all the previous moves by the other players (including Nature). The equilibria can then be computed as pairs of strategies (based on what each player knows) such that each player maximises his expected payoff, given that the other is using a particular strategy.[5]

As for Williamson's output restriction rule, note that it is as underinclu-

---

[5] The interested reader is referred to Milgrom and Roberts (1982b) for further details.

sive as the Areeda–Turner rule. There is no reason why a predator, as defined here, should necessarily violate it, that is, should necessarily expand output above its pre-entry level. It is also worth recalling that such a rule is likely to facilitate tacit collusion, as shown in the Isaac–Smith experiment. Conversely, as noted by Baumol (1979, p. 3, note 8), the rule prevents entry from serving its purpose of forcing price reductions upon the incumbent and 'inhibits price wars among large incumbent firms, who are constrained, in effect, to retain their initial market shares, at least for the immediate post-entry period'.

Baumol (1979) therefore proposes a rule that, instead of preventing output increases, forbids price increases after the entrant has been forced to cease operations. In this way, price reductions are made 'quasi-permanent'. Though left free to respond to entry by a price cut, in contrast to Williamson's output restriction rule, the established firm can no longer do so without fear of long-term repercussions, because it must take the long-run cost of a permanent reduction in price into account. This quasi-permanence rule could be supplemented, according to Baumol, with a test like the Areeda–Turner test to determine whether profits on other outputs or markets are used to subsidise predatory prices. Of course, the defendant should be allowed to provide evidence that a post-entry increase is justified by cost increases or by other autonomous developments. The burden of proof should thus be on the defendant.

Baumol's quasi-permanency rule is deemed consistent with the requirements of allocative efficiency because it closely approximates the optimality properties of stationary limit pricing. This type of limit pricing, in turn, is possible only if the incumbent is a natural monopoly, that is, if several firms cannot produce the industry's output at least as cheaply. Indeed, in that situation, stationary limit prices are such that entry can be prevented without changing them in response to an attempted entrant's moves. The incumbent 'can sit back and await the entrant's financial failure' (Baumol 1979, p. 18). When a prospective predator, who, by definition, is not a natural monopoly, knows that it cannot raise its price after a predatory campaign, it will automatically abandon the idea of preying upon an entrant!

Baumol's rule is thus embedded in a particular form of limit pricing. No game-theoretic explanation on how such pricing could occur in equilibrium is given. Awaiting such explanation, the critiques formulated above against traditional limit pricing apply. In addition, this rule is as underinclusive as Williamson's (predation does not necessarily induce exit and a subsequent rise in prices) and is equally likely to facilitate collusion.

Abuse of a dominant position

I must conclude that none of the per se rules under discussion can be adopted as a useful weapon against predatory pricing. The only available alternative seems to be to use a rule of reason, that is, to establish predation with all available evidence at hand. In the case of the Treaty of Rome, this amounts to treating predatory pricing as a case of 'abuse of a dominant position' in application of Article 86 of the Treaty.

From our discussion it should be clear that proof, by the defendant, that the allegedly predatory price is above marginal cost or average variable cost should be treated as inconclusive and discarded. In a similar vein, discussions about whether a post-entry price increase (or sales expansion) by the predator was justified by cost increases (or decreases) can and should be avoided. The same is true, more generally, for arguments cast in terms of limit pricing. The only way out is to collect evidence that is related to the game-theoretic arguments presented.

Game theory admittedly requires a great deal of sophistication. Its implications, however, are clear and simple, at least in principle. The negative implications are that it is immaterial whether the alleged victim was forced out of the market it entered into and whether its cash flow (current profits) remained positive. As for the alleged predator, when this turns out to be a single-market firm, the presumption should be that predation is irrational.

The positive implication is that the plaintiff (or the antitrust authority) should provide evidence to the effect that an alleged predatory price cut turned a positive entry value into a negative one for the alleged victim. It should be shown that the present value of future profits is larger than the fixed sunk entry costs of the victim under normal competition and that the price cut made this value smaller than the fixed sunk entry cost. In simple words, this amounts to showing that, without the price cut, there was room in the market for an additional firm under normal competition, that is, in a non-cooperative Nash equilibrium. And that, as a result of the price cutting, the price went below the non-cooperative Nash equilibrium price.

The difficulty is that such proof is hard to provide in practice, because predation can occur only when there is uncertainty about whether the price cutting is the result of normal competition, that is, whether the post-entry non-cooperative Nash equilibrium implies a negative entry value, or not. The alleged predator will inevitably argue that its price is the non-cooperative Nash equilibrium price (so that it is normal competition that made the entrant's entry value negative) while the alleged victim will pretend it is not. Nevertheless, I wish to emphasise that the post-entry non-cooperative Nash equilibrium, with the implied price (or prices, if the commodity is non-homogeneous) and market shares (for the incumbent and the entrant), should be the theoretical yardstick. The discussion should be on the issue whether this equilibrium leaves room for the entrant, in the sense that entry is profitable in the long run under normal competition.

One might object that, in addition to the inherent uncertainty about the predatory nature of a price cut, information about the competitors' cost and demand is generally incomplete (how could the victim know the predator's profits in its different markets?), so the relevant Nash equilibrium cannot be computed. This objection will not do. It is well established and well known[6] that it can, even if the competitors are not perfectly informed about each other's profits, costs and/or demands. In fact, the non-cooperative equilibrium is the natural outcome of oligopolistic competition under incomplete information! The entrant and the alleged predator *are* therefore able to say what the post-entry competitive price is, in the market in which entry occurred, in the absence of predation, and what the corresponding market shares are. The least the Commission should do is to ask that these numbers be revealed.

In particular, the victim should be asked to show (a) that its post-entry equilibrium market share and the equilibrium price(s) are, in this market, such that its entry value was positive and (b) that, at the predator's price, this value became negative. The alleged predator's defense would be to show that its post-entry price, in the local market in which entry occurred, is the non-cooperative equilibrium price in this market.

13.2 Informational requirements

The conclusions of the preceding section about what sort of questions are to be asked by the antitrust authority and what sort of data are to be provided by the plaintiff and the defence are rather precise. Unfortunately, once all this is well understood, a further practical difficulty is to be faced. Given that the authority is at an informational disadvantage relative to the firms under investigation – it has to obtain the relevant information from the firms themselves! – the latter can easily misrepresent the situation. Indeed, the defence (the incumbent) can make predatory prices and sales appear as non-cooperative Cournot outcomes that are not objectionable. Alternatively, the plaintiff (the entrant) can make a fight by the incumbent to remain the price leader appear as predatory behaviour. These are the points made by Normann (1994b). They parallel the discussion of the Harstad–Phlips indistinguishability theorem in case of tacit collusion in section 8.1.

Normann simplifies the discussion by considering only static one-shot

[6] See section 5.1.

games, to avoid considerations about future profits and discounting. He first shows how an incumbent can make predatory pricing appear as a non-cooperative Cournot equilibrium. He then shows how the reactions of 'innocent' price leaders can be construed by an entrant, who engages in Stackelberg warfare, to appear as predatory. Let us consider these two cases in turn.

Predation or Cournot?[7]

Consider a quantity setting duopoly consisting of an incumbent firm i and an entrant e protected from further entry. Inverse demand is assumed to be linear

$$p = a - b(q_i + q_e). \tag{13.1}$$

Firms produce at constant marginal cost c_i, c_e and a fixed cost K_i, K_e which might differ between the incumbent and the entrant. The entrant has to pay an entry cost which shall not be specified further. Profit functions are

$$\Pi_i = (a - b(q_i + q_e) - c_i)q_i - K_i, \tag{13.2}$$

$$\Pi_e = (a - b(q_i + q_e) - c_e)q_e - K_e. \tag{13.3}$$

The non-cooperative Cournot equilibrium will serve as a benchmark for 'permitted' non-predatory behaviour. It is straightforward to compute from (13.2) and (13.3):

$$q_i^C = \frac{a - 2c_i + c_e}{3b}, \tag{13.4}$$

$$q_e^C = \frac{a - 2c_e + c_i}{3b}, \tag{13.5}$$

$$p^C = \frac{a + c_i + c_e}{3}. \tag{13.6}$$

Equilibrium profits are

$$\Pi_i^C = \frac{(a - 2c_i + c_e)^2}{9b} - K_i \tag{13.7}$$

$$\Pi_e^C = \frac{(a - 2c_e + c_i)^2}{9b} - K_e \tag{13.8}$$

which are assumed to be positive. Both competitors know all parameters.

---

[7] The following pages are taken from Normann (1994b) with minor expositional changes.

In the model of predation used the predator sells a quantity such that the entrant makes at best zero profit. So this model certainly matches the above definition of predation: a positive entry value is turned into a negative one because sunk entry costs cannot be regained. Given the predator's sales q_i^P the entrant produces $q_e^P = (a - bq_i^P - c_e)/2b$ as an optimal response. The entrant's profit function (13.3) can be rewritten as

$$\Pi_e^P(q_i^P) = \left(\frac{a - bq_i^P - c_e}{2}\right)^2 \cdot \frac{1}{b} - K_e = 0. \tag{13.9}$$

Solving this for q_i^P one gets the outcomes

$$q_i^P = \frac{a - c_e}{b} - 2\sqrt{K_e/b}, \tag{13.10}$$

$$q_e^P = \sqrt{K_e/b}, \tag{13.11}$$

$$p^P = \sqrt{K_e b} + c_e. \tag{13.12}$$

Only the entrant's costs (c_e and K_e) appear in these equations, because driving its profit to zero depends only on its costs. These quantities and the price give profits of

$$\Pi_i^P = q_i^P(p^P - c_i) - K_i, \tag{13.13}$$

and

$$\Pi_e^P = 0. \tag{13.14}$$

The model has six parameters $z = (z_1, \ldots, z_6) = (a, b, c_i, c_e, K_i, K_e)$ of which the competition authority is assumed to know only a subset. Parameters reported by firms to the authority are indicated as $\hat{z}$. The strong assumptions are made that (a) the authority knows that demand and costs are linear, (b) a fixed cost for operating in the market is involved and (c) firms compete in quantities. The authority observes the quantities produced by the two firms and the market price.

Proposition 1: If the authority does not know the incumbent's marginal cost c_i, an actual predatory outcome cannot be distinguished from the Cournot–Nash equilibrium.

Proof: To make the predatory quantity q_i^P appear as Cournot behaviour, the right-hand side of (13.4) has to be equal to the right-hand side of (13.10), or

$$\frac{(a - c_e)}{b} - 2\sqrt{K_e/b} = \frac{a - 2\hat{c}_i + c_e}{3b}. \tag{13.15}$$

This simplifies to

$$\hat{c}_i = 3\sqrt{K_e b} + 2c_e - a. \tag{13.16}$$

Given non-negativity of $\hat{c}_i$, also q_e^P, p^P appear as resulting from Cournot behaviour when $\hat{c}_i$ is used to compute q_e^C and p^C using (13.5) and (13.6).

The proposition states that the incumbent, by misrepresenting its marginal cost as indicated in the proof, can make the predatory outcome appear as Cournot behaviour. To report $\hat{c}_i$ as in (13.16) implies understating the true value of c_i. In this apparent Cournot equilibrium the entrant makes zero profits, though. Consequently, the incumbent should argue that the plaintiff should not have entered the market, since sunk entry costs cannot be regained.

As an illustration, consider a numerical example with true values $a = 10$, $b = 1$, $c_i = c_e = 3$, $K_i = K_e = 4$. The predatory outcome for these values is $q_i^P = 3$, $q_e^P = 2$ and $p^P = 5$ according to equations (13.10) to (13.12). If the incumbent reports that his marginal cost is $\hat{c}_i = 2$, the observed quantities and prices appear as a Cournot equilibrium. (With equal costs, both producers have equal sales in a Cournot equilibrium – see equations (13.4) and (13.5). By reporting a lower cost, the incumbent justifies his larger sales.)

Proposition 2: If the authority does not know the demand parameters a, b the incumbent's predatory quantity q_i^P cannot be distinguished from the Cournot quantity q_i^C.

Proof: The predatory price (13.12) has to be claimed as resulting from $p = \hat{a} - \hat{b}(q_i^P + q_e^P)$. Solving for $\hat{a}$ gives

$$\hat{a} = \sqrt{K_e b} + c_e + \hat{b}((a - c_e)/b - \sqrt{K_e/b}). \tag{13.17}$$

To justify q_i^P as Cournot behaviour, the right-hand sides of (13.10) and (13.4) have again to be equal, or

$$\frac{(a - c_e)}{b} - 2\sqrt{K_e b} = \frac{\hat{a} - 2c_i + c_e}{3\hat{b}}. \tag{13.18}$$

Using $\hat{a}$ gives

$$\hat{b} = \frac{b(\sqrt{K_e b} + 2(c_e - c_i))}{2(a - c_e) - 5\sqrt{K_e b}}. \tag{13.19}$$

For the incumbent to justify its own sales as Cournot it suffices to understate both the intercept and the slope of the inverse demand function. In contrast to proposition 1, here the entrant's observed quantity does not appear as an optimal response when using $\hat{a}$ and $\hat{b}$. However, the incumbent can claim that the entrant chose the wrong entry level of production by mistake.

The same numerical example as above may be used, as an illustration. The triple $q_i^P = 3$, $q_e^P = 2$, $p^P = 5$ is observed. According to the data available to the authority this could be, but is not necessarily a case of predation. Now the incumbent reports $\hat{a} = 7.5$ and $\hat{b} = 0.5$. Then q_i appears as a result of Cournot behaviour and the observed price does not contradict this claim. The entrant's quantity q_e appears as mistaken: according to $\hat{a}, \hat{b}$ the entrant should have produced a higher output $q_e = q_i = 3$. Although at that output a lower equilibrium price of $p^P = 4.5$ would have resulted, the entrant would have made a small positive profit.

Predation or Stackelberg warfare?

Stackelberg warfare is a strategic fight for market leadership. Normann (1994a) shows that Stackelberg warfare can occur as an equilibrium choice in a reputation game[8] for the following scenario: one firm (here the incumbent) plays Stackelberg leader. The other firm (here the entrant) could operate profitably in the market as a follower. However, it does not accept to do so in the long run. It engages in warfare to discipline the first firm and make it withdraw from its leader position. Thus, it is the entrant's own action that turns its market value into a negative one.

The incumbent produces the quantity of a Stackelberg leader $q_i = (a - 2c_i + c_e)/2b$. This quantity is not predatory and profitable entry is possible if an upper restriction on K_e is imposed such that

$$K_e < \frac{(a + 2c_i - 3c_e)^2}{16b}. \tag{13.20}$$

The entrant plays Stackelberg warfare: it chooses the quantity q_e such that the incumbent makes zero profit.[9] The incumbent's profit (13.2) can be expressed in terms of q_e taking the Stackelberg leader quantity q_i as given

$$\Pi_i = \left(\frac{a - 2c_i + c_e}{2b}\right)\left(\frac{a - c_e}{2} - bq_e\right) - K_i = 0. \tag{13.21}$$

---

[8] Inspired by the Kreps–Wilson model discussed in section 11.4.

[9] Any quantity q_e may discipline the incumbent if it pushes the incumbent's profit below the Cournot level: then the incumbent does better settling the conflict by withdrawing from its Stackelberg leader position (see Normann, 1994a). Here the zero profit level is assumed for analytical convenience.

Solving for q_e gives

$$q_i^W = \frac{(a - 2c_i + c_e)}{2b}, \tag{13.22}$$

$$q_e^W = \frac{a - c_e}{2b} - \frac{2K_i}{a - 2c_i + c_e}, \tag{13.23}$$

$$p^W = \frac{2K_i b}{a - 2c_i + c_e} + c_i. \tag{13.24}$$

In this constellation the incumbent makes zero profit and the entrant deliberately makes losses

$$\Pi_i^W = 0, \tag{13.25}$$

$$\Pi_e^W = q_e^W (p^W - c_e) - K_e < 0. \tag{13.26}$$

Proposition 3: If the authority lacks information about
(i) the entrant's marginal cost c_e or
(ii) the entrant's fixed cost parameter K_e,
the incumbent's (non-predatory) Stackelberg leader quantity q_i^W cannot be distinguished from the predatory output q_i^P.

Proof: To make q_i^W appear as predatory, the right-hand sides of (13.22) and (13.10) have to be equal

$$\frac{a - 2c_i + c_e}{2b} = \frac{a - \hat{c}_e}{b} - 2\sqrt{K_e/b} \tag{13.27}$$

if c_e is unknown to the authority. Solving for $\hat{c}_e$ gives

$$\hat{c}_e = \frac{a + 2c_i - c_e}{2} - 2\sqrt{K_e b}. \tag{13.28}$$

Similarly

$$\hat{K}_e = \frac{(a + 2c_i - 3c_e)^2}{16b} \tag{13.29}$$

leads to the same indistinguishability result if $\hat{K}_e$ is unknown in (13.27) rather than $\hat{c}_e$.

In this case it is the entrant which misrepresents the data to its advantage. Although it was the entrant which made the market unprofitable by engaging in Stackelberg warfare, the data reported by the entrant makes the incumbent appear as the aggressor. The entrant has to overstate its marginal cost or its fixed entry cost. In this case, the fact that q_e^W is not profit maximising (or more precisely not loss minimising) is beside the point. According to the entrant's report the incumbent turned a profitable entry possibility into a negative one – and that is predation.

Consider a different numerical example: $a = 10$, $b = 1$, $c_i = c_e = 2$, $K_i = K_e = 3$. Condition (13.20) holds so the market is profitable for the entrant as a Stackelberg follower. A market outcome of $q_i = 4$, $q_e = 3.25$, $p = 2.75$ is observed. The limited information available to the authority indicates a case of Stackelberg warfare. However, if the entrant reports $\hat{c}_e = 6 - 2\sqrt{3} \approx 2.53$ then the incumbent's quantity appears as predatory. If K_e is unknown to the authority, reporting $\hat{K}_e = 4$ leads to the same result. Since the authority does not know either c_e or K_e it cannot distinguish the two outcomes.

The competition authority might try to make use of other sources to detect predation. Of such sources three are discussed here.

The information of the opposing firm In the cases related to proposition 1 and proposition 2 the incumbent misrepresents data to its advantage. The entrant does the same in the case related to proposition 3. Can the authority rely on the information reported by the opposing firm in each case?

The answer is no. The authority cannot rely on the entrant's report in the cases related to propositions 1 and 2. The entrant will report things in its own interest. If predation actually happened, the entrant will report the missing parameter(s) truthfully and will attempt to convince the authority that a Cournot equilibrium is not a correct description of the situation. But if the incumbent's report was correct and apparent predatory behaviour was actually a Cournot outcome, then the entrant would misrepresent c_i such that a Cournot equilibrium could not have been the case. By the same token the incumbent firm's information is not reliable in the case described in proposition 3, if predation is the true outcome.

Observing preceding monopoly outcomes The authority could try to infer lacking data by analysing the monopoly output and price before the entrant comes into play. The incumbent maximises monopoly profits by producing $q_i = (a - c_i)/2b$ at a price of $p = (a + c_i)/2$. From this outcome the authority could easily get to know, e.g., the incumbent's marginal cost c_i or the demand parameters a, b.

However, unconstrained profit-maximising monopolies hardly exist in the real world. Monopolies protected from further entry generally face regulatory constraints so that observing pre-entry outcomes provides little information to the authorities. If the monopolistic market is deregulated, there is usually a transition phase before the market is opened to further entrants. This phase may be used by the incumbent to make production more efficient. In addition, price and output may be used strategically to signal cost and demand structures to potential entrants as well as to the authorities.[10] Whatever the incumbent might undertake, the pre-entry market outcomes do not give an unbiased representation of cost and demand in the market.

Detection possibilities via econometric inference are also very limited, as indicated at the end of section 8.2, to which the reader is referred.

13.3 The AKZO decision[11]

In December 1985, a fine of 10 million ECU, payable in guilders, was imposed on AKZO Chemie BV by the Commission of the European Economic Communities[12] for infringement of Article 86 of the Roman Treaty, that is, for abuse of a dominant position. AKZO allegedly abused the dominant position which it holds in the EEC organic peroxides market by a policy of selective and below-cost price cutting designed to damage the business of Engineering and Chemical Supplies Ltd (ECS), a small producer of organic benzoyl peroxide in the United Kingdom, and to exclude it as a competitor. Although the concept of 'predatory pricing' is not used explicitly by the Commission, it is clear from the arguments used that the Commission did consider the alleged abuse as predatory. Is this a correct interpretation of the facts (as described in the decision)? We argue that it is not.[13]

The facts[14]

AKZO Chemie, a division of the Dutch multinational chemical and fibres group AKZO NV, is a multimarket, multiproduct firm, for which the UK

---

[10] It is not the purpose of this section to analyse how much information (or misleading information) such signalling can provide. See Roberts (1986) for such an analysis.

[11] This section is based on Phlips and Moras (1993).

[12] *Official Journal of the European Communities (O.J.)*, No. L374 of 31 December 1985.

[13] An appeal by AKZO was rejected on 3 July 1991 by the Court of Justice of the Communities. See *Recueil de la Jurisprudence de la Cour et du Tribunal de première instance*, 1991, vol. 7, part I, pages I-3439–77. The Advocate-General of the Court, C.O. Lenz, had concluded on 19 April 1989 that AKZO's appeal should be accepted on the grounds that the Commission did not prove that AKZO had a dominant position (see pages I-3396–438 of the same *Recueil*) nor give sufficient proof of a number of alleged abuses.

[14] In this section the facts, as reported by the Commission, are put in a chronological order. In the published decision, facts are reported in the order necessary to corroborate the different arguments advanced to prove abuse of a dominant position with reference to Article 86 of the Roman Treaty.

market for flour additives – on which the alleged aggression occurred – is a relatively small submarket. ECS, on the other hand, is a small privately owned company whose principal activity is the production of flour additives including benzoyl-peroxide-based bleaching agents. In the EEC, the use of this particular bleaching agent for flour is authorised only in the United Kingdom and Ireland. There is therefore a well-delineated local market for this particular flour additive.

However, benzoyl peroxide (BP) is also (and mainly) used as an initiator in the polymer industry. Let us denote this use as the 'plastics market'. In 1979, ECS began to produce benzoyl peroxide products for the bulk polymer industry and to sell these in the UK. By September 1979, a first shipment was dispatched to BASF of Ludwigshafen (Germany), one of AKZO's major customers in the polymer industry, at a price 15 per cent to 20 per cent below AKZO's then price. ECS thus first entered AKZO's UK submarket for plastics and then entered one of AKZO's continental plastics markets, which AKZO shared with smaller suppliers.[15]

What was AKZO's reaction? Its first reaction was a series of threats, which the Commission describes as follows (*O.J.*, L374/7, K 26):

ECS alleged that the AKZO reaction to its expansion was swift. On or about 14 November 1979 senior AKZO UK representatives had requested an urgent meeting with ECS which was scheduled for two days later. ECS alleged that in this first meeting direct threats were made by AKZO UK, that unless ECS withdrew from the plastics market retaliation from AKZO UK would follow in the form of both overall price reductions and selective cuts aimed at ECS's customers. These price reductions would be concentrated in the flour additives sector as it would cause the most harm to ECS. AKZO UK had said it was prepared to go down to below cost if necessary, the more profitable side of its business supporting the price reduction venture.... An alternative possibility canvassed by AKZO was that it might even buy out ECS so as to neutralize the competition. ECS also alleged that a second meeting took place about a fortnight later when the AKZO UK representatives were joined by the head office product manager from AKZO Chemie in the Netherlands and the threats were repeated. A few days later ECS applied for and was granted an injunction under Article 86 of the EEC Treaty in an *ex parte* hearing in the High Court in London.

From a legal point of view, these threats are important, since they can be (and were) used by the antitrust authority to establish predatory intent, the more so as they were directed to the flour additives market rather than the plastics market. For the economist, the interesting question (not considered

---

[15] The scenario strongly resembles the one imagined by Easley *et al.* (1985) – see section 11.5 – except that AKZO did not have the monopoly of the submarkets in which entry occurred.

by the Commission) is whether AKZO's threat was a credible one.[16] It occurred after two successive entries in AKZO's British and German submarkets for plastics. The fact that the fight would have been located in the UK market for flour additives, ECS's main market, rather than in the plastics markets where the entries occurred, implied more harm to ECS and smaller costs to AKZO, and thus did not reduce its entry-deterring nature. From a game-theoretic point of view, we have a repeated-game situation of the chain store paradox type. However, it is well known that in perfect subgame equilibrium, threats of this nature are not credible in such games when information is perfect and complete. On the one hand, AKZO was perfectly informed about the entrant's moves. On the other hand, given the long history of friendly collaboration between the two firms in the UK market for flour additives,[17] it is unlikely that there was (that Mother Nature had chosen) a positive probability that AKZO was a predator – as in Kreps and Wilson (1982a) – so that information can be considered 'complete'.

At any rate, whether the threat was credible or not, a settlement was reached out of court. AKZO agreed to pay ECS's legal costs and undertook not to reduce its normal selling prices for benzoyl peroxide in the UK or elsewhere for either plastics or flour additives. In the game-theoretic jargon, AKZO made a binding commitment to eliminate predation from its action set, thus indicating that it was willing to collaborate. AKZO probably expected ECS to remain a price follower on the flour additives market. That this is a reasonable explanation is confirmed by the fact that AKZO again increased its prices for flour additives to its UK customers by 10 per cent in early 1980, that is, right after the settlement.

The preceding sets the stage for the events to come. ECS's complaint to the EEC Commission (in June 1982) was indeed based on the claim that AKZO had attempted to put it out of business by a sustained and systematic campaign of price cutting *since the end of 1980*.

In order to be able to follow the story of this price undercutting, it is

---

[16] AKZO claims that the meetings had been a mere 'communications exercise' to explain that a 'more competitive' sales policy for flour additives would be adopted. According to the Advocate-General of the Court, a senior sales manager of AKZO UK wrote a note stating that he thought the threats were 'vain' (menaces 'vaines') since AKZO had admitted previously that its flour additives branch was not profitable. This manager also indicated that he did not think AKZO would (or intended to) launch a price war and that it wanted ECS out of the flour additives market. See *Recueil de la Jurisprudence de la Cour* ... 1991, vol. 7, part I, pages I-3419–20.

[17] All through the seventies, AKZO had in fact fixed the UK prices for flour additives (with regular increments of 10 per cent) and ECS had always followed these increases.

necessary to describe the structure of the flour additives market in the UK and Ireland on both the supply and the demand side. There were three suppliers of a full range of flour additives, with the following market shares[18] (in 1982):

AKZO UK: 52%
ECS: 35%
Diaflex: 13%.

(Note that Diaflex bought its raw material, concentrated benzoyl peroxide, from AKZO.) The customers and their buying shares were:

RHM, Spillers and Allied Mills: 85%
'Large independents':   10%
'Small independents':   5%

with RHM, Spillers and Allied Mills of roughly comparable size. These customers were supplied as follows:

RHM: by AKZO and Diaflex;
Spillers: by AKZO and, in second order until 1982, by Diaflex;
Allied Mills: by ECS (and one of the mills by AKZO);
Independent mills: ECS had 2/3 and AKZO 1/3 until 1982. (From 1982 onwards, AKZO had 2/3 and ECS 1/3.)

In other words, ECS did not supply RHM or Spillers. Its prices to Allied Mills, its sole major customer, were generally about 10 per cent below AKZO UK's prices to the two other majors. Its prices to the independent mills were also substantially below AKZO UK's. In spite of this price differential, AKZO UK had been able to maintain its share of the market, including the larger part of the business of RHM and Spillers. ECS maintained that its production costs were lower than AKZO UK's and stated that it obtained reasonable profit margins before AKZO's subsequent price undercutting.

When AKZO UK increased its prices to its usual UK customers in early 1980, ECS *did not react*, as it had done over the past decade, by following the price increase. Instead, it kept its 1979 price, so that the customary price gap between ECS and AKZO widened. AKZO's two main customers (the milling groups Spillers and RHM) then asked ECS for a quotation for supplying flour additives. The Commission describes ECS's answer as follows (*O.J.*, L374/9, §36 and 37):

In March 1980 ECS quoted to Spillers prices of £532 per tonne for BP 16% and £336 per tonne for PB (potassium bromate) 10%. (These quotes corresponded exactly

---

[18] According to the Advocate General, these numbers can be questioned. Alternative estimates are 34 per cent for AKZO and 53 per cent for ECS. See footnote 20 of the Advocate General's conclusions.

with the prices then offered by ECS to Allied Mills (its main customer) while AKZO UK's prices to Spillers were then £605 and £405, respectively.) The response of AKZO UK (whose representative was shown the ECS quotation) was that it did not wish to lose any business whatever to ECS and it adjusted its price downwards to match the ECS quote.

Later in the year (towards October) Spillers requested quotations for a fixed price contract of six or 12 months' duration from all three suppliers of flour additives. ECS again quoted for its standard product the same prices as it had offered earlier in the year, but at the request of Spillers reduced prices of £512 and £309 were offered for a special cheap mixture using only gypsum instead of the normal inert filler. Later the offer for the cheap mix was increased by ECS by £5.90 to cover the cost of an additive to ensure better flow characteristics. Diaflex also quoted, initially, £530 and £335 per tonne; then a reduced offer of £517 and £327 for 12 months or £490 and £310 for a six months' contract. (The Diaflex product uses the cheaper gypsum filler.)

Spillers again gave AKZO UK full details (including copy correspondence) of the quotes received from both the other suppliers. With the knowledge of what the other suppliers had offered, AKZO UK quoted for its standard formulation £489 and £309 (thus undercutting by £1 per tonne the lowest price which had been offered by either of the other suppliers for a cheap mix) and took the business on the basis that Spillers obtained its total requirements from AKZO UK.

AKZO's other main customer (the milling group RHM) almost simultaneously made similar moves and received similar quotations from ECS, which were matched by AKZO. However, in late 1980 AKZO did launch a counter-attack, by approaching ECS's main customer (Allied Mills) – first as a group and then through its individual members – with new prices of £517.90 and £314.90. In December 1980, AKZO also approached the independent mills with special offers. The end of the story is this (*O.J.*, L374/11, §41):

'The result of these systematic low price offers from AKZO UK – which were assiduously followed up – was that ECS gradually lost the business of its three most important large independent customers plus several individual Allied Mills. The custom of the remaining mills was only kept by price reductions to match the AKZO UK quotes. In about January 1983 AKZO UK lowered its price offers to the Allied Mills and to the independents still further, and ECS to retain its customers was again obliged to decrease its prices despite substantial cost increases for labour and raw materials.

In July 1983, minimum prices for flour additives were imposed on AKZO by the Commission (Decision 83/462/CEE of 29 July 1983) as a provisional measure.

Predatory pricing or active competition?

Is this a story of predatory pricing or of active competition? The conclusions of chapter 11 imply that predatory pricing occurs only if a number of conditions are simultaneously met. First, the aggressor is a multimarket firm (possibly a multiproduct firm). If we assume that AKZO was the aggressor, then this first condition is obviously met. Second, the predator attacks after entry has occurred in one of its markets. At the end of 1979, ECS did enter AKZO's plastic market, both in the UK and in Germany. AKZO's reaction to this entry was a series of threats, followed by an increase in its prices for flour additives to its UK customers by 10 per cent. It was a 'regular' price increase: for years, AKZO had been increasing its prices every year by 10 per cent. This is the behaviour of a dominant firm, convinced that it still is the price leader. No predation so far!

In fact, it was ECS that started cutting prices by not following the price leader, with the result that the customary price differential between ECS and AKZO widened. Even more, ECS went as far as to make offers at its earlier prices to some of AKZO's main UK customers. Clearly, ECS turned into a price-setter and started a price war to get the price below the new price quoted by AKZO. Given the settlement reached in 1979, ECS could expect AKZO's hands to be bound.

AKZO had no choice but to follow by adjusting its prices to the quotations made by ECS. In what was practically a duopoly situation – Diaflex did not count much – the only price it could adjust to was the competitor's price. It is hard to understand, therefore, in what sense the Commission objects in §40 of its decision to AKZO's not calculating its low prices 'by reference to a market price or the price then being paid by the customer'. (When, later on, ECS had to adjust to quotations made by AKZO, the Commission did not find this objectionable.) To construe AKZO's price adjustment as a case of predatory pricing, one would first have to establish a direct link between ECS's 1979 entry into the plastics market and an attack by AKZO. We do not see any such link.[19] AKZO's 'counter-attack' (around December 1980) appears as the reaction of a dominant firm that lost its price leadership and tries to discipline a deviant. Since this sort of discipline, as displayed by ECS in the seventies, is not objected to by the Commission, it is difficult to find efforts to restore it objectionable, the more so as in the event these efforts led to more price competition.

Our reasoning, in the preceding paragraphs, is based on the assumption that ECS had acquired a sufficiently large cost advantage to become the

---

[19] The Advocate-General arrived at the same conclusion.

Table 13.1. *AKZO's costs*

Year	1981	1982	1983
Total average cost	557.9	578.1	519.2
Variable cost	298.3	324.7	314.1

Source: Judgement of the Court of Justice, *Recueil*,
Articles 89, 97.

price leader, its small size notwithstanding. Note, indeed, that the price
leader is not necessarily the firm that has the largest market share (see the
discussion of figure 7.1 in section 7.1). AKZO does not seem to have
understood this. Nor did it understand that, if ECS was truly the new price
leader, it was in AKZO's interest to become a follower (as shown by Ono,
1978). AKZO's counter-attack on ECS is thus to be interpreted as a case of
Stackelberg warfare.

In Article 1 of its decision, the Commission makes the point that AKZO
infringed Article 86 of the Roman Treaty by offering flour additives to the
customers of ECS, in its counter-attack, 'at unreasonably low prices
designed to damage ECS's business viability in that ECS was obliged either
to abandon the customer to AKZO Chemie BV or to match a loss-making
price in order to retain the customer'. It would be rather tedious to go
through a detailed comparison of the individual price quotations. The
following remarks raise serious doubts about the Commission's claim:
(1) since ECS did not follow AKZO's 10 per cent price increase, it may be
thought that the 1979 prices were profitable enough for ECS (possibly
because of its declared cost advantage); (2) if ECS's cost advantage was of
the order of 10 per cent, then AKZO's undercutting could not have been too
damaging: its price quotations were of the order of 2 per cent, 5 per cent, 8
per cent or 11 per cent below those of ECS, depending on whether the
customer was its own or that of its competitor; (3) by January 1983, ECS
was still resisting the price cutting, retaining at least 70 per cent of its 1980
sales level.

Strikingly, though it is the central point of the Commission's decision,
just one out of its 101 paragraphs of roughly equal length in the official
documentation concerns the damage or elimination of ECS business
(paragraph 50). Even more strikingly, the Commission considered it
superfluous to investigate ECS's cost.[20]

[20] It is hard to understand why the Court of Justice decided that an analysis of ECS's cost
advantage is irrelevant (No. 74 of the judgement), notwithstanding the opinion to the
contrary of the Advocate-General (Nos. 34–6 of his conclusions).

Table 13.2. *ECS's estimated total average cost*

Year	1981 £	1982 £	1983 £
scenario 1	502.1	520.3	467.3
scenario 2	557.9	578.1	519.2
scenario 3	583.9	603.4	539.7

Normann (1994b) estimates ECS's costs using information about AKZO's costs. He makes two preliminary points. First, ECS was apparently the more efficient firm. ECS itself claims so. Furthermore, ECS always had prices of about 10 per cent below those of AKZO before the price war started. Second, since ECS's business had declined by 1984, it had less sales to cover its fixed cost. Did it therefore have higher total average costs than AKZO? No. There was a sharp decline in the demand for white bread and therefore also in the demand for flour and its additives between 1980 and 1984, that is, during the time of the conflict. But AKZO also had to accept a decrease in sales, namely from £393,000 in 1980 to £301,000 in 1983 (i.e., a decline down to 76 per cent of its 1980 business) so that market shares of AKZO and ECS changed only slightly between 1980 and 1983.[21] In addition, note that in the polymer market (the one ECS invaded successfully in 1979) the same main substance (benzoyl peroxide) is used as in the flour additives market. Consequently ECS might have covered some of its fixed costs by engaging in this new business – at the disadvantage of AKZO. Summarising these conjectures about ECS's costs one has to conclude lower rather than higher total average cost for ECS.

In order to show how crucially judgements about the damage of AKZO's pricing policy depend on ECS's costs, the following three scenarios are considered. In the first, ECS is assumed to have a cost advantage of 10 per cent in comparison to AKZO's total cost. In the second, both are assumed to be equally efficient. In the third – in contradiction to what is concluded above – ECS is assumed to have a cost disadvantage of 10 per cent in fixed cost and to be equally efficient in variable costs. One obtains the following values for ECS's total average cost.

These conjectures have to be compared with the alleged predatory price

[21] Market shares were 35 per cent for ECS and 52 per cent for AKZO in 1980 and 30 per cent and 55 per cent in 1983 respectively. See Article 103 of the judgement of Court of Justice in the *Recueil*. Other estimates indicate a higher market share for ECS but no significant change in the market shares.

of £517.9.[22] In the first scenario (and even in the second) serious damage to ECS's business can hardly be claimed. Whatever ECS's true costs were, the fact that the Commission did not investigate them makes its statements about prices and costs worthless: information about the preyed firm's costs is essential for the identification of predation (see equations (13.10)–(13.12)).

Even if the Commission had investigated ECS's costs, a judgement would presumably have been difficult. As shown, the answer to the question whether ECS business was 'damaged' or not changes within a small range of ECS's costs. This range is such that ECS, by slightly overstating its costs (see proposition 3), could have pretended that AKZO's policy was damaging when it in fact was not. Even after a complete investigation the Commission would have faced indistinguishability problems.

---

[22] This is the price offered between 1980 and 1983 to Allied Mills for benzoyl peroxide (BP 16%) by AKZO.

References

Abreu, D. (1986), 'External equilibria of oligopolistic supergames', *Journal of Economic Theory*, 39, 191–225.
  (1988), 'On the theory of infinitely repeated games with discounting', *Econometrica*, 56, 383–96.
Abreu, D., D. Pearce and E. Stacchetti (1986), 'Optimal cartel equilibria with imperfect monitoring', *Journal of Economic Theory*, 39, 251–69.
Albaek, S. (1990), 'Stackelberg leadership as a natural solution under cost uncertainty', *Journal of Industrial Economics*, 38, 335–47.
Andersen, T.M. and M. Hviid (1994), 'Acquisition and dissemination of information in imperfectly competitive markets', *Economic Inquiry*, 32, 498–510.
Anderson, S. (1987), 'Spatial competition and price leadership', *International Journal of Industrial Organization*, 5, 369–98.
Areeda, P. and D.F. Turner (1975), 'Predatory pricing and related practices under Section 2 of the Sherman Act', *Harvard Law Review*, 88, 697–733.
Ash, P. and J. Seneca (1976), 'Is collusion profitable?', *Review of Economics and Statistics*, 58, 1–12.
Aumann, R.J. (1960), 'Acceptable points in games of perfect information', *Pacific Journal of Mathematics*, 10, 381–417.
Basar, T. and Y.C. Ho (1974), 'Informational properties of the Nash solutions of two nonzero-sum games', *Journal of Economic Theory*, 7, 370–87.
Baumol, W.J. (1979), 'Quasi-performance of price reductions: a policy for prevention of predatory pricing', *Yale Law Journal*, 89, 1–26.
Baumol, W.J., J.C. Panzar and R.D. Willig (1982), *Contestable Markets and the Theory of Industry Structure*, New York, Harcourt, Brace, Jovanovich.
Beath, J., Y. Katsoulacos and D. Ulph (1989), 'Strategic R&D policy', *Economic Journal*, Supplement, 99, 74–83.
Benoit, J.P. and V. Krishna (1987), 'Dynamic duopoly: prices and quantities', *Review of Economic Studies*, 54, 23–36.
Bernheim, B.D. and Whinston M.D. (1990), 'Multimarket contact and collusive behaviour', *Rand Journal of Economics*, 21(1), 1–26.
Bloch, K. (1932), 'On German cartels', *Journal of Business*, 5, 213–22.
Böhnlein, B. (1994a), 'The soda-ash market in Europe: multi-market contact with

256

collusive and competitive equilibria', EUI Working Paper ECO no. 94/42, Florence.

(1994b), 'Multimarket contact, collusion and market structure', Ph.D. dissertation, European University Institute, Florence.

Bork, R.H. (1967), 'The goals of antitrust policy', *American Economic Review*, 57, Papers and Proceedings, 242–53.

(1978), *The Antitrust Paradox*, New York, Basic Books.

Bourdet, Y. (1988), *International Integration, Market Structure and Prices*, London and New York, Routledge.

Boyer, M. and M. Moreaux (1986), 'Rationnement, anticipations rationelles et équilibre de Stackelberg', *Annales d'économie et de statistique*, 1, 55–73.

(1987), 'Being a leader or a follower', *International Journal of Industrial Organization*, 5, 175–92.

Branco, F. (1992), 'The design of multidimensional auctions', Paper presented at the 1992 Asset meeting in Toulouse.

Cabral, L.M.B. and M.H. Riordan (1994), 'The learning curve, market dominance, and predatory pricing', *Econometrica*, 62, 1115–40.

Choi, J.P. (1989), 'An analysis of cooperative R&D', Working Paper, Department of Economics, Harvard University.

Clarke, R.N. (1983a), 'Duopolists don't wish to share information', *Economics Letters*, 11, 33–6.

(1983b), 'Collusion and the incentives for information sharing', *Bell Journal of Economics*, 14, 383–94.

Cooper, T.E. (1986), 'Most-favored-customer pricing and tacit collusion', *Rand Journal of Economics*, 17, 377–88.

Cramton, P.C. and T.R. Palfrey (1990), 'Cartel enforcement with uncertainty about costs', *International Economic Review*, 31, 17–47.

Crawford, V. and J. Sobel (1982), 'Strategic information transmission', *Econometrica*, 50, 1431–51.

Cummings, F.J. and W.E. Ruther (1979), 'The Northern Pacific case', *Journal of Law and Economics*, 22, 329–50.

d'Aspremont, C. and A. Jacquemin (1988), 'Cooperative and noncooperative R&D in duopoly with spillovers', *American Economic Review*, 78, 1133–7.

(1990), 'Cooperative and noncooperative R&D in duopoly with spillovers: erratum', *American Economic Review*, 80, 1641–2.

d'Aspremont, C., A. Jacquemin, J. Gabszewicz and J. Weymark (1983), 'On the stability of collusive price leadership', *Canadian Journal of Economics*, 16, 17–25.

David, H.A. (1981), *Order Statistics*, New York, John Wiley and Sons Inc.

Davidson, C. and R. Deneckere (1990), 'Excess capacity and collusion', *International Economic Review*, 31, 521–42.

De Bondt, R. and I. Henriques (1994), 'Strategic investment with asymmetric spillovers', *Canadian Journal of Economics*, forthcoming.

De Bondt, R., P. Slaets and B. Cassiman (1992), 'The degree of spillovers and the number of rivals for maximum effective R&D', *International Journal of Industrial Organization*, 10, 35–54.

De Bondt, R. and R. Veugelers (1991), 'Strategic investment with spillovers', *European Journal of Political Economy*, 7, 345–66.

Deneckere, R. and D. Kovenock (1992), 'Price leadership', *Review of Economic Studies*, 59, 143–62.

Deneckere, R., D. Kovenock and R. Lee (1992), 'A model of price leadership based on consumer loyalty', *Journal of Industrial Economics*, 40, 147–56.

Dickson, V. (1988), 'Price leadership and welfare losses in US manufacturing: comment', *American Economic Review*, 78, 285–7.

Dobson, P.W. and C.D. Sinclair (1990), 'On the possibility of price wars when firms use a "tit-for-tat" strategy', *Economics Letters*, 32, 115–19.

Dodgson, J.S., Y. Katsoulacos and C.R. Newton (1992), 'A modelling framework for the empirical analysis of predatory behaviour in the bus service industry', *Regional Science and Urban Economics*, 22, 51–70.

(1993), 'An application of the economic modelling approach to the investigation of predation', *Journal of Transport Economics and Policy*, 153–70.

Dolbear, F., L. Lave and G. Bowman (1968), 'Collusion in oligopoly: an experiment on the effect of numbers and information', *Quarterly Journal of Economics*, 82, 240–59.

Dowrick, S. (1986), 'von Stackelberg and Cournot duopoly: choosing roles', *Rand Journal of Economics*, 17, 251–60.

Easley, D., R.T. Masson and R.J. Reynolds (1985), 'Preying for time', *Journal of Industrial Economics*, 33, 445–60.

Eckard, E. (1982), 'Firm market share, price flexibility, and imperfect information', *Economic Inquiry*, 20, 388–92.

Edgeworth, F. (1897) 'La teoria pura del monopolio', *Giornale degli Economisti*, 40, 13–31. Reprinted in English as 'The pure theory of monopoly', in F. Edgeworth, *Papers Relating to Political Economy*, London, Macmillan, 1925, 111–42.

Eisenberg, B.S. (1980), 'Information exchange among competitors: the issue of relative value scales for physicians' services', *Journal of Law and Economics*, 23, 441–60.

Esposito, F.F. and L. Esposito (1974), 'Excess capacity and market structure', *Review of Economics and Statistics*, 56, 188–94.

Fehl, U. and W. Güth (1987), 'Internal and external stability of bidder cartels in auctions and public tenders', *International Journal of Industrial Organization*, 5, 303–13.

Feinberg, R.M. and T.A. Husted (1993), 'An experimental test of discount-rate effects on collusive behaviour in duopoly markets', *Journal of Industrial Economics*, 61, 153–60.

Fellner, W. (1960), *Competition Among the Few*, Reprints of Economic Classics, New York, A.M. Kelley.

Fershtman, C. and N. Gandal (1994), 'Disadvantageous semicollusion', *International Journal of Industrial Organization*, 12, 141–54.

Fershtman, C. and E. Muller (1986), 'Capital investments and price agreements in semicollusive markets', *Rand Journal of Economics*, 17, 214–26.

Fog, B. (1960), *Industrial Pricing Policies*, Amsterdam, North-Holland.

Fouraker, L. and S. Siegel (1963), *Bargaining Behavior*, New York, McGraw-Hill.

Fraas, A. and D. Greer (1977), 'Market structure and price collusion: an empirical analysis', *Journal of Industrial Economics*, 26, 29–33.

Fried, D. (1984), 'Incentives for information production and disclosure in a duopolistic environment', *Quarterly Journal of Economics*, 99, 367–81.

Friedman, J.W. (1963), 'Individual behavior in oligopolistic markets: an experimental study', *Yale Economic Essays*, 3, 359–417.

(1969), 'On experimental research in oligopoly', *Review of Economic Studies*, 36, 399–415.

(1970), 'Equal profit as a fair division', in H. Sauermann (ed.), *Beiträge zur experimentellen Wirtschaftsforschung*, vol. II, Tübingen, 19–32.

(1971), 'A non-cooperative equilibrium for supergames', *Review of Economic Studies*, 38, 1–12.

(1972), 'On the structure of oligopoly models with differentiated products', in H. Sauerman (ed.), *Beiträge zur experimentellen Wirtschaftsforschung*, vol. III, J.C.B. Mohr (Paul Siebeck), Tübingen, 28–63.

(1977), *Oligopoly and the Theory of Games*, Amsterdam, North-Holland.

(1979), 'On entry preventing behavior', in S.J. Brams, A. Schotter and G. Schwödiauer (eds.), *Applied Game Theory*, Vienna, Physica Verlag, 236–53.

(1983), *Oligopoly Theory*, Cambridge, Cambridge University Press.

Friedman, J.W. and A.C. Hoggatt (1980), *An Experiment in Non-Cooperative Oligopoly*, Greenwich, Connecticut, JAI Press.

Friedman, J.W. and J.-F. Thisse (1993), 'Partial collusion fosters minimum product differentiation', *Rand Journal of Economics*, 24, 631–45.

Fudenberg, D. and E. Maskin (1986), 'The folk theorem in repeated games with discounting or with incomplete information', *Econometrica*, 54, 533–54.

Fudenberg, D. and J. Tirole (1986a), *Dynamic Models of Oligopoly*, New York, Harwood Academics.

(1986b), 'A "signal-jamming" theory of predation', *Rand Journal of Economics*, 17, 366–76.

(1989), 'Noncooperative game theory for industrial organisation: an introduction and overview', in R. Schmalensee and R. Willig (eds.), *Handbook of Industrial Organisation*, vol. I, Amsterdam, North-Holland, chapter 5.

Gal-Or, E. (1985a), 'First and second mover advantages', *International Economic Review*, 26, 649–53.

(1985b), 'Information sharing in oligopoly', *Econometrica*, 53, 329–43.

(1986), 'Information transmission – Cournot and Bertrand equilibria', *Review of Economic Studies*, 53, 85–92.

(1987), 'First mover disadvantages with private information', *Review of Economic Studies*, 54, 279–92.

Gandal, N. and S. Scotchmer (1989), 'Coordinating research through research joint ventures', Working Paper, Domestic Studies Program, Hoover Institution, Stanford University.

Gaskins, D. (1971), 'Dynamic limit pricing: optimal pricing under threat of entry', *Journal of Economic Theory*, 2, 306–22.

Gisser, M. (1984), 'Price leadership and dynamic aspects of oligopoly in U.S.

manufacturing', *Journal of Political Economy*, 92, 1035–47.

(1986), 'Price leadership and welfare losses in U.S. manufacturing', *American Economic Review*, 76, 756–67.

(1988), 'Price leadership and welfare losses in U.S. manufacturing: reply', *American Economic Review*, 78, 288–9.

(1989), 'Price leadership and welfare losses in U.S. manufacturing: reply', *American Economic Review*, 79, 610–13.

Graham, D.A. and R.C. Marshall (1987), 'Collusive bidder behaviour at single-object second-price and English auctions', *Journal of Political Economy*, 95(6), 1217–39.

Graham, D.A., R.C. Marshall and J.F. Richard (1990), 'Differential payments within a bidder coalition and the Shapley value', *American Economic Review*, 80(3), 493–510.

Green, E.J. and R.H. Potter (1984), 'Noncooperative collusion under imperfect price information', *Econometrica*, 52, 87–100.

Greenhut, J.G. and M.L. Greenhut (1975); 'Spatial price discrimination, competition and locational effects', *Economica*, 42, 401–19.

Greenhut, M.L., C.S. Lee and Y. Mansur (1991), 'Spatial discrimination, Bertrand vs. Cournot: comment'; *Regional Science and Urban Economics*, 21, 127–34.

Greer, D.F. (1979), 'A critique of Areeda's and Turner's standards for predatory practicing', *The Antitrust Bulletin*, 24, 233–61.

Güth, W. and B. Peleg (1993), 'On ring formation in auctions', Discussion Paper CentER no. 9357, Tilburg University.

Hamilton, J., Thisse J.-F. and A. Weskamp (1989), 'Spatial discrimination: Bertrand versus Cournot in a model of location choice', *Regional Science and Urban Economics*, 19, 87–102.

Hamilton, J.S. and S.M. Slutsky (1990), 'Endogenous timing in duopoly games: Stackelberg or Cournot equilibria', *Games and Economic Behavior*, 2, 29–46.

Harstad, R.M. and L. Phlips (1994); 'Informational requirements of collusion detection: simple seasonal markets', mimeo, European University Institute, Florence.

Hay, G. (1982), 'Oligopoly, shared monopoly, and antitrust law', *Cornell Law Review*, 67, 439–81.

Hay, G. and D. Kelley (1974), 'An empirical survey of price-fixing conspiracies', *Journal of Law and Economics*, 17, 13–38.

Henriques, J. (1990), 'Cooperative and noncooperative R&D with spillovers: comment', *American Economic Review*, 80, 638–40.

Higgins, R.S., W.F. Shughart II and R.D. Tollison (1989), 'Price leadership with incomplete information', *Journal of Economic Behavior and Organization*, 11, 423–9.

Hinloopen, J. (1994), 'Subsidising cooperative and non-cooperative R&D in duopoly with spillovers', EUI Working Paper ECO no. 94/25, Florence.

Hoggatt, A.C. (1959), 'An experimental business game', *Behavioral Science*, 4, 192–203.

(1967), 'Measuring the cooperativeness of behavior in quantity variation duopoly games', *Behavioral Science*, 12, 109–21.

Holahan, W.L. (1978), 'Cartel problems: comment', *American Economic Review*, 68, 942–6.

Holt, C.A. and D.T. Scheffman (1987), 'Facilitating practices: the effects of advance notice and best-price policies', *Rand Journal of Economics*, 17, 187–97.

Holthausen, D. (1979), 'Kinky demand, risk aversion and price leadership', *International Economic Review*, 20, 123–37.

Isaac, R.M. and V.L. Smith (1985), 'In search of predatory pricing', *Journal of Political Economy*, 93, 320–45.

Jacquemin, A. (1988), 'Cooperative agreements in R&D and European antitrust policy', *European Economic Review*, 32, 551–60.

Johansen, L. (1982), 'On the status of the Nash type of noncooperative equilibrium in economic theory', *Scandinavian Journal of Economics*, 84, 421–41.

Judd, K.L. (1985), 'Credible spatial preemption', *Rand Journal of Economics*, 16(2), 153–66.

Jung, Y.J., J.H. Kagel and D. Levin (1994), 'On the existence of predatory pricing: An experimental study of reputation and entry deterrence in the chain-store game', *The Rand Journal of Economics*, 25, 72–93.

Kamien, M.I., E. Muller and I. Zang (1992), 'Research joint ventures and R&D cartels', *American Economic Review*, 82, 1293–306.

Kamien, M.I. and N. Schwartz (1971), 'Limit pricing under uncertain entry', *Econometrica*, 39, 441–54.

Kamien, M.I. and I. Zang (1993), 'Competing research joint ventures', *Journal of Economics & Management Strategy*, 2, 23–40.

Karikari, J.A. (1988), 'Tariffs and international price leadership', *Quarterly Review of Economics and Business*, 28, 53–66.

Kihlstrom, R.E. and X. Vives (1989), 'Collusion by asymmetrically informed duopolists', *European Journal of Political Economy*, 5, 371–402.

(1992), 'Collusion by asymmetrically informed firms', *Journal of Economics and Management Strategy*, 1, 371–96.

Kirman, A. and L. Phlips (1993), 'Empirical studies of product markets', EUI Working Paper ECO no. 93/4, Florence.

Kirman, A. and N. Schueller (1990), 'Price leadership and discrimination in the European car market', *Journal of Industrial Economics*, 39, 69–91.

Koller, R.H. (1971), 'The myth of predatory pricing: an empirical study', *Antitrust Law and Economics Review*, 4, 105–23.

Kreps, D.M. (1990), *A Course in Microeconomic Theory*, New York, Harvester Wheatsheaf.

Kreps, D.M. and J.A. Scheinkman (1983), 'Quantity precommitment and Bertrand competition yield Cournot outcomes', *Bell Journal of Economics*, 14, 326–37.

Kreps, D.M. and R. Wilson (1982a), 'Reputation and imperfect information', *Journal of Economic Theory*, 27, 253–79.

(1982b), 'Sequential equilibria', *Econometrica*, 50, 863–94.

Kuehn, K.-U., P. Seabright and A. Smith (1992), *Competition Policy Research: Where Do We Stand?*, CEPR Occasional Paper no. 8, Centre for Economic Policy Research, London.

Laffont, J.J. and J. Tirole (1987), 'Auctioning incentive contracts', *Journal of*

Political Economy, 95, 921–37.

(1993), *A Theory of Incentives in Procurement and Regulation*, Cambridge, Mass., MIT Press.

Lambson, V.E. (1987), 'Optimal penal codes in price-setting supergames with capacity constraints', *Review of Economic Studies*, 54, 385–97.

Lanzillotti, R.F. (1957), 'Competitive price leadership: a critique of price leadership models', *Review of Economics and Statistics*, 39, 56–64.

Logan, J.W. and R.W. Lutter (1989), 'Guaranteed lowest prices: do they facilitate collusion?', *Economics Letters*, 31, 189–92.

Luce, R.D. and H. Raiffa (1957), *Games and Decisions*, New York, John Wiley.

MacLeod, W.B. (1984), 'The core and oligopoly theory', revision version of CORE Discussion Paper no. 8331, Louvain-La-Neuve.

(1985), 'A theory of conscious parallelism', *European Economic Review*, 27, 25–44.

Mann, H.M., J.W. Meehan and G.A. Ramsey (1979), 'Market structure and excess capacity: a look at theory and some evidence', *Review of Economics and Statistics*, 61, 156–60.

Markham, J. (1951), 'The nature and significance of price leadership', *American Economic Review*, 41, 891–905.

Martin, S. (1993a), *Advanced Industrial Economics*, Oxford, Basil Blackwell.

(1993b), 'On the divergence between the legal and economic meanings of collusion', mimeo, European University Institute, November.

Matsui, A. (1989), 'Consumer-benefitted cartels under strategic capital investment competition', *International Journal of Industrial Organization*, 7, 451–70.

McAfee, R.P. and J. McMillan (1986), 'Bidding for contracts: a principal-agent analysis', *Rand Journal of Economics*, 17, 326–8.

(1987), 'Auctions and bidding', *Journal of Economic Literature*, 25, 699–738.

(1988), *Incentives in Government Contracting*, University of Toronto Press.

(1992), 'Bidding rings', *American Economic Review*, 82, 579–99.

McGee, J.S. (1958), 'Predatory price cutting: the Standard Oil (N.J.) case', *Journal of Law and Economics*, 1, 137–69.

(1960), 'Ocean freight rate conferences and the American Merchant Marine', *University of Chicago Law Review*, 27, 191 sq.

(1964), 'Government intervention in the Spanish sugar industry', *Journal of Law and Economics*, 7, 121 sq.

(1980), 'Predatory pricing revisited', *Journal of Law and Economics*, 23, 238–330.

Merrilees, W.J. (1983), 'Anatomy of a price leadership challenge: an evaluation of pricing strategies in the Australian newspaper industry', *Journal of Industrial Economics*, 31, 291–311.

Milgrom, P. and J. Roberts (1982a), 'Predation and entry deterrence', *Journal of Economic Theory*, 27, 280–312.

(1982b), 'Limit pricing and entry', *Econometrica*, 50, 443–59.

(1987), 'Informational asymmetries, strategic behavior, and industrial organization', *American Economic Review*, 77 (Papers and Proceedings), 184–93.

Modigliani, F. (1958), 'New developments on the oligopoly front', *Journal of Political Economy*, 66, 215 sq.

Monopolies and Mergers Commission (1990), *Highland Scottish Omnibuses Ltd.*, HMSO.

Mood, A.M., F.A. Graybill and D.C. Boes (1974), *Introduction to the Theory of Statistics*, McGraw Hill International Editions.

Mougeot, M. and F. Naegelen (1993), *Les marchés publics*, Paris, Economica.

Nash, J.F. (1950), 'The bargaining problem', *Econometrica*, 18, 155–62.

(1951), 'Noncooperative games', *Annals of Mathematics*, 45, 286–95.

Nermuth, M. (1982), *Information Structures in Economics*, Studies in the Theory of Markets with Imperfect Information, Lecture Notes in Economics and Mathematical Systems, no. 196, Berlin, Springer-Verlag.

Neven, D., R. Nuttall and P. Seabright (1993), *Merger in Daylight: The Economics and Politics of European Merger Control*, Centre for Economic Policy Research, London.

Neven, D. and L. Phlips (1985), 'Discriminating oligopolists and common markets', *Journal of Industrial Economics*, 34, 133–49.

Normann, H.-T. (1994a), 'Stackelberg warfare as an equilibrium choice in a game with reputation effects', EUI Working Paper ECO no. 94/43, Florence.

(1994b), 'Informational requirements of predation detection', Mimeo, EUI, Department of Economics, Florence.

Novshek, W. (1984), 'Finding all n-firm Cournot equilibria', *International Economic Review*, 25, 61–70.

Novshek, W. and H. Sonnenschein (1978), 'Cournot and Walras equilibrium', *Journal of Economic Theory*, 19, 223–66.

(1982), 'Fulfilled expectations, Cournot duopoly with information acquisition and release', *Bell Journal of Economics*, 13, 214–18.

OECD, (1989), *Predatory Pricing*, Paris.

(1994), *Competition Policy and Vertical Restraints*, Paris.

Office of Fair Trading (1989a), 'West Yorkshire Road Car Company Limited: Fares policy on certain routes between Bradford and Skipton', *Office of Fair Trading*, London.

(1989b), 'Highland Scottish Omnibuses Ltd.: Local bus services in Inverness', *Office of Fair Trading*, London.

(1989c), 'South Yorkshire Transport Ltd.: Registration and operation of Service 74 between High Green and Sheffield', *Office of Fair Trading*, London.

(1990), 'Kingston upon Hull City Transport Ltd.: Local bus services in Kingston upon Hull', *Office of Fair Trading*, London.

(1992), 'Southdown Motor Services Ltd.: The registration and operation of Services 262 and 242 in Bognor Regis', *Office of Fair Trading*, London.

Okada, A. (1982), 'Information exchange between duopolistic firms', *Journal of the Operations Research Society of Japan*, 25, 58–75.

(1983), 'Coalition formation of oligopolistic firms for information exchange', *Mathematical Social Sciences*, 6, 337–51.

Ono, Y. (1978), 'The equilibrium of duopoly in a market of homogeneous goods', *Economica*, 45, 287–95.

(1982), 'Price leadership: A theoretical analysis', *Economica*, 49, 11–20.

Osborne, K.D. (1976), 'Cartel problems', *American Economic Review*, 66, 835–44.

Osborne, M.J. and C. Pitchik (1983), 'Profit-sharing in a collusive industry', *European Economic Review*, 22, 59–74.

(1986), 'Price competition in a capacity-constrained duopoly', *Journal of Economic Theory*, 38, 238–60.

(1987), 'Cartels, profits and excess capacity', *International Economic Review*, 28, 413–28.

Oxenfeldt, A. (1952), 'Professor Markham on price leadership', *American Economic Review*, 42, 380–4.

Palfrey, T.R. (1982), 'Risk advantages and information acquisition', *Bell Journal of Economics*, 13, 219–4.

Patinkin, D. (1947), 'Multi-plant firms, cartels and imperfect competition', *Quarterly Journal of Economics*, 61, 173–205.

Peterman, J.L. (1979), 'The *International Salt* case', *Journal of Law and Economics*, 22, 351–64.

Phlips, L. (1962), *De l'intégration des marchés*, Louvain and Paris, Nauwelaerts.

(1983), *The Economics of Price Discrimination*, Cambridge, Cambridge University Press.

(1988a), 'Price discrimination: a survey of the theory', *Journal of Economic Surveys*, 2, 135–67.

(1988b), *The Economics of Imperfect Information*, Cambridge, Cambridge University Press.

(1993), 'Basing point pricing, competition and market integration', in H. Ohta and J.-F. Thisse (eds.), *Does Economic Space Matter? Essays in Honor of M.L. Greenhut*, St. Martin's Press, 303–15.

(1994), 'Price leadership and conscious parallelism', in S. Martin (ed.), *The Construction of Europe*, Essays in Honour of Emile Noël, Dordrecht, Kluwer Academic Publishers.

Phlips, L. and I.M. Moras (1993), 'The AKZO decision: a case of predatory pricing?' *Journal of Industrial Economics*, 41 (3, September), 315–21.

Phlips, L. and J.F. Richard (1989), 'A dynamic oligopoly model with demand inertia and inventories', *Mathematical Social Sciences*, 18, 1–32.

Phlips, L. and J.-F. Thisse (1981), 'Pricing, distribution and the supply of storage', *European Economic Review*, 15, 225–43.

Plott, C.R. (1982), 'Industrial organization theory and experimental economics', *Journal of Economic Literature*, 20, 1485–527.

(1989), 'An updated review of industrial organization: applications of experimental methods', in R. Schmalensee and R.D. Willig (eds.), *Handbook of Industrial Organization*, vol. II, Amsterdam, North-Holland, chapter 19.

Png, I.P.L. and D. Hirschleifer (1987), 'Price discrimination through offers to match price', *Journal of Business*, 60, 365–83.

Ponssard, J.-P. (1979), 'The strategic role of information on the demand function in an oligopolistic market', *Management Science*, 25, 243–50.

Porter, R.H. (1983a), 'Optimal cartel trigger price strategies', *Journal of Economic Theory*, 29, 313–38.

(1983b), 'A study of cartel stability: the Joint Executive Committee', *Bell Journal of Economics*, 14, 301–14.

Posner, R.A. (1976), *Antitrust Law: An Economic Perspective*, Chicago, University of Chicago Press.

Pyatt, G. (1971), 'Profit maximization and the threat of new entry', *Economic Journal*, 81, 242–55.

Rees, R. (1985), 'Cheating in a duopoly supergame', *Journal of Industrial Economics*, 33, 387–400.

—— (1991), 'Collusive equilibrium in the great salt duopoly', mimeo.

—— (1993a), 'Tacit collusion', *Oxford Review of Economic Policy*, 9, 27–40.

—— (1993b), 'Collusive equilibrium in the great salt duopoly', *Economic Journal*, 103, 833–48.

Roberts, J. (1986), 'A signalling model of predatory pricing', *Oxford Economic Papers*, 38 (Supplement), 75–93.

Roberts, K. (1985), 'Cartel behaviour and adverse selection', *Journal of Industrial Economics*, 33, 401–13.

Rosenbaum, D.I. (1989), 'An empirical test of the effect of excess capacity in price setting, capacity-constrained supergames', *International Journal of Industrial Organization*, 7, 231–41.

Rotemberg, J.J. and G. Saloner (1990), 'Collusive price leadership', *Journal of Industrial Economics*, 39, 93–110.

Rothschild, R. (1981), 'Cartel problems: note', *American Economic Review*, 71, 179–81.

Sakai, Y. (1990, 1991), 'Information sharing in oligopoly: overview and evaluation', *Keio Economic Studies*, 27 (1990), 17–41 and 28 (1991), 51–71.

Salop, S.C. (1979), 'Strategic entry deterrence', *American Economic Review*, 69, 335–8.

—— (1981) (ed.), *Strategy, Predation and Antitrust Analysis*, Federal Trade Commission, Bureau of Economics, Bureau of Competition, Washington, DC.

—— (1986), 'Practices that (credibly) facilitate oligopoly coordination', in *New Developments in the Analysis of Market Structure*, ed. by J. Stiglitz and I. Matthewson, London, Macmillan.

Salop, S.C. and L.J. White (1988), 'Private antitrust litigation: an introduction and framework', in L.J. White (ed.), *Private Antitrust Litigation: New Evidence, New Learning*, Cambridge, Mass., MIT Press.

Sauermann, H. and R. Selten (1967), 'Ein oligopolexperiment', in H. Sauermann (ed.), *Beiträge zur experimentellen Wirtschaftsforschung*, vol. I, Tübingen, 9–59.

Scharfstein, D. (1984), 'A policy to prevent rational test-market predation', *Rand Journal of Economics*, 15, 229–43.

Scherer, F.M. (1980), *Industrial Market Structure and Economic Performance*, 2nd edition, Chicago, Rand McNally College Publishing Co.

Seidmann, D.J. (1987), 'Incentives for information production and disclosure: comment', *Quarterly Journal of Economics*, 102, 445–52.

Selten, R. (1965), 'Spieltheoretische Behandlung eines Oligopolmodells mit Nachfrageträgheit', *Zeitschrift für die Gesamte Staatswissenschaft*, 121, 301–24 and 667–89.

—— (1973), 'A simple model of imperfect competition where four are few and six are many', *International Journal of Game Theory*, 2, 141–201, reprinted in R. Selten, *Models of Strategic Rationality*, Kluwer Academic Publishers, 1988, 95–155.

(1978), 'The chain store paradox', *Theory and Decision*, 9, 127–59.

(1979), 'Experimentelle Wirtschaftsforschung', *Rheinisch-Westfälische Akademie der Wissenschaften*, Vorträge no. 287, 41–72.

(1984), 'Are cartel laws bad for business?', in Hauptman *et al.* (eds.), *Operations Research and Economic Theory*, Springer-Verlag, reprinted in R. Selten, *Models of Strategic Rationality*, Kluwer Academic Publishers, 1988, 183–215.

Sevy, D. (1992), 'Faut-il réguler la R&D?', Document de travail 371, Laboratoire d'économétrie de l'Ecole Polytechnique, Paris.

Shaked, A. and J. Sutton (1987), 'Product differentiation and industrial structure', *Journal of Industrial Economics*, 34, 131–46.

Shapiro, C. (1986), 'Exchanges of cost information in oligopoly', *Review of Economic Studies*, 53, 433–46.

(1989), 'Theories of oligopoly behavior', in R. Schmalensee and R. Willig (eds.), *Handbook of Industrial Organisation*, vol. I, Amsterdam, North-Holland, chapter 6.

Shaw, R.W. (1974), 'Price leadership and the effect of new entry on the U.K. retail petrol supply market', *Journal of Industrial Economics*, 23, 65–79.

Shubik, M. (1980), *Market Structure and Behaviour*, Cambridge, Mass., Harvard University Press.

(1982), *Game Theory in the Social Sciences, Concepts and Solution*, Cambridge, Mass., MIT Press.

Simpson, R.D. and N.S. Vonortas (1994), 'Cournot equilibrium with imperfectly appropriable R&D', *Journal of Industrial Economics*, 42, 79–92.

Slade, M.E. (1987), 'Interfirm rivalry in a repeated game: an empirical test of tacit collusion', *Journal of Industrial Economics*, 35, 499–516.

Sleuwaegen, L. (1986), 'On the nature and significance of collusive price leadership', *International Journal of Industrial Organization*, 4, 177–88.

Smith, R.A. (1961), 'The incredible electrical conspiracy', *Fortune*, 63, 164–210.

Spence, A.M. (1978), 'Tacit co-ordination and imperfect information', *Canadian Journal of Economics*, 11, 490–505.

(1981), 'Competition, entry and antitrust policy', in Salop S.C. (ed.), *Strategy, Predation and Antitrust Analysis*, Federal Trade Commission, Bureau of Economics, Bureau of Competition, Washington, DC, 45–88.

Stahl, K. (1982), 'Location and spatial pricing theory with nonconvex transportation cost schedules', *Bell Journal of Economics*, 13(2), 575–82.

Stenbacka, R.L., (1990), 'Collusion in dynamic oligopolies in the presence of entry threats', *Journal of Industrial Economics*, 39, 147–54.

Stigler, G.J. (1964), 'A theory of oligopoly', *Journal of Political Economy*, 72, 44–61.

(1966), *The Theory of Price*, 3rd edition, New York, Macmillan.

Stoecker, R. (1980), *Experimentelle Untersuchung des Entscheidungs-verhaltens im Bertrand-Oligopol*, Bielefeld, Pfeffersche Buch-handlung.

Sultan, R.G.M. (1974), *Pricing in the Electrical Oligopoly*, 2 vols., Cambridge, Mass., Harvard University Press.

Suzumura, K. (1992), 'Cooperative and noncooperative R&D in an oligopoly with spillovers', *American Economic Review*, 82, 1307–20.

Sylos-Labini, P. (1962), *Oligopoly and Technical Progress*, Cambridge, Mass., Harvard University Press.

Telser, L.G. (1966), 'Cutthroat competition and the long purse', *Journal of Law and Economics*, 9, 259–77.

Thisse, J.-F. and X. Vives (1988), 'On the strategic choice of spatial price policy', *American Economic Review*, 78(1), 122–37.

Tirole, J. (1988), *The Theory of Industrial Organization*, Cambridge, Mass., MIT Press.

Van Bael, I. and J.-F. Bellis (1990), *Competition Law of the EEC*, 2nd edition, Bicester, CCH Editions Ltd.

Vickrey, W. (1961), 'Counterspeculation, auctions, and competitive sealed tenders', *Journal of Finance*, 16, 8–37.

Vives, X. (1984), 'Duopoly information equilibrium: Cournot and Bertrand', *Journal of Economic Theory*, 34, 71–94.

(1990), 'Trade association disclosure rules, incentives to share information and welfare', *Rand Journal of Economics*, 21, 409–30.

Williamson, O.E. (1977), 'Predatory pricing: a strategic and welfare analysis', *Yale Law Journal*, 87, 284–340.

Willner, J. (1989), 'Price leadership and welfare losses in U.S. manufacturing: comment', *American Economic Review*, 79, 603–8.

Yamey, B.S. (1972), 'Predatory price cutting: notes and comments', *Journal of Law and Economics*, 15, 129–42.

Ziss, S. (1994), 'Strategic R&D with spillovers, collusion and welfare', *Journal of Industrial Economics*, 62, 375–93.

Index

Abreu D., 99
abuse of a dominant position, 2, 239–40
active competition, *see* normal
    competition
adverse selection, 56, 56n
AKZO Chemie BV, 247–55
AKZO decision, 3, 20, 222, 229,
    247–55
Albaek S., 113
Alexanders Ltd., 224, 229
alignment, 107, 118–23
Anderson S., 108n
antitrust litigation, 215–19
Areeda P., 231–4
auctions
    collusion in, 67–78
    English, 74n
    first-price sealed bid, 67–72
    knock-out, 77
    prior, 76
    private value, 63, 68
    procurement, 17, 67–78
    second-price, 57, 74n
    Vickrey, 57, 68
Aumann R.J., 94n

backward map, 27n
backward reaction mapping, 27n
Baniak A., 86n
Basar T., 87
basing point, 119–23
Baumol W.J. 238
Bellis J.-F., 1n, 4
Benoit J.P., 169n
best reply, 5
bidding
    in auctions, 67–78
    ring, 67–8, 74–8
    rotating, 73n
Bloch K., 153

Böhnlein B., 136n
Boes D.C., 77n
Bork R.H., 216
Bourdet Y., 106n
Bowman G., 82
Boyer M., 109–11
Branco F., 69n
Brenner S., 4n
British Salt, 101–5
bus war, 221–9

cartel
    bargaining, 23–46
    cast-iron pipe, 77
    contract, 58
    enforcement with imperfect
        information, 49–56
    enforcement with incomplete
        information, 56–66
    export, 133
    in public procurement markets, 66–78
    laws, *see* competition law
    soda-ash, 137
    strong, 75–7
    weak, 75–6
chain store paradox, 189–93, 209–14
cheating, 47, 49–56, 90, 96, 169
Choi J.P., 179n
Clarke R.N., 87–9
collective dominance, 106n
collusion
    detection, 124–47, 164–8
    explicit, 2, 10, 21–78
    in procurement auction, 67–78
    tacit, 2, 3, 7, 10, 75–6, 79–148
Commission (of the European
    Communities), 3, 240
competition
    active, 8–16
    normal, 8–16

competition law
  in the EC, 1–3
  in general, 39–40
  in the Member States, 3n
  in the US, 2n, 124n
competition policy in the EC, 8–16
concerted practice, 2, 7, 118, 118n, 121
conscious parallelism, 15, 117–19
consistency, 7
Cooper T.E., 91, 91n, 92
cost
  common, 66, 88
  private, 56–66, 69, 74, 88
Cournot duopoly, 6, 69, 74, 88
Cramton P.C., 61–6
Crawford V., 87n
cross-hauling, 123
Cummings F.J., 89
customer loyalty, 113–15

Darmon M., 132n
d'Aspremont C., 24, 106n, 174–80
Davidson C., 152, 168–9
De Bondt R., 179n
Deneckere R., 113–15, 152, 168–9
DG IV, 2, 8, 18, 124, 126
Diaflex, 250
Dickson V., 106n
Dodgson J.S., 221–9
Dolbear F., 82
dominant firm, 109, 112
Dowrick S., 107
duopoly
  Bertrand, 18, 82, 87–8
  Cournot, 6, 82–9, 241–7
  salt, 101–5, 166–8
  with price leadership, 107–17
DuPont, 90

Easley D., 198–202, 233, 248n
econometric evidence, 130, 169–72, 247
EC decisions
  AKZO, 3, 20, 222, 229, 247–55
  flat glass, 106n
  ICI-Solvay, 3, 18, 126, 137
  wood pulp, 3, 18, 119, 126, 131–6
Eckard E., 111, 113
Edgeworth F., 154
Einpassungsfunktion, 27
Eisenberg B.S., 87n
Electrical Conspiracy, 73, 76n
Engineering and Chemical Supplies Ltd.,
  247–55
equilibrium
  balanced temptation, 97, 99
  fulfilled expectations, 84

non-cooperative Nash, *see* Nash
  equilibrium
  sequential, 199n
  subgame perfect, 7, 12, 26, 33, 40, 100,
  127, 175, 191
Esposito F.F., 169
Esposito L., 169
Ethyl, 90
European Coal and Steel Community
  (ECSC), 18, 107, 119–23
European Court of Justice, 3, 118n, 126,
  132, 247n, 253
excess capacity, 150–72
experiments
  information and collusion, 82
  predation, 206–14

Feinberg R.M., 97n
Fellner W., 52n
Fershtman C., 152, 162n, 180
Fichera V., 66n
fighting brands, 216
fighting ships, 220
fitting-in function, 27–9
Fog B., 106n
folk theorem, 99–105
Fouraker L., 82
Fraas A., 93n
franchising, 4
Fried D., 89
Friedman J.W., 5n, 18, 48n, 82, 94–8, 110,
  152, 198, 236
Fudenberg D., 98n, 99, 102, 194n

Gal-Or E., 87n, 89, 107, 113
Gandal N., 152, 180
Gaskins D., 235n
General Electric, 76n, 91n, 92
Gisser M., 106n
Graham D.A., 74n
Graybill F.A., 77n
Green E.J., 98
Greenhut J.G., 144
Greenhut M.L., 144
Greer D.F., 93n, 231

Hamilton J.S., 108
Harstad R.M., 18, 124n
Hay G., 91n, 93
Henriques J., 174, 179n
Higgins R.S., 112
Highland Scottish Omnibuses, 224
Hinloopen J., 179n
Ho Y.C., 87
Hoggatt A.C., 82, 94n
Holahan W.L., 53n

Holt C.A., 90n
Holthauser D., 113n
Hotelling H., 52n, 108n, 223n
Husted T.A., 97n

ICI, 136–48
ICI-Solvay decision, 3, 18, 126, 137
ICI Weston Point, 101–5
incentive compatibility, 58–60, 62
indistinguishability, 125–48, 242–7, 255
individual rationality, 60–2, 64–5
industry
    aluminium, 170–2
    automobile, 106n, 110, 111n
    bus services, 222–9
    cement, 153
    coal and steel, 119–23
    flat glass, 106n
    newspaper, 106n
    nitrogen fertilizer, 153
    organic peroxides, 247–55
    petrol, 106n
    photographic products, 106n
    salt, 101–5, 166–8
    shipping, 220
    soda-ash, 3, 18, 126, 136–48
    wood pulp, 3, 18, 119, 126, 131–6
information
    complete, 13, 58–9, 74, 97, 107–11
    imperfect, 9, 13, 17, 23, 49–56
    incomplete, 13, 17, 23, 56–66, 74–8,
        83–9, 111–15
    perfect, 9, 13–14, 25–6, 40, 47, 116
    social value of, 88
information acquisition, 14, 85–7, 112
information revelation, 56–66
information sharing, 14, 17, 81–93
information transmission, 9, 85–7
informational disadvantage, 125
informational requirements, 124–48,
    240–7
International Salt, 90
inventories, 98n, 128–9
Inverness bus market, 224–9
Inverness Traction Ltd., 224
Isaac R.M., 207–11

Jacquemin A., 173, 174–80
Johansen L., 5n
joint profit maximisation, 48–9
joint ventures in R&D, 2–3, 173–80
Jung Y.J., 209–14

Kagel J.H., 209–14
Kamien M.I., 179, 235n
Katsoulacos Y., 221–9

Kelley D., 93n
Kihlstrom R.E., 57–61
Kirman A., 106n
Koller R.H., 216
Kovenock D., 113–15
Kreps D.M., 82n, 154–9, 194, 199n, 212,
    249
Krishna V., 169n

Laffont J.-J., 69n
Lambson V.E., 101n
Lanzillotti R.F., 106n
Lave L., 82
Lee R., 113–15
Lenz C.O., 247n
Levin D., 209–14
limit pricing, 232, 234–8
Logan J.W., 90n
Lutter R.W., 90

Magicbus Ltd., 224, 229
Mann H.M., 169
McAfee R.P., 67, 69n, 74–8
McGee J.S., 186–9, 202, 230–1, 236
MacLeod W.B., 18, 82n, 117–19, 133
McMillan J., 67, 69n, 74–8
market transparency, 9
Markham J., 106n
Martin S., 24, 124n, 127n
Maskin E.S., 99, 102
Masson R.T., 198–202
Matsui A., 180n
mechanism design, 67
Meehan J.W., 169
meet competition clause, 82
merger control, 4
Merrilees W.J., 106n
Milgrom P.R., 192–8, 194n, 237
minimax profit, 99, 159
minimax strategy, 99–105
Modigliani F., 234
Mongeot M., 71n
Monopolies and Mergers Commission,
    224
Mood A.M., 77n
moral hazard, 56, 56n
Moras I., 247n
Moreaux M., 109–11
most favoured customer clause, 82, 91–3
Muller E., 162n, 179

Naegelen F., 71n
Nash J.F., 5, 160–1
Nash equilibrium
    Bayesian, 70, 87
    Bertrand, 93

collusive, 96, 118–19
Cournot, 6, 10, 26, 62, 64, 82–5
defined, 5
discriminatory, 203
normal competition, 11
Osborne's rule, 54
post-entry, 221–9, 239–40
predation, 198–202, 239–40
Nermuth M., 5
Neven D., 4, 188n, 203n
Newton C.R., 221–9
normal competition, 8–16
Normann H.-T., 240–7
Northern Pacific, 89
Novshek W., 17, 27n, 83–7
Nuttall, R., 4

Office of Fair Trading, 224
Okada A., 89
Ono Y., 108–11, 112
OPEC, 14, 52, 55–6
order statistics, 77n
Osborne K.D., 49, 52–6, 94, 95, 97, 152, 154–64
Oxenfeldt A., 106n

Palfrey T.R., 61–6, 87n
parallel pricing, 10, 15, 101, 115–19
Pareto optimality, 48
Patinkin D., 52n
payoff, 5
Peterman J.L., 90
Phlips L., 15n, 52n, 57n, 68n, 69n, 98n, 106n, 119n, 144n, 152–3, 188n, 203n, 204n, 223n, 233n, 247n
Pitchik C., 154–64
Plott C.R., 82, 82n, 206n
pooling
of information, *see* information sharing
of revenues, *see* side-payments
Porter R.J., 98
Posner R.A., 231n
predatory pricing, 2, 19–20, 185–255
price
delivered, 120n
fob-mill, 120n
franco, 120n
price discrimination, 2, 3n, 8, 144–7, 202–4
price leadership
group, 106n
in basing-point system, 121
individual, 101, 106–23
national, 115
price wars, 2, 13, 98, 116

prisoner's dilemma, 49–51, 90, 91, 96, 98
probability distribution
of costs, 57, 61, 63
of market size and monopoly profit, 45
of signals, 83
of types of entrants, 195
of types of monopolists, 199
procurement, 66–78
profit frontier, 48, 51, 95
Pyatt G., 235n

Ramsey G.A., 169
rationing, 110
reaction function, 6, 27–8, 99, 113, 226–9
Rees R., 54n, 93, 94n, 101–5, 106n, 166
repeated game, 6, 78, 94–105, 115–19, 127
reputation, 194–8
Rey P., 4n
Reynolds R.J., 198–202
Richard J.-F., 98n
Roberts J., 192–8, 194n, 237, 247n
Roberts K., 56
Roman Treaty, *see* Treaty of Rome
Rosenbaum D.I., 170–2
Rotemberg J.J., 115–17
Rothschild R., 53n
Ruther W.E., 89

Sakai Y., 88n
Saloner G., 115–17
Salop S.C., 90, 91, 215–19, 235n
Sauermann H., 82
Scharfsgtein D., 194n
Scheffman D.T., 90n
Scheinkman J.A., 82n, 154–9
Scherer F.M., 76, 106n
Schueller N., 106n
Schwartz N., 235n
Seabright P., 4
seasonal variations, 126–36
secret rebates, 8, 13
Selten R., 7, 16, 23–46, 82, 82n, 98, 189–92
semicollusion, 2, 19, 149–81
Sevy D., 180n
Shaked A., 12n
Shapiro R.D., 89
Shaw R.W., 106n
Shubik M., 5n, 49
side-payments, 52, 57–61, 75–7, 164
Siegel S., 82
signal, 83–8, 118
Simpson R.D., 179n
Slade M.E., 98n
Sleuwaegen L., 106n
Slutsky S.M., 108

Smith R.A., 73n, 76n
Smith V.L., 207–11
Sobel J., 87n
Solvay, 136–48
Sonnenschein H., 17, 27n, 83–7
Spence A.M., 231
spillover effect, 174
Stackelberg
    leader, 106
    Natural Stackelberg Solution, 113
    warfare, 20, 109, 244–7
Standard Oil, 186–8
Stigler G.J., 54, 77
Stoecker R., 82
strategy
    Bertrand, 82, 94n, 95, 102,. 136–48,
        144n, 154–9
    Cournot, 82, 95, 126–36
    defined, 5
    dominant, 51, 88
    minimax, 99–105
    mixed, 158, 160
    price, *see* Bertrand
    quantity, *see* Cournot
    stick and carrot, 99, 124
    trigger, 99, 124, 133
Sultan R.G.M., 91n
Sutton J., 12n
Suzumura K., 179n

tangentopoli, 72n
Telser L.G., 203
Thisse J.-F., 15n, 144n, 152

Tirole J., 69n, 98n, 194n
trade association, 93
Treaty of Rome, 1–2, 119, 137, 173, 247n
trigger price, 98
Turner D.F., 231–4
tying clause, 89

uncertainty
    cost, 23, 88–9
    demand, 83–8

Van Bael I., 1n, 4
values
    common, 18
    private, 18
vertical restraints, 4
Veugelers R., 179n
Vickrey W., 57, 68
Vives X., 17, 57–61, 87–8, 93, 144n
Vonortas N.S., 179n

Westinghouse, 76n, 92
White L.J., 215–19
Williamson O.E., 234, 235n, 237
Willner J., 106n
Wilson R., 194, 199n, 212, 249
wood pulp decision, 3, 18, 119, 126, 131–6

Yamey B.S., 216–21

Zang I., 179
Ziss S., 179n